nebraska symposium on motivation
1965

Nebraska Symposium on Motivation, 1965, is Volume XIII in the series on CURRENT THEORY AND RESEARCH IN MOTIVATION

nebraska symposium on motivation
1965

DAVID LEVINE, Editor

Howard H. Kendler	Professor of Psychology *University of California, Santa Barbara*
Robert Ward Leeper	Professor of Psychology *University of Oregon*
David Premack	Professor of Psychology *University of Missouri*
J. McV. Hunt	Professor of Psychology *University of Illinois*
Donald T. Campbell	Professor of Psychology *Northwestern University*
J. P. Guilford	Professor of Psychology *University of Southern California*

university of nebraska press

lincoln

1965

Publishers on the Plains

UNP

Copyright © 1965 by the University of Nebraska Press
Library of Congress Catalog Card Number: 53–11655
Manufactured in the United States of America

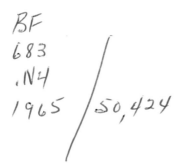

Contents

Introduction

The papers in this book were delivered at the two sections of the thirteenth annual Nebraska Symposium on Motivation held in Lincoln, Nebraska, on December 3 and 4, 1964, and April 8 and 9, 1965. In a series of this kind, one may legitimately ask if any trends have been noted over the years, and if so, what the implications of these trends might be: for theory and research in motivation; for theoretical psychology in general; and for the application of psychological knowledge to individual and social problems.

One trend which has been emerging clearly in recent papers is an increased emphasis on mediational, cognitive, or central processes in theories of motivation. Human beings almost certainly and probably some animals do think. Although evident from the start of the series, this emphasis is being voiced more clearly and more vigorously. In this year's volume, the papers by J. McV. Hunt, J. P. Guilford, and Robert Leeper continue to stress the importance of these kinds of concepts. The role of mediational constructs is a crucial aspect of a psychologist's theoretical stance and directs the kinds of research he will undertake. During the discussion period this year, Donald Campbell commented on this shift by many behaviorists who now include some kind of feedback mechanism in their model of behavior. He suggests that they might be called "cyberno-behaviorists" by future historians of science.

The implications of this trend are also of great importance in the applied fields of psychology. L. Breger and J. L. McGaugh, in the *Psychological Bulletin* (May 1965), have discussed the critical implications of these notions for developments in psychotherapy or behavior modification. They note that the newly evolving school of "behavior therapy," which claims to be based on modern learning theory, has not taken into account the increasing emphasis on mediational processes in learning and problem solving.

In addition to furnishing a continuing forum for the exploration of current theory and research in motivation, the Nebraska Symposia on Motivation fill a void which R. Nevitt Sanford has recently bemoaned. In the March, 1965, issue of the *American Psychologist* he writes: "The accent today is on the production of knowledge rather than on its organization. There are few attempts at systematization of the sort that would put particular facts in perspective and show their significance." Leeper's paper is a clear example of this kind of systematization. He has drawn from history, anthropology, early behaviorism, Gestalt psychology, psychoanalysis, recent research in learning theory, the work of foreign psychologists and neoanalysts, physiology, philosophy, and comparative psychology. In his closely reasoned paper, Leeper presents a convincing argument for his position that "emotions are motives, and ... emotional processes, along with all other motives, are perceptual or representational processes." After indicating the research and theoretical implications of this position, Leeper goes on to mention its social implications: "It is not surprising that we emphasize the ills that emotional processes can produce and fail to recognize the constructive possibilities in the emotional constitution which is so important in all of the higher vertebrates, particularly in the higher primates and man."

Although Leeper presented his paper at the December, 1964, section of the Symposium, Campbell's paper, delivered in April, 1965 (without his having seen Leeper's), is relevant to the same discussion. Campbell refers to his own paper as "a self-directed protest against the overly individualistic assumption as to human motivation which is dominant in social psychology today." He continues: "This assumption can be called *skin-surface hedonism,* the notion that all human activity has as its goal the pleasurable activation of taste receptors and other erogenous zones, the reinforcements of food, sex, and pain avoidance." Drawing on the work of biology and genetics, as well as social psychology, he raises the hypothesis that "biological and sociocultural evolution ... have produced in both man and termite motivational dispositions furthering group life and reflecting its advantages, as in the economy of cognition, division of labor, and mutual defense."

Hunt's paper, like Leeper's, demonstrates the enormous gain which is to be achieved through a careful, scholarly review of great breadth. Although presaged by his recent volume *Intelligence and Experience* and his paper in O. J. Harvey's *Motivation and Social Interaction,* the contribution which Hunt has prepared for this volume develops in somewhat greater detail his position that the organism's informational interaction with the environment is relevant to its motivational processes. The theoretical debt to Jean Piaget is clear, but, like Leeper, Hunt has drawn from many disciplines. His integration of this information and his description of his own recent experiments make his paper an important contribution to this series.

Guilford presents a review of his theoretical position which also emphasizes informational variables. He reviews the problems presented by motivational phenomena and then presents a model of behavior which accounts for behavior generally considered motivational. When a psychologist who has worked so carefully in an area seemingly unrelated to motivation is able to integrate his findings with the most recent work in motivation, one may begin to hope for a useful comprehensive theory of behavior.

Howard Kendler's comments concerning three levels of discourse are reminiscent of Ernest Hilgard's discussion of the three clusters of papers in these volumes. Kendler's "worlds" of physiology, phenomenal experience, and inferred behavior determinants parallel Hilgard's three clusters: physiological-hormonal, personality-social, and S-R drive-reduction learning theory. Is the number "three" mystical, or is it possible that there are three fundamentally unique avenues to knowledge about behavior? Or is it simply a historical accident?

Kendler's paper, in any event, clarifies considerably what is meant by S-R theories and indicates what some of the other papers develop more fully, namely, the importance of mediational variables for a complete theory of motivation. As background reading for his paper, Kendler recommended to our students a book on modern British philosophy by G. J. Warnock, a work which devotes considerable space to the views of Ludwig Wittgenstein. The end of philosophy, says Wittgenstein, is to clarify verbal confusion: "to let the fly out of the bottle." Kendler has done much to let some flies out of the bottle: the problem of the relation between motivational and nonmotivational concepts; the problem of determining a motivational unit of behavior; and the problem of distinguishing between primary and secondary drives.

In his paper, David Premack undertakes a sweepingly new approach to the difficult problem of reinforcement with the generalization that "for any pair of responses, the more probable one will reinforce the less probable one" and discusses his series of experiments to explore this generalization. Along the way, Premack presents some highly cogent criticisms of the more traditional views of reinforcement theory. The style of his paper is illustrated by the following few sentences: "First, the basic assumptions of the traditional account [of reinforcement] appear to be empirical propositions with a confirmation status so high that further test is unnecessary; actually, the assumptions were little more than common sense, which is to say, they were never tested. Second, when tested, they proved to be invalid. . . . They appear to be propositions involving empirical claims, claims so weak as to be essentially trivial. It is only when the propositions are seen to be nonempirical that they become nontrivial." Premack goes on to question the logical and empirical status of the traditional account of reinforcement. He is finally able to demonstrate that a response which functions as a reinforcement in one situation may function as the response to be reinforced in another situation, or, as he puts it, "the response which had been instrumental could be made reinforcing and vice versa."

These papers have been presented with the continuing financial support of the National Institute of Mental Health. I would like to voice, on behalf of the Department of Psychology, our thanks to NIMH for this support; to the Administration of the University of Nebraska for their understanding and cooperation; to Mrs. Dee Hughes, Mrs. Molly Hardt, Mrs. Peggy Nelson, and

Mrs. Lorraine Rains for their prompt and efficient secretarial assistance; and to the participants, who continue to expend effort beyond the call of duty in an attempt to make this series an educational and scientific success.

DAVID LEVINE

Lincoln, Nebraska
June 2, 1965

Motivation and Behavior[1]

HOWARD H. KENDLER

University of California, Santa Barbara

Although it may be inappropriate to begin an analysis of the concept of motivation with a personal confession, such a course of action does have the advantage of spelling out the aims of this paper.

My first inclination after receiving an invitation to participate in this symposium was to decline, because, unlike most participants over the years, I possessed no compelling set of data or integrative conceptualizations that demanded immediate attention or, for that matter, even circulation. But in spite of my initial reluctance, I could not ignore the challenge of the invitation. At that time, a year had not quite passed since I had finished an introductory textbook (Kendler, 1963) which was based on the assumption that the science of psychology possessed an intrinsic structure instead of representing a fortuitous conglomeration of problem areas. Accepting the decision that psychology is the science of behavior—and by behavior I mean publicly observable acts and movements ranging from responses that are defined in terms of their achievements to specific muscular contractions and glandular secretions[2]—I conceptualized behavior

---

[1] The preparation of this paper was assisted by grants from the National Science Foundation (GB-1447) and the Office of Naval Research (Nonr-4222[04]). Acknowledgment is made to Dr. Tracy S. Kendler and Dr. Robert W. Leeper for many helpful suggestions.

[2] I would prefer to emphasize the inclusiveness, instead of the exclusiveness, of the response concept. Defining responses in terms of publicly observable events does not exclude phenomenal experience. Two general methods exist for incorporating phenomenal experience within behavioristic psychology. The first is to infer conscious experience from behavior, as is the case when the verbal report of a subject is assumed to reflect his inner experience. The second is to convert phenomenal experience into a publicly observable event.

1

as reflecting the operation of four basic and relatively independent processes: sensation, learning, perception, and motivation. The problem I set for myself was to present the principles that governed both the operation of these four fundamental processes as well as the manner in which they interacted in more complex forms of behavior, e.g., problem solving, conflict, language, etc. My task was difficult, more difficult than initially anticipated, especially when dealing with the problems of motivation. Although I do not feel compelled to offer any apologies for the results of my efforts, I must confess that my initial aspiration to present the psychology of motivation as a nice, neat, orderly array of facts and principles was not fully realized. I would like to believe that the fault was not entirely my own but was due in part to the refractory quality of motivation. It is apparent to me that the topic of motivation is more confusing, more disorderly, more vexing than are the fields of sensation, learning, and perception. Why do we psychologists have so much difficulty with the problems of motivation? Why does motivation represent a backward area of psychology? What can be done? These are the questions I would like to consider, with the hope of clarifying some of the associated historical, methodological, and conceptual problems.

Motivation and Everyday Language

We are often victims of our past in the sense of being committed to a course of action without having the opportunity to judge its implications. Our ordinary language system reeks of motivational concepts. Even in early childhood we begin to think about the cause and effect of behavior in terms of motivation and rewards. No explanation of human action is deemed satisfactory unless some reference is made to psychological dis-

---

Although this is not now possible, the difficulty represents a technical problem, not a logical one. Conceivably, technological developments could make it possible for one person to observe directly another person's phenomenal experience. This position obviously implies that the mind-body problem possesses empirical components and therefore is not exclusively a philosophical and semantic issue.

positions directed at achieving some goal. No matter what their theoretical bent, psychologists find it difficult to escape from this frame of reference. When dealing with the realities of existence, such as coping with one's offspring who has packed sand in his ear or destroyed a new toy, it seems eminently reasonable to ask the question "Why did you do that?" or more elegantly, "What motivated you to behave in such a pathological manner?"

The pervasiveness of the motivational-reward model of behavior in our ordinary language is mentioned neither to disparage everyday language as a tool of psychological analysis nor to deny the validity of the motivational-reward model of behavior. Not at all! To avoid misunderstanding, let me comment about each point separately.

1. Although the relative merits of ordinary language as opposed to a logically pure and operationally based language (Warnock, 1958) represents a complex problem well beyond the scope of this paper, I would like to warn against the easy acceptance of *a priori* judgments in dealing with this problem. Experimental psychologists, in their attempt to convince others, as well as themselves, about the scientific status of their subject matter, have looked with disdain and suspicion on any ordinary-language analysis of a psychological problem. Simultaneously, they seem to endorse the principle that theoretical formulations must be expressed in a logically elegant fashion. Such a prejudgment confuses ends with means. I share the hope and the goal that some day all psychological theory will be expressed in a rigorous mathematical fashion. But our ultimate aims do not necessarily dictate the methods by which these aims are to be achieved. For example, we should not commit ourselves to the position that mathematical representation is necessary at every stage of theoretical development. Look at the form in which Darwin's theory of evolution was expressed and compare it to the demands some of us set for all psychological theory.

In contrast to the conventional view of the experimental psychologist is the attitude shared by many philosophers, and some psychologists, that ordinary language possesses a rich mine of psychological information. Although I cannot argue against

Scriven's counsel that "it would do psychologists no harm, though they are likely to find the suggestion objectionable, to mine the resources of ordinary language considerably more thoroughly than they have" (1964, p. 175), it should be recognized that the quality of the psychological principles excavated from common language will be at best crude, requiring both theoretical refinement and empirical supplementation to transform them into significant psychological truths.

The gist of my remarks, therefore, is to warn against prejudging the usefulness, or the harm, of the psychological principles imbedded in ordinary language. Ideas from ordinary language can be evaluated by the same methods we use to evaluate any idea—by experimenting and theorizing.

2. The ready intuitive acceptance of a motivational-reward model of behavior represents both its weakness and its strength. One of the distinctive characteristics of scientific principles is that they recognize their limits, i.e., what phenomena they do *not* apply to. The ordinary-language motivational-reward model is often applied indiscriminately and without qualifications to all forms of behavior, thus attenuating, and often eliminating, its formal explanatory capacity. Nevertheless, the model does persist. Why? It offers the common man some intuitive understanding of the behavior of others. The basic question is whether this sense of understanding is false and illusory, on a par with the primitive superstition that supernatural spirits control the behavior of mortal man, or whether, in fact, it is real in the sense that it does predict human and animal behavior. The second alternative seems to be the more reasonable one, and if accepted, it suggests that instead of rejecting the motivational-reward model of behavior because of its theoretical and empirical limitations, we should try to translate it into a more acceptable epistemological form and supplement it by experimental facts and conceptual precision. Fortunately, throughout the history of psychology, intellectually talented and sophisticated individuals have argued convincingly the case for a motivational-reward model of behavior. However, as we all know, the proper chord has yet to be struck to produce a motivational psychology appeal-

ing to a majority of psychologists. I would like to comment on some of the reasons for this.

My remarks will be restricted primarily to the motivational component of the motivational-reward model. First I will consider the problems raised by the different kinds of observations, or what may be said more precisely, the different modes of discourse with which we describe and discuss psychological phenomena. Then I will discuss the general problem of relationship between motivation and behavior with specific reference to current S-R analysis of behavior. The reason for limiting my discussion to this kind of conceptualization will become obvious later.

THREE MODES OF PSYCHOLOGICAL DISCOURSE

In the analysis of behavior, psychologists, for the most part, have not faced up to the problems created by different modes of discourse with which psychological events are described and discussed. One can describe motivational processes in terms of (1) *conscious feelings of urges,* (2) *physiological conditions of the body,* and (3) *hypothesized environmental-behavioral relationships* (or what some prefer to describe as *inferred behavior determinants*). It can be, and has been, argued that one of these three approaches possesses certain advantages over the others as the starting point for the analysis of motivation. Reasonable arguments can be offered in support of all three orientations, but no method exists, except perhaps the test of history, to decide which approach is superior. I would maintain that the choice among these three alternatives represents a volitional decision (Reichenbach, 1938) and therefore the argument about their relative merits and demerits cannot be resolved by any appeal to truth or validity.

Regardless of the choice made, ultimately, an analysis—and hopefully an integration—of the concept of motivation on all three "levels" would be achieved. But it would be unstrategic, as well as arbitrary, to assume that analysis of motivation with one mode of discourse would provide the same picture of motivation as revealed by analysis with another mode of discourse. To accept a simple isomorphism of this sort would be foolish;

it would essentially prejudge issues instead of solving them. We have seen already in our history the confusions and difficulties encountered when it was assumed that our hunger urge was in some manner isomorphic with the physiology of hunger. Similarly, today we are cognizant of the enormous difficulties of integrating the concept of drive as defined by physiological processes, on the one hand, with environmental conditions, deprivation conditions, and incentives, on the other. Although prescriptions about how to deal with these different levels of discourse are easy to offer and difficult to evaluate, I cannot help but believe that a more cautious approach has advantages over an ambitious effort that tries to integrate in bold but vague terms the motivational components of conscious experience, physiology, and inferred behavior determinants. Perhaps blinders are needed to protect both the researcher and theorist from being seduced by an unmanageable amount of information. This is not to deny the potential goal of a general behavior theory, but instead to warn against the temptation to explain everything before explaining anything.

Again I feel compelled to protect myself against possible misinterpretation. In psychology, even in the absence of requests, we are offered methodological prescriptions that must be observed faithfully. My suggestion that it is legitimate, and perhaps even strategic, to restrict one's efforts to one mode of discourse is not a prescription but an "antiprescription." It argues against two related methodological attitudes that are too willingly and uncritically accepted: (1) the worlds of physiology, phenomenal experience, and inferred behavior determinants are conceptually isomorphic, and (2) the facts of physiology, phenomenal experience, and environmental-behavioral relationships dovetail with each other.

These are not necessarily so! My questioning these two assumptions does not, however, argue against *any* attempt to span the three different modes of psychological discourse. Quite obviously, numerous legitimate and important problems, capable of being investigated, exist between these different areas. One of many examples that can be offered is the work of

Penfield and Roberts (1959), which seeks to relate cortical processes with phenomenal experiences. The fact that such "inter-
discourse" research is possible does not mean that it should serve
as a model for all psychological research and theory.

It has also been argued that if one chooses to approach motivation in terms of a phenomenal, physiological, or environmental-
behavioral approach, the conception formulated should be consistent with the evidence from other approaches. Although
seemingly reasonable, this intellectual gambit has been over-
played for two reasons. The first is that a conception of motivation based, for example, upon an environmental-behavioral analysis can be physiologically and phenomenally neutral, as I will
try to indicate in my analysis of the concept of an S-R association. The second reason is that our knowledge and theories on
one level are not so permanent as to justify the abandonment of
fruitful conceptions because of apparent contradictions that may
well disappear with time. The formulation of a conceptually
consistent interpretation of one kind of data—phenomenal, physiological, or environmental-behavioral—represents a reasonable
aim for the time being.

MOTIVATION, A COMPONENT OF BEHAVIOR

Up to this point I have tried to give an overview of some
important orienting attitudes and methodological considerations
that have complicated our understanding of motivation. Let us
now turn our attention to the fundamental issue of the relationship between motivation and behavior. In dealing with this relationship, I accept two assumptions which should attract universal
assent. The first is that these two terms are not equivalent. Motivation, to me, can be conceived on the empirical level to represent a group of variables (e.g., deprivation conditions) or on the
theoretical level to represent a process (e.g., energizing, steering)
that influences behavior. In either case, there is more to behavior
than motivation; there are nonmotivational variables and there
are nonmotivational processes that are related to behavior. This
leads to the second assumption: Motivation, whether it be conceived as a group of experimental variables or as a theoretical

process, is not *the sole* cause of behavior. I do not think any psychologist today would seriously defend the extreme position that motivation is the sole cause of behavior, but I do get the impression that even though it fails to receive formal recognition, it often operates as a working assumption. The psychoanalytical analysis of behavior tends to view motivation, if not as the sole cause of behavior, at least as the paramount one.

Emphasizing motivation—or perhaps it should be said, over-emphasizing motivation—has typically led to a blurring of the differences between motivational and nonmotivational factors. Maslow's stricture that "sound motivational theory should... assume that motivation is constant, never ending, fluctuating, and complex, and that it is an almost universal characteristic of practically every organismic state of affairs" (1954, p. 69) is an example of a kind of motivational conception which, although not equating the concepts of motivation and behavior, does little to disentangle them.

Failing to consider motivation within some framework of behavior attenuates the meaning and significance of any motivational conception. It fact, it can be argued that many of the confusions surrounding the state of motivational theory stem from the failure of motivational theorists to express their formulations within a clearly defined behavioral structure. While denying that motivation is equivalent to behavior and that motivation is the sole cause of behavior, I am also insisting that a conception of motivation without one of behavior is at best futile and at worst meaningless.

THE STIMULUS-RESPONSE CONCEPTION OF BEHAVIOR

There are many advantages to discussing behavior within a stimulus-response (S-R) framework. I do not see any virtue in arguing in favor of an S-R analysis over other conceptions, since all such arguments, in a certain sense, revolve about rationalizations of one's own predilections. I do, however, perceive a very great need to illuminate the concept of an S-R association. Since my undergraduate days I have heard and read such a wide variety of statements about S-R associationism, pro and con, passionate and dispassionate, that it becomes difficult to see how a student can arrive at a reasonable understanding of this controversial concept. A sound epistemological analysis of this concept will do much to clarify the historical development of experimental psychology over the past four decades.

In order to understand S-R associationism, we must understand its development and philosophical commitments. The origins of S-R associationism are deep in the past, certainly antedating the beginnings of experimental psychology. In fact, one can speculate that associationism had its roots in the phenomenal experience of the people who originally started worrying about how they behaved. Associative events occur frequently in phenomenal experience: we are often reminded of the past by what we experience in the present; we learn new words by associating them with old ones. Perhaps the Greek philosophers' concern with associative processes was an expression of the universality of associative events in phenomenal experience.

Aristotle (1948) suggested that the recall of past events was generated, according to predetermined principles, by a series of associations. These principles which linked the associated events were *similarity, contrast,* and *contiguity*.

The British Associationists, with their introspectively based rationalism, extended and systematized associationism by considering two questions that every associationistic doctrine must cope with. What is associated? How is it associated? *Ideas* was the general answer to the first question, and various combinations of *contiguity, similarity,* and/or *contrast* were the answers offered to the second question.

Associationism was incorporated into an experimental approach to psychology by the Structuralists. With their analytic introspection, they sought "to analyze the structure of mind; to ravel out the elemental processes from the tangle of consciousness ... to isolate the constituents in the given conscious formation" (Titchener, 1898). The basic elements of consciousness for Titchener were *sensations, images,* and *feelings,* and although he did not pay too much attention to the problem of how the elementary events of conscious experience were organized, Titchener concluded that "the law of contiguity can, with a little forcing, be translated into our general law of association" (Titchener, 1910, pp. 378–379).

When psychologists started paying more attention to behavior than to mental events, the problem of what is associated took on new significance. Since early behaviorally oriented psychologists conceptualized their problems within a physiological framework, it is not surprising that the stimulus-response association paradigm was adopted. Reflex physiology illustrated how direct stimulation of certain receptors will trigger motor events. Only one step was needed to project an S-R associationistic framework on behavior, and that step required an experimental technique that would reveal, in an objective fashion, the formation and strengthening of S-R associations. Classical conditioning was that technique. It illustrated how a new association could be formed between an environmental event, represented by the term "conditioned stimulus," and a behavioral event, represented by the term "unconditioned response." In short, conditioning represented the final turn in the historical development of associationism from phenomenal events to objectively defined environmental-behavioral relationships. Although the methodological commitments of behaviorism do not demand a stimulus-response associationism (witness Tolman's purposive behaviorism) the contemporaneity of the early conditioning experiments and the behavioristic revolution ensured the central role which stimulus-response associationism played in the development of behaviorism.

With so many historical antecedents, it is not surprising that S-R associationism cannot be thought of as a simple, unitary conception. Actually, it consists of four major, *relatively* independent components: (1) a technical language, (2) a methodological orientation, (3) a pretheoretical model, and (4) a group of theories. I would like to describe each briefly in order to dispel some widely held misconceptions.

1. The most general interpretation of S-R associationism, and the one I personally favor since it is the least controversial, is that it represents a technical language system, analogous to

notations used to represent moves in a chess game or events in a chemistry laboratory. In relation to this last example, the comments of Toulmin are particularly relevant: "We do not *find* light atomized into individual rays; we represent it as consisting of such rays" (1953, p. 29). Applying the same idea to S-R associationism as a *language* would result in the following statement: "We do not *find* behavior atomized into individual S-R associations; we represent it as consisting of such associations."

The essence of this stimulus-response language is represented by the widely publicized S-R paradigm, which functions, in a limited way, as a model of behavior. Accordingly, there are three important sets of theoretical variables in psychology: stimuli, responses, and the association (the —) between them. The stimulus, which functions as a cue, is defined in terms of some property of the environment.[3] The response refers to some characteristic of behavior. The dash between the S and the R represents some functional relationship between the two, expressed

[3] Any brief definition of the concept *stimulus* must be incomplete and can be misleading. Certainly S-R psychologists are not in complete agreement about the defining characteristics of a *stimulus*. One of the major areas of controversy is whether a stimulus should be defined independently of behavior or in relation to it. I favor the former alternative. In order to achieve the status of an empirical law, an S-R relationship must be stated in terms of two *independently* defined concepts. Both clarity of meaning and elegance of expression are achieved when stimulus and response terms are defined independently. To define them as independent events does not deny that some organisms respond to some stimuli but not to others. A light wave, for example, is a stimulus even though a blind person cannot respond to it. Sensitivity to stimulation is an empirical problem, not a definitional issue. Experimentation determines which stimuli are *effective* in controlling behavior and which are not.

Much of the confusion surrounding the term *stimulus* can be eliminated by distinguishing, as Koch (1954) has done, between stimuli as *experimental independent variables* and as *systematic* (theoretical) *independent variables*. The *conditioned stimulus* (tone) in classical conditioning is an experimental independent variable because it is defined (observed) directly as a property of the environmental situation. The response-produced cue (e.g., s_g), in some mediational sequence, is a systematic independent variable because it is not directly observed but instead is inferred. The working assumption behind designating an inferred event as a *stimulus* is that it possesses functional characteristics similar to a stimulus defined as an experimental independent variable.

either in terms of an empirical relationship or a theoretical concept (e.g., habit).

I would maintain that this language is neutral with regard to the physiological correlates of behavior. It does not imply a telephone-switchboard conception of the nervous system, nor does it rule out associations between sensory areas of the cerebral hemispheres. It merely represents a set of notations that can be used to characterize environmental-behavioral events.

Another point should be made clear in anticipation of future discussion. An S-R linguistic analysis of psychological events does not preclude the inclusion of other theoretical variables in conceptualizing behavior. Although for some theorists (e.g., Guthrie, 1952) the concepts of stimulus, response, and association are sufficient to represent all forms of behavior, for others (e.g., Hull, 1943), additional concepts have to be added.

2. Another way of perceiving stimulus-response associationism is to consider it as a methodological orientation. Although S-R associationists differ about many methodological issues (e.g., the nature of, as well as the need for, theory), they do share a common behavioristic orientation which can be succintly characterized as physicalistic, operational, and experimental (Estes, 1959). Stimulus-response psychologists have a preference for carrying over the goals and accepting the methods of the natural sciences. They aspire to clear-cut operational definitions of the concepts they use. And finally they demand experimental evidence to prove their points—or disprove somebody else's point. Evidence from natural observation, clinical experience, and personal experience is neither convincing nor conclusive and is often viewed with suspicion and distrust.

3. In addition to being conceived as a technical language and a methodological orientation, S-R psychology can be considered as a pretheoretical model. By pretheoretical model I mean an informal conception that operates as an analogy (Lachman, 1960). For example, in my own work in the field of classificatory and problem-solving behavior (Kendler & Kendler, 1962), I have assumed that these complex forms of behavior are in certain ways analogous to responses in simple discrimination situations.

To some extent, an S-R pretheoretical orientation prejudges empirical problems by focusing attention on variables that have been demonstrated to be important in conditioning and selective-learning experimental situations. The merit of such prejudgments can only be ascertained by the fruitfulness of their consequences.

4. The final conception of S-R associationism, and the one that requires the least amount of exposition, is that it represents a group of theories. Anybody who knows anything about the psychology of learning is aware that S-R theorists disagree about a wide variety of topics: the manner of defining a stimulus, the associative process, the nature of the response, etc. If nothing else, their differences of opinion should shatter forever the naïveté of sentences which begin: "S-R theory states...." To consider S-R associationism as one theory, with one set of assumptions, with one set of predictions, is simply a sign of ignorance.

Now to tidy up some loose ends. Who is, and who is not, an S-R psychologist? The answer depends on what characteristic of S-R psychology one is referring to. If we consider S-R associationism as a technical language system, then we shall have to draw the apparently trivial conclusion that an S-R psychologist is one who uses S-R language. Actually, the conclusion is not trivial. Although the Whorfian hypothesis which assumes that thinking is shaped by the language of the user is open to question, it does seem to have some validity when applied to the current psychological scene. The technical language system used by a psychologist has a strong impact on the manner in which he structures psychological phenomena. Stimulus-response language *forces* its user to analyze behavior into stimulus, response, and associative components. The resulting analysis is strikingly different from the one that a psychoanalytic or Gestalt language system would generate.

If we view S-R associationism as a methodological orientation, then we shall be forced to identify some psychologists as S-R psychologists even though they never use the language system. Tolman (1932) not only can be classified as an S-R methodologist, but also must be recognized as one of the most powerful forces in converting rigid Watsonian behaviorism into a more liberal, sophisticated neobehaviorism—in spite of the fact that S-R language was, to him, an anathema.[4]

MOTIVATION AND S-R ASSOCIATIONISM

The adoption of a stimulus-response language to represent psychological events does not involve any particular motivational assumptions. Many alternatives exist. One radical treatment is to deny its theoretical significance by assuming that the concepts of stimulus, response, and association are sufficient to explain behavior (Guthrie, 1952; Estes, 1958) without reference to any concept of motivation with unique properties. Such an assumption, it should be clear, does not deny either the phenomenal experience or the physiological correlates of hunger. It merely represents an attempt to systematize behavioral phenomena associated with hunger. There are no compelling reasons to deny the possibility that different physiological events, such as the stimulation of the eye by light waves and the biochemical correlates of food deprivation, can have similar functional properties in a behavioral analysis.

Aside from the broad generalities of Guthrie's analysis of behavior, the conceptualization of motivation as exclusively a stimulus process has for the most part been limited to a narrow range of experimental phenomena. The S-R psychologists who have tried to cope with a wider variety of experimental phenomena, including the so-called "acquired drives," have felt compelled to add motivational concepts onto the S-R framework.

[4] The distinction between S-R associations as a *language* and a *pretheoretical model* can be clarified at this point. Although S-R language helps to analyze psychological phenomena into stimulus, response, and associative events, it does not suggest any necessary relationships between them. For example, an S-R contiguity theorist, when analyzing some novel phenomenon, might very well make the same linguistic analysis, in the sense of identifying the stimulus, response, and associative components, as would an S-R reinforcement theorist, but the pretheoretical model they would apply would determine how they explained it. The S-R contiguity theorist would emphasize the importance of the cues which occurred contiguously with the response, while the S-R reinforcement theorist, in addition, would stress the conditions of reinforcement that followed the response.

The two most important concepts are *drive* and *drive stimulus*. It is important to recognize that these two concepts have emerged primarily from an analysis of the effects of food deprivation on behavior in instrumental-conditioning and selective-learning situations (Hull, 1933; Leeper, 1935; Perin, 1942). The theoretical analysis of the behavior exhibited in these experiments has served as a model for other behavior. *Drive* has been conceptualized as an energizer that operates upon the association between a stimulus and a response. *Drive stimulus* has been conceptualized as a cue that can become associated to instrumental responses. These two concepts have been described functionally as the energizing and steering attributes of motivation. This simple motivational model of drive as an energizer and as a cue has been extended to a variety of situations with experimental operations quite different from those used with food deprivation. The acquired fear drive (Miller, 1948), incentive motivation (Spence, 1956), frustration drive (Amsel, 1958), and emotional drive (Spence, 1956; Taylor, 1951) are all examples of the energizing conception of drive being applied to new sets of phenomena. The strategy behind these extensions is both simple and widely used. A new phenomenon is conceptualized *as if* it obeyed the principles of an old one. Such an assumption does not deny the possibility of other reasonable or perhaps even potentially superior conceptions. But these extensions do at least raise a challenge that other formulations must meet: viz., a "motivational" explanation must be couched in a behavioral framework. In some manner, a motivational process, no matter how important one believes it is, must possess a behavioral consequence. I feel compelled to point out once again that the "validity" of the hypothesized energizing effect of food deprivation, fear, incentives, frustration, and manifest anxiety is not to be denied by an absence of any physiological mechanism common to all five events or, for that matter, a similarity among the phenomenal experiences they produce. The energizing conception of drive is offered to account for environmental-behavioral relationships and it should be evaluated in terms of how well it does its job.

PROBLEMS OF MOTIVATION
WITHIN A STIMULUS-RESPONSE FRAMEWORK

Conceptualizing behavior in terms of stimulus-response associations offers a wide latitude of motivational interpretations. No one conceptualization is demanded by the nature of the language system. Nevertheless, there are goals of empirical generality and logical consistency to strive for. I would like to consider some of the obstacles and problems associated with reaching these objectives.

The Independence of Motivational and
Nonmotivational Concepts

Drive as an energizer is assumed to operate on the associative connection between a stimulus and response. Conceptually, the meaning of drive as an energizer is clear; operationally, it can be ambiguous. Experimental manipulations that presumably affect the strength of a drive can influence stimulus and associative processes. When a single experimental operation has multiple theoretical consequences, it becomes difficult to disentangle their independent influences. For example, the size of food in the goal box of a T maze can have stimulus (cue), associative (habit), and motivational (drive) consequences. A large piece of food, contrasted with a small one, will produce, according to neobehavioristic theory (Spence, 1956), a more vigorous anticipatory goal response (r_g). This has three consequences: the large-reward group will develop more distinctive cues $(s_g\text{'s})$ at the choice point, a stronger drive (by increasing K, *incentive motivation*), and a stronger anticipatory goal-response habit. Although all of these factors would enhance the performance of the large-reward group, the exact contribution of each factor could not be identified. Some of these individual contributions can be teased out by clever experimental designs, but at the present time it would be the height of theoretical devotion to believe that the major motivational and nonmotivational assumptions of neobehavioristic theory are separate and distinct. Although this logical inadequacy has led some to become disenchanted with this approach, I would like to offer the observation that those who have tried to avoid similar difficulties have chosen to eschew theory or to deal with a more limited range of phenomena. These comments are offered, not to deny the importance of the logical independence of the primary assumptions in a theory of behavior, but, instead, to emphasize the difficulties and hardships in developing a general theory of behavior.

I will not hazard a guess about how the problem of the independence of the motivational and nonmotivational assumptions will be solved. I suspect that the problem will even become more difficult when serious consideration is given to the possibility that in addition to activating the stimulus-response association, motivation can perhaps energize behavior by lowering stimulus thresholds (Fuster, 1958) and by facilitating response evocation (e.g., Amsel, 1958). But whatever difficulties confront the behavior theorist, the goal should remain clear: motivational processes must be operationally distinguishable from nonmotivational processes.

A Motivational Unit of Behavior

Muenzinger argues in favor of adopting a descriptive unit of behavior involving a motivational sequence. He suggests that an appropriate unit of description is the start-to-end unit, a unit that is characterized by a starting-phase, a constant direction, and an end-phase. Illustrative of such a start-to-end unit would be the behavior of a hungry organism moving toward food: "The beginning of the movement, the stage where hunger initiates food-seeking, we may call the *starting-phase*, and the eating of the food, the *end-phase* of this particular cycle of his behavior" (1939, p. 21).

A stimulus-response association differs in two major ways from Muenzinger's start-to-end unit. First, although essentially representing a unit of behavior, a stimulus-response association does not necessarily possess a motivational component. Second, a stimulus-response association can, and often does, represent an isolated component of behavior without reference to what the organism has just been doing or will be doing. A classical conditioned response is often described in such a disembodied way.

The distinction between Muenzinger's start-to-end behavioral unit and S-R associations was not discussed in order to evaluate their relative merits. Both serve a useful purpose. A fine-grain analysis of discrete classical conditioned responses has supplied much information about the formation and strengthening of individual S-R associations. An extended behavioral analysis as suggested by Muenzinger, and actually used by many S-R psychologists (e.g., Miller's analysis of conflict behavior, 1959), provides insights into principles governing the sequential organization (chaining) of successive S-R associations. This kind of extended analysis in S-R psychology is *often* overlooked, and as a consequence, important motivational factors are ignored. In this connection, it is interesting to note that very little work has been done relating motivational variables to cognitive processes. Perhaps this state reflects our intuitive feeling that motivational processes interfere with problem-solving behavior, a feeling that does have some basis in fact (e.g., Glucksberg, 1962). But in my opinion, one of the most important factors in cognitive behavior is the motivation that directs people to try to solve a problem or encourages them to escape from such challenges. It is possible to distinguish between *intellectual ability* and *intellectual activity*, the former referring to the intellectual capacity of an individual and the latter, a motivational-type concept, referring to an individual's tendency to indulge in intellectual behavior. In experimental situations designed to investigate problem-solving behavior, we do not typically offer the subject any alternative but to cooperate with the experimenter by attempting to solve the problem. The experimental situation does not possess the temporal extensity that exists in everyday intellectual activities. One reason why motivational factors have not proved to be of great importance in intellectual problems is simply because we have sampled, for the most part, a very narrow range. If we desire to understand more about the relationship between motivation and cognitive processes, then we must devise experimental situations in which subjects are given a choice of avoiding or participating in intellectual activities. The degree of importance of motivation in cognitive activites may very well be related to our success in coping with larger start-to-end behavioral units.

Primary and Secondary Drives

The distinction between primary and secondary drives has caused much confusion and controversy, partly because of the tendency to discuss each with a different mode of discourse. Typically, a primary drive, often described as a physiological or unlearned drive, is defined in terms of such physiological conditions as tissue deficits or physiochemical states. A secondary drive, sometimes referred to as an acquired or learned drive, is considered to be a product of learning. Although obvious, the following two points need mentioning.

First, if assigning motivational characteristics to both primary and secondary drives is to have any meaning, then they must share some common conceptual property. In neobehavioristic theory, both primary and secondary drives have both energizing and cue properties. Second, both primary and secondary drives must have physiological underpinnings. Because the physiological properties of primary drives have been stressed while those of the secondary drives have been ignored, it would be unfortunate to consider a secondary drive as nonphysiological. Quite obviously, learning has physiological correlates, although we are not quite sure what they are. The only meaningful way to differentiate between primary and secondary drives *on the physiological level* is to specify the different *kinds* of physiological events to which each is correlated.

The distinction between primary and secondary drives is clear enough when this simple two-category classification is applied to the differences between hunger, thirst, and sex, on the one hand, and learned fear, on the other. This categorical division becomes strained, however, when we try to force other kinds of drives into the same mold. For example, the curiosity drive (Berlyne, 1955) or the manipulatory drive (Harlow, Blazek, & McClearn, 1956) must not necessarily fit into one or the other of these two categories. The physiological correlates of such drives do not necessarily have to be the same as the life-maintaining or life-reproducing physiological mechanisms of hunger, thirst, or sex or the learned physiological correlates of the fear drive. Conceivably, they *could* have physiological correlates similar in some respects to hunger, thirst, sex, or fear, but I am arguing they do not *have* to. One possibility is that the curiosity, manipulatory, and similar drives are dependent upon certain kinds of past experiences, but not of the types that fit our conventional learning paradigms, as is the case for some forms of instinctive behavior. Eibl-Eibesfeldt (1955, 1956) reports that female rats who failed to develop an attachment to any particular place in their cage failed to build nests during pregnancy, even though nest-building material was available to them.

Secondary drives have been distinguished from primary drives on the basis that the former are aroused by external stimuli. Such a distinction is questionable at best. Certainly an analysis of behavior in terms of an environmental-behavioral relationship indicates that even primary drives, such as hunger and sex, can be aroused by stimuli external to the organism. Perhaps it can be argued that secondary drives can *only* be aroused by external stimuli but primary drives do not have to be.

My conclusion, after this brief discussion of the distinction between primary and secondary drives, is that at present the classification is confused because a primary drive is largely defined in terms of physiological events while a secondary drive is defined by environmental-behavioral relationships. An adequate classification of drives will have to include *for each drive* the environmental-behavioral relationships associated with its development within the maturing organism as well as its physiological correlates. And probably other factors will have to be included in the classificatory schema. In any case, the simple two-category classification of drives, primary *versus* secondary or physiological *versus* acquired, has outlived its usefulness.

SUMMARY

I have tried, in a detached and distant but not disinterested way, to offer an overview of the relationship between motivation and behavior.

Our thinking about motivation has been influenced by the presence of a motivational-reward model of behavior that is implicit in our everyday language. The pervasiveness of this model does not justify its acceptance or rejection. If it possesses any degree of validity—and I believe it does—then the problem becomes one of refining it to meet the standards of science. In order to accomplish this, it is necessary to realize that psychological events, such as motivational processes, can be described in three ways: phenomenal, physiological, and environmental-behavioral. The choice of which mode of discourse one should use to represent psychological events represents an example of a volitional decision.

An analysis of motivation, regardless of the mode of discourse which is used, must be presented within some behavioral framework. I have suggested that one possible behavioral framework is represented by stimulus-response (S-R) associationism. An epistemological analysis of S-R associationism reveals four major components: (1) a technical language system that represents environmental-behavioral events and is both physiologically and phenomenally neutral, (2) a methodological orientation that is essentially behavioristic, (3) a pretheoretical model, and (4) a group of theories.

The adoption of an S-R language to represent psychological events does not involve any particular motivational assumptions. Some S-R theorists believe that no special motivational concepts are required, since motivational factors can be represented adequately by stimulus processes. Others believe that it is necessary to conceptualize motivation in terms of both energizing and steering functions. Both of these S-R conceptions, motivation as a stimulus and motivation as an energizer and cue, have to be evaluated in terms of their adequacy to account for environmental-behavioral relationships and not physiological and phenomenal events.

Three major problems of a motivational theory within an S-R framework were discussed. These were (1) the independence of motivational and nonmotivational concepts, (2) a motivational unit of behavior, and (3) the distinction between primary and secondary drives.

REFERENCES

Amsel, A. The role of frustrative nonreward in noncontinuous reward situations. *Psychol. Bull.*, 1958, **55**, 102–119.

Aristotle. On memory and recollection. In W. Dennis (Ed.), *Readings in the history of psychology*. New York: Appleton-Century-Crofts, 1948.

Berlyne, D. E. The arousal and satiation of perceptual curiosity in the rat. *J. comp. physiol. Psychol.*, 1955, **48**, 238–247.

Eibl-Eibesfeldt, I. Angeborenes und Erworbenes im Nestbauverhalten der Wanderatte. *Naturwissenschaften*, 1955, **42**, 633–634.

Eibl-Eibesfeldt, I. Fortschritte der vergleichenden Verhaltensforschung. *Naturw. Rdsch.*, 1956, **86–90**, 136–142.

Estes, W. K. Stimulus-response theory of drive. In M. R. Jones (Ed.), *Nebraska Symposium on Motivation: 1958*. Lincoln: Univ. of Nebraska Press, 1958.

Estes, W. K. The statistical approach to learning theory. In S. Koch (Ed.), *Psychology: a study of a science*. Vol. 2. New York: McGraw-Hill, 1959. Pp. 380–491.

Fuster, J. M. Effects of stimulation of brain stem on tachistoscopic perception. *Science*, 1958, **127**, 150.

Glucksberg, S. The influence of strength of drive on functional fixedness and perceptual recognition. *J. exp. Psychol.*, 1962, **63**, 36–41.

Guthrie, E. R. *The psychology of learning*. New York: Harper & Row, 1952.

Harlow, H. F., Blazek, N. C., & McClearn, G. E. Manipulatory motivation in the infant rhesus monkey. *J. comp. physiol. Psychol.*, 1956, **49**, 444–448.

Hull, C. L. Differential habituation to internal stimuli in the albino rat. *J. comp. Psychol.*, 1933, **16**, 255–273.

Hull, C. L. *Principles of behavior*. New York: Appleton-Century-Crofts, 1943.

Kendler, H. H. *Basic psychology*. New York: Appleton-Century-Crofts, 1963.

Kendler, H. H., & Kendler, T. S. Vertical and horizontal processes in problem solving. *Psychol. Rev.*, 1962, **69**, 1–16.

Koch, S. Clark L. Hull. In W. K. Estes, S. Koch, K. MacCorquodale, P. E. Meehl, C. G. Mueller, Jr., W. S. Schoenfeld, & W. S. Verplanck, *Modern learning theory*. New York: Appleton-Century-Crofts, 1954.

Lachman, R. The model in theory construction. *Psychol. Rev.*, 1960, **67**, 113–129.

Leeper, R. W. The role of motivation in learning: a study of the phenomenon of differential motivational control of the utilization of habits. *J. genet. Psychol.*, 1935, **46**, 3–40.

Maslow, A. H. *Motivation and personality*. New York: Harper, 1954.

Miller, N. E. Studies of fear as an acquirable drive: I. Fear as motivation and fear-reduction as reinforcement in the learning of new responses. *J. exp. Psychol.*, 1948, 38, 89–101.

Miller, N. E. Liberalization of basic S-R concepts: extensions to conflict behavior, motivation, and social learning. In S. Koch (Ed.), *Psychology: a study of a science*. Vol. 2. New York: McGraw-Hill, 1959. Pp. 196–292.

Muenzinger, K. F. *Psychology: the science of behavior.* New York: Harper, 1939.

Penfield, W., & Roberts, L. *Speech and brain-mechanisms.* Princeton: Princeton Univ. Press, 1959.

Perin, C. T. Behavior potentiality as a joint function of the amount of training and the degree of hunger at the time of extinction. *J. exp. Psychol.*, 1942, 30, 93–103.

Reichenbach, H. R. *Experience and prediction.* Chicago: Univ. of Chicago Press, 1938.

Scriven, M. Views of human nature. In T. W. Wann (Ed.), *Behaviorism and phenomenology.* Chicago: Univ. of Chicago Press, 1964.

Spence, K. W. *Behavior theory and conditioning.* New Haven: Yale Univ. Press, 1956.

Taylor, J. A. The relationship of anxiety to the conditioned eyelid response. *J. exp. Psychol.*, 1951, 41, 81–92.

Titchener, E. B. The postulates of a structural psychology. *Phil. Rev.*, 1898, 7, 449–465.

Titchener, E. B. *Text-book of psychology.* New York: Macmillan, 1910.

Tolman, E. C. *Purposive behavior in animals and men.* New York: Appleton-Century-Crofts, 1932.

Toulmin, S. *The philosophy of science.* London: Hutchinson Univ. Library, 1953.

Warnock, G. J. *English philosophy since 1900.* London: Oxford Univ. Press, 1958.

Some Needed Developments in the Motivational Theory of Emotions

ROBERT WARD LEEPER

University of Oregon

This whole paper will center on the question "What is the nature of emotions (or, as I would prefer to say, of emotional processes)?" I assume that this is not only an appropriate but also a basic psychological problem, provided we respect certain cautions that Howard Kendler presented in a paper before the New York Academy of Sciences in 1950. Kendler entitled his paper " 'What Is Learned?'—A Theoretical Blind Alley." This title seems to suggest that Kendler was denouncing any attempts to develop concepts about intervening variables or mediating processes. Actually, however, the theme of his paper was that any effort to determine the nature of some psychological factor or process is a blind alley only when we imagine that we can learn about the nature of such factors or processes *as such*. When we develop constructs about the nature of any factor or process, Kendler said, we need to remember that "the only function they serve is . . . the economical description of the known empirical relationships, and the prediction of new phenomena" (1950, pp. 74–75). These are two fairly important functions, of course. Hence, despite the seemingly sweeping condemnation of constructs about intervening variables expressed by Kendler's title at that time, we presumably can stay on safe ground in the quest that follows, provided we are careful.

Another clarification should be given before we proceed further. What I mean by "emotions" or "emotional processes" is not what I assume is meant by "emotional behavior" by psychologists such as Bindra (1955, 1959) and Duffy (1962), who prefer to make this their key term. I assume that by "emotional behavior" such authors mean the effector activities and the overt interactions with the environment that occur when organisms are afraid, angry, playful, and so on. If that is the meaning they intend, emotional processes as I want to discuss them are not "emotional behavior," but are the processes that lie back of such publicly observable phenomena. They are processes that have a physiological character, of course, as I assume all psychological processes have. In some cases, too, they are conscious processes and can be studied partly through subjective reports; in other cases, I assume, they are identifiable only by inference from objective data. In either type of case, they are mediating processes rather than something that is directly observable by objective means.

With regard to such emotional processes, the main ideas of the discussion which follows will be these:

1. In the development of concepts in any field, the concepts that develop first tend to be those dealing with relatively palpable factors and relationships. Even when scientific work starts from the previous concepts developed in everyday life, it begins with a stress on palpable material. Indeed, the early work in any science may accentuate such palpabilistic tendencies because of the difficulties, originally, of explicit concepts and of empirical research dealing with anything other than such relatively palpable factors and relationships.

2. Both within prescientific thinking and within scientific work, there are some other factors, however, that favor a development of concepts about less palpable factors as well.

3. The development of any science has to come partly through learning to deal with highly impalpable factors as well as with the factors with which its work tended to start. The impalpable factors are often among the most powerful factors, practically speaking, and they are often among the most significant factors, theoretically or scientifically speaking.

4. The history of concepts about emotional processes illustrates the above propositions. Both in prescientific thought and within the early development of psychology, there have been

very strong tendencies to develop and emphasize merely those concepts about emotions that were suggested by relatively palpable factors and relationships. There also have been some lines of thought derived from less palpable material as well. In consequence, the conceptions about emotional processes have been a conglomeration of strikingly contradictory propositions.

5. Our thinking about such problems can be helped by various metatheoretical and heuristic principles, however, such as, particularly, the need to deal in science with hierarchical conceptual systems rather than in dichotomies in which emphasis is placed merely on differences in properties of different sets of phenomena.

6. Using such principles to help us, we can eventually see that (a) emotional processes are a part of a larger continuum of motivational processes and, indeed, are unusually important motives in higher species, and (b) emotions or emotional processes, along with other motives, ought not to continue to be seen as some lower-level processes as compared with perceptual or representational processes. Instead, they need to be seen as a part of a larger continuum which ranges from motivationally neutral representational processes at one end to motivationally very powerful representational processes at the other end of the continuum.

7. Such altered concepts about emotional processes have the value, not only of organizing efficiently what we now know about emotions, but also of opening out a whole series of important implications regarding both the determinants and the effects of emotional processes in the lives of relatively complex organisms.

WHAT BASIC CONCEPTS ABOUT EMOTIONS HAVE DEVELOPED IN THE PAST, AND WHY

Any survey of current writing about emotion is certain to impress us with the great differences of opinion that now prevail regarding the nature and influences of emotional processes. Furthermore, these differences do not come merely from differences of focus of interest within the total area of emotion. Many of them are differences between basically contradictory conceptions about emotions. Great is the confusion and chaos that prevails in this part of psychology. It behooves us, therefore, to proceed with special care when we undertake, in this paper, to examine the basic theoretical problems of this field.

Palpabilistic Trends in Thinking About Emotions

The general tendency toward palpabilistic conceptions on all matters.—To help us re-examine the basic theories of emotion, our approach might well be through some historical analysis. As Howard Kendler has said in his paper in the present symposium, psychologists did not originate most of the basic concepts that they use with regard to motivation. Instead, they came on a scene where a whole host of concepts already had been developed. He vividly described our situation: "Our ordinary language system reeks of motivational concepts. . . . No matter what their theoretical bent, psychologists find it difficult to escape from [the] frame of reference [set by such traditional motivational concepts]."

This statement about motivation also applies to our concepts about emotion. Psychologists came on a scene where concepts about emotions were already rife. They inherited a whole gamut of principles woven into the very texture of our culture. There is a serious probability that this heritage may have been affecting our supposedly technical thinking about emotion more than we have realized. Accordingly, it may be wise for us to start our discussion some distance back, rather than beginning with current discussions of emotions. Indeed, there may be some real gains through starting, not with the problem of how concepts about emotions developed, but with a more general consideration of how knowledge or concepts develop in human history as a whole.

It seems quite certain that knowledge or understanding develops at quite different rates on different matters. For instance, according to the physical anthropologists, the use of fire goes back at least to ancient Peking man, about a quarter of a million years ago. But even though ancient man must often have had difficulty finding food adapted to his needs, it was not until about fifteen thousand years ago, perhaps, that people learned that they could decide what plants would grow in a particular area, and thus got the basis for a settled agriculture. Only at the beginning of the present century was it learned that malaria and yellow fever are caused, not by swamp air, but by the transmission of these diseases from one person to another by mosquitoes, so that these diseases could be controlled by eliminating breeding sites for these insects. And beyond that, in our own day it seems all too clear that we still have not learned how to deal with problems of war and peace and that, indeed, mankind generally has not come to view these problems as calling for careful research and disciplined thinking such as we respect so highly on technological problems and in the areas of natural science.

What are the reasons for such inequalities in the rate at which knowledge develops on different matters? Is it merely a matter of chance? Perhaps in part. But if we can locate some principles that would account systematically for such differences of timing, this would restrict the degree to which we would credit such unevenness to chance factors. Is the unevenness due to factors of motivation and reward? Does knowledge proceed most rapidly with those questions where there are urgent practical needs for some better understanding? We can get some evidence of this influence, of course. But the surprising thing is that early knowledge in any field of study is so frequently concerned with matters of little practical significance. Modern medical research, for example, started with the careful studies of human anatomy that Vesalius published in 1543, not with studies of such urgent medical problems as those of smallpox, scurvy, typhus, cholera, diphtheria, Saint Anthony's fire, or rickets. Experimental work on psychological problems started with studies of reaction time, psychophysical judgments, sensory perception, and rote memorizing. One could hardly claim that these problems were chosen for study because of some strong social demand for work in these areas.

Are the differences of timing due to a need for prior development of certain other knowledge which would lay the basis for further discoveries? We can think of examples of this. There are certainly various parts of knowledge that required the prior development of specialized tools and techniques such as optical or electron microscopes, methods of spectrographic analysis, or special mathematical techniques. But this is not the whole story, surely. It would have required no technical knowledge of chemistry to have discovered more quickly that the use of unpolished brown rice could prevent or cure the terrible disease of beriberi in the Orient. Similarly, a knowledge of bacteria might have helped physicians to discover more quickly the causes of puerperal or childbed fever, which sometimes cost the lives of up to 30 per cent of the women who came to the hospitals of the early 1800's to give birth to their infants. But this knowledge was not indispensable, because Ignatz Semmelweiss solved the practical problem in the 1840's, decades before the work of Pasteur and Koch. His explanation was partly fanciful, because he came to believe that such cases were due to "blood poisoning" carried by physicians from one woman to another. He had come to realize that childbed fever occurred in cases where physicians had first conducted autopsies on the bodies of women who had died of childbed fever and had then gone, without careful cleaning of their hands, to make pelvic examinations of other women who were in labor in the maternity wards. His explanation was fanciful, but it was sufficient, nevertheless, to help him virtually to eradicate this problem in a hospital where there had been several thousand deaths from this cause in preceding years. It is interesting to note that Semmelweiss' term "blood poisoning" still persists in our speech despite the more sophisticated knowledge we now have about the causal factors involved. The term is a monument to his demonstration that important and practically valuable knowledge often can be developed even in the absence of other knowledge that would facilitate such discoveries.

What other factors do we have to take into account, then, if the above-mentioned factors do not furnish a sufficient explanation of why some conceptions develop before others? If we survey a considerable range of historical data, I believe we can come to the conclusion that the following factors are also very important.

In brief, we may summarize them by saying that knowledge tends to develop first on relatively palpable matters. This summary statement cannot mean very much until it is translated into some more specific and testable propositions, but we can at least formulate the following four principles:

1. Concepts tend to develop more quickly regarding those objects or events where (a) the objects or events are relatively tangible—that is, directly perceptible rather than knowable only inferentially (and perhaps tangible also in the sense that they are attention-commanding, as would be true of a forest fire or an eclipse of the sun or the symptoms of smallpox), (b) there are close temporal relationships between the directly perceptible causes and effects, and (c) the effects are highly invariable either in a purely cyclical sense, as with eclipses, or in the causal relationship between a particular observable cause and a particular observable effect.

These factors of relative tangibility, close temporal relationships of observable causes and effects, and high invariability are, as a group, what I mean by palpable factors. Their influence might be illustrated by many different examples. Thus, old Neanderthal man probably knew that mosquitoes produce the little bumps we call mosquito bites. The three above-mentioned factors should have helped him grasp this relationship. But the relationship of mosquito bites to malaria remained a mystery until the twentieth century. In this case, the mosquitoes are tangible enough, and the disease of malaria is tangible, not, merely in some minor sense, but also in an attention-commanding sense. But only mosquitoes of certain species transmit malaria or yellow fever and then only if they have previously drawn blood from an infected person. So there is no high invariability in the relationship between the directly perceptible causes and effects. Even so, the responsibility could have been pinpointed if the malaria had developed almost immediately, as does the pain from touching a burning ember.

Many other examples could be given. But this is not a treatise on the history of science, so I shall leave it to the reader to decide whether this first principle seems reasonable and move on to several other propositions.

2. When scientific work starts in any subject area, these same factors of tangibility, close temporal relationships, and high invariability tend to operate in this scientific work, just as they did in earlier prescientific thinking, and tend to decide what problems are worked on first and what theoretical interpretations get developed first. Scientific work does not start with factors and relationships mainly on the basis of their practical significance nor on the basis of their ultimate theoretical interest. Scientific work more or less necessarily starts with what is manageable, both experimentally and conceptually. Thus, physics started with mechanics, modern medicine with anatomy, embryology with anatomical developments rather than with chemical embryology, psychopathology with the study of psychoses and then with hysteria rather than with defective patterns of interpersonal relationships.

3. Both within everyday thought and within scientific thinking, a further factor tends to increase the extent to which conceptions get developed around those factors that are relatively tangible, relatively close temporally, and relatively invariable. Whatever perception or conception gets developed first will tend to obstruct the development of other perceptions or conceptions which, except for the prior developments of thought, might readily have developed from further empirical observations.

In other words, an effect occurs in complex thought which has been demonstrated in simpler sensory perceptions, as by the research of Anna Douglas (1947) and Bruner and Potter (1964). These investigators asked their subjects to try to identify pictures of ordinary objects and scenes, starting with very brief tachistoscopic exposures for each picture and then gradually increasing the exposure time on successive trials. Under these circumstances, the subjects frequently formed perceptual organizations with the brief exposures and then, even when these original "perceptual hypotheses" were seriously erroneous, found difficulty in escaping from these, even on later trials where the exposure time ought to have made correct perceptions very easy.

In their discussions of the history of science, both Conant (1947) and Kuhn (1962) have emphasized the principle that scientific thought shows this same obstructing influence. It took a very long time, for instance, before the concept could be revised that some continuing external force must be operating on a body if its motion is to continue. This conception was based, of course, on some reasonable observations, such as that a wagon will stop moving on level ground if the horse stops pulling. But this conception kept physicists from using other reasonable observations that might easily have suggested the contrary view which Galileo finally developed. For, after all, it was also common knowledge that, after the same initial push, an object would slide much farther over a smooth floor or over an expanse of ice than it would slide over some dry earth. It therefore seems rather puzzling that it took so long before the older conception of continued motion as due to external forces was replaced by the concept that movement would continue except as *diminished* by external forces. Puzzling, however, only if we disregard the principle that the achievement of any new conception is likely to be much more difficult if it requires a drastic reorganization of a conception already developed on the basis of more palpable factors.

4. A fourth factor also seems to contribute to any continued emphasis on relatively tangible factors, etc.—to wit, many people have learned proclivities favoring relatively palpable factors. There is a great deal of worthwhile knowledge that deals with the highly tangible factors in the world. A focus on such material has a facilitating effect in the early development of any science. Hence, it should not be at all surprising that some persons should develop strong predispositions for believing that any problems that still defy prediction and control must ultimately prove understandable in terms of relatively tangible factors. It should not be surprising that some persons get the enduring conviction that any thinking that is "really rigorous," etc., will deal only with factors and methods of study of the sort that yields big returns in the early period of any science's development.

In the preceding four points, we have recognized only some

of the factors that tend to govern the earlier conceptions of any subject matter. The account is incomplete because it disregards certain other factors that tend to produce some other conceptions that take relatively impalpable factors and relationships into account, too. Before we consider those, however, let us see what kinds of conceptions about emotions would have tended to develop out of the factors which we have examined thus far.

Palpabilistic thinking in prescientific thinking about emotions.—If the earliest conceptions about emotions tended to be governed by such factors as we have described above, we might expect several consequences, as follows:

First of all, if emotional processes can operate either consciously or unconsciously, it could be expected that early conceptions of emotions would be phrased solely in terms of emotions that are clearly conscious. Such conscious experiences are not palpable or tangible in the root meaning of either of these words, because they are not something that can be touched or explored tactually. But in the sense that developed from that original meaning, such conscious experiences are relatively tangible. They can be experienced directly, just as negative after-images can be, rather than having to be known inferentially, as proactive and retroactive inhibitions must be. And, in fact, this is what the popular tradition about emotional processes has assumed—that emotions definitely are always conscious experiences.

Second, we would expect that attention would focus more naturally on very intense emotions rather than on any milder version. Even if there is some continuing emotional activity of a mild sort that provides the basis for all of a person's ordinary life activities, we would not expect that such milder processes would be emphasized or even recognized by prescientific conceptions of personality or of emotion. And, in fact, the popular thinking about emotions generally has concerned merely the stronger emotional processes.

Third, with such an emphasis on strong emotional processes, we might have anticipated, too, that the main emotions that would be used as paradigms in everyday thought would be such emotions as fear, anger, and grief, which are particularly capable of appearing in spectacularly strong forms. This meant that emotions came to be conceived of primarily in terms of the negative or aversive emotions. There were also some positive emotional processes that would have been emphasized, like joy over some surprising good fortune and like "falling in love." But the positive emotions are less related to crisis situations, and the emphasis on intense emotional reactions naturally focused attention on the negative emotions as the paradigms.

Fourth, some of the effects of emotions which are most palpable, furthermore, are the reflex effects that occur, particularly with strong emotional processes. Such things as trembling, dilated pupils, and paling of the face are easily observed. In order to make clear that I am not unattentive to such effects, I might mention an experience I had when I presented my first paper at a scientific meeting—to a group of about twenty-five psychologists at the Kansas Academy of Science in 1931. I could tell, when my paper was coming due, that I was somewhat nervous. I took out my watch and timed my pulse. It was going 165 a minute, which I assure you is much more than I usually can muster. In a case like that, it would be hard for a person to judge how the fear reactions were affecting the more complex phases of his thinking and behavior, but it is easy to tell that there are some unusual autonomic effects. And the popular tradition about emotion from time immemorial has placed marked emphasis on such effects.

Fifth, insofar as emotions were seen as producing effects on the behavior of the individual, the most palpable effects were the greater intensity and duration of relatively primitive sorts of behavior. People were more apt to engage in physical combat when they were angry and were more apt to fight in reckless, strenuous fashion. Such things were easy to recognize. Emotions, therefore, came to be thought of partly as processes that tended to make people engage in relatively primitive reactions rather than in more sophisticated or culturally elaborated ways.

Sixth, another relatively palpable effect of strong emotions was their frequent role in producing attitudes or behavior at odds with people's social responsibilities. Fears could obviously keep soldiers from doing "what they were supposed to do." The stirring up of various other emotions could help produce lynchings, pogroms, bitter religious persecutions, social movements like the Nazi and Fascist movements, "anti-intellectualism," and the like. Particularly as the Western world developed into a more complex technological and scientifically oriented culture, a contrast tended to be drawn increasingly between emotions, on the one hand, and intelligent, rational, well-adjusted intellectual functioning, on the other. The modern world called for persons who could be counted on to do things "by the clock"—in disciplined, standardized ways consistent with objective criteria. Only in this way could the social group have the advantage of highly developed technical skills and a high degree of specialization and interdependence. Emotional processes seemed alien to such functioning, and people came to set emotion and intellectual processes as the antitheses of each other. "I was too mad to think straight." "I knew what I ought to do, but my emotions got the better of me." "He's too emotional to be counted on." Such everyday expressions are symptomatic of the view that developed.

Cast in more abstract terms, the conception of emotions that developed was that of rationalism. Basically, this was the conception that man is properly *Homo sapiens*—the *knowing* creature. According to the rationalistic interpretation, human nature is most fittingly represented by rational, intellectual processes such as are involved in our clearest reasoning processes. Immanuel Kant, for example, argued that any generous or kindly act performed because the person felt affection or friendliness or sympathy for the other person was not truly an ethical act. Ethical acts, according to Kant, are only those that arise out of a consideration of broad rational principles.

This rationalistic view also recognized that human beings have some deep "animal passions" that tend to prevent people from living and acting as they should. But these are destructive forces. The hope of achieving a stable, prosperous, peaceful world, according to the rationalist view, depends on finding means of curbing and minimizing the emotional elements of life and on replacing them with the calm, cool, dispassionate life of reason. The jealousy of an Othello, the emotional turmoils of a Hamlet, or the terrible ambitions and sense of guilt of a Lady Macbeth might be interesting fare for a Shakespeare or a Dostoevski or a Verdi, but such dramatic materials were seen as portraying the forces that threatened disaster to individual persons and to society rather than as illustrating something required as a constructive basis for civilized living.

Palpabilistic elements in scientific thinking about emotions.— Psychologists tend to emphasize the "great contrasts" between everyday thought, on the one hand, and the "scientifically based concepts" of their own field, on the other. However, it is remarkable how many parallels may be found between much of the technical psychological portrayal of emotions and the everyday interpretation of emotions, as summarized above. Thus:

First, although most psychotherapeutically based interpretations of emotional processes place great emphasis on unconscious emotional processes, and hence have gone beyond the first emphasis that marked popular conceptions, it is only slowly and gradually that academic psychologists, more generally, have moved over to the view that emotional processes might be either conscious or unconscious processes. A good many psychologists still take for granted that emotions necessarily are conscious experiences.

Second, there still are widespread tendencies to think of emotions as solely strong experiences. Thus P. T. Young, in his recent volume on *Motivation and Emotion,* says: "An emotion is here defined as an acutely disturbed affective state" (1961, p. 355; see also pp. 352, 357–359, 409, and 597). This equating of emotions and strong reactions is found even in the remarkably fine recent booklet on *Motivation and Emotion* by Edward J. Murray. He introduces his chapter on "Emotional Motives" by describing the successive experiences of a person in a serious automobile accident and then by saying: "We are talking here about emotions—powerful reactions that have motivating effects on behavior" (1964, p. 49).

Third, the emotions most emphasized by psychologists are still the negative or aversive emotions most easily recognized by prescientific thinkers. Thus, although the neo-Hullians have made some real changes from older psychological discussions of emotion in their discussions of emotions as "acquired drives," the only "drives" that are thus discussed are fear or anxiety and sometimes hostility. In orthodox Freudian theory, the same was true. Unless the sex motive is treated as an emotional motive rather than as a physiologically based drive, the only fundamental emotional motives which Freud recognized were hostility (the death instinct) and anxiety.

Fourth, many psychologists have conceived of emotions as primarily either the consciousness of visceral changes or even the visceral reactions themselves. The old James-Lange theory was, to a great extent, in this tradition. It still persists. Thus, at the conclusion of his recent ambitious essay on emotion, George Mandler says: "We might speculate that the reason why people have for centuries tended to lump the different emotional states together may be found in the common visceral background of most emotions. . . . In everyday life, we probably know that we are emotional because of some slight awareness of or response to the state of our guts" (1962, pp. 338–339).

John B. Watson, of course, felt that he made the conception of emotions more scientific by proclaiming that emotions are not some consciousness of visceral reactions, but *are* the visceral reactions. Somewhat the same basic view lingers on to produce a confusing touch in what is generally, I believe, a really epochal recent volume on motivation by John W. Atkinson. In his concluding chapter, Atkinson makes considerable reference to the experiment by Solomon, Kamin, and Wynne (1953; Solomon & Wynne, 1953). In this experiment, dogs were trained to respond to a signal by jumping over a hurdle to the other side of a shuttle box to escape an electric shock from the floor. The dogs soon learned to jump with complete regularity and within about 1.0 to 1.5 seconds after the presentation of the conditioned stimulus. Solomon and his collaborators saw this quick reaction time as rather puzzling. They noted that if the jumps had been responses to visceral reactions or to arousal effects from subcortical mechanisms, the minimum latencies of the jumps should have been about 2.4 to 3.4 seconds. Hence, these investigators said, "Obviously, the animals at this point *could not* have been responding to their own emotional reactions" (Solomon, Kamin, & Wynne, 1953, p. 298). Atkinson accepts this interpretation. As he expresses the matter: "The latency of the avoidance response is so short that the animal already has performed it before having time to be afraid.... avoidant responses occur too rapidly to be explained by the concept of fear as an acquired drive" (1964, pp. 288, 290). With these authors, in other words, we have merely a modernized version of the James-Lange theory. Emotions are treated as something to be inferred, not from behavioral observations, but from hypothesized somatic reactions. If there was not sufficient time for the latter to have occurred, there could have been no emotion. Palpable visceral reactions may not wag the dog, but they certainly seem to wag the conceptualizations in such discussions!

Fifth, there is still much use of the concept that emotions basically are antithetical to realistic, adaptive functioning. P. T. Young, who has long been a classical spokesman for this view, puts the matter in these words in the recent revision of his earlier book: *"When an individual is affectively disturbed by the environmental situation to such an extent that his cerebral control is weakened or lost and subcortical patterns and visceral changes appear, that individual is emotional"* (1961, p. 358; italics in the original).

There is no American monopoly on this view. The same emphasis on visceral responses and on emotion as a maladaptive alternative to effective functioning is seen in the chapter on emotions by Paul Fraisse, former president of the French Psychological Society, in the important *Traité de Psychologie Expérimentale*. At the conclusion of the chapter, Professor Fraisse makes the following statement, if I translate him correctly: As the child matures, his emotions become more differentiated. "But what is still more important... is the diminution of absolute frequency of the emotions. The child is unarmed before a physical world full of surprises.... The adult [in contrast] anticipates situations which can confront him, and he is capable of adapting his reactions to such situations in larger measure than the child can. ... even if he cannot always evade the emotions, he is at least able to inhibit the motor reactions ... which depend on voluntary control" (1963, p. 148).

There seem to be many respects, therefore, in which the technical conceptions of psychology resemble prescientific conceptions in portraying emotions in terms of those factors and relationships which have been most tangible and attention-commanding, most closely linked temporally, and apparently most invariable. It would require an elaborate sampling study to say this with complete confidence, but it seems fairly safe to say that the predominant thinking about emotions, both in psychology and in the long experience of humanity before psychology developed, has been a palpabilistic kind of thinking about emotional processes.

The Gradual Shift to a Recognition Also of Relatively Impalpable Material

Some factors that bring recognition of impalpable factors in general.—Let us start by quoting one of the dictionary meanings of the word "impalpable": "too slight or subtle to be grasped easily by the mind." What we now need to consider is that our survey of past conceptions about emotions would be one-sided if we left the discussion with the proposition that all of the thinking about emotions has emphasized merely the palpable factors and relationships described above. The historical picture has been a more complex one, because there are certain factors that tend to bring some recognition of impalpable factors and relationships as well. At least the three following factors need to be recognized:

1. Even though some factors and relationships are "too slight or subtle to be grasped easily by the mind," these factors and relationships can be of terrific practical importance. They can account for effects that are so directly perceptible and so attention-commanding that people are driven to a continued concern with the question of what might be responsible for these effects.

The efforts to discover such causes may be frustrated for very long periods, as with efforts to discover the sources of scurvy, typhus, smallpox, and other diseases, or as with our modern efforts to get some good understanding of the origins of war or the origins of the widespread restlessness that pervades modern society. But the effects of impalpable factors can be so serious that they tend to keep people searching for explanations and for means of control even though they have not been able to find these from a consideration of relatively palpable factors.

2. Some impalpable factors and relationships come to be grasped because some circumstances occur where the observable causes and effects are cast into a more easily grasped combination. This occurred in the case of Semmelweiss and the problem of the causes of childbed fever. One of his fellow physicians, after cutting his hand with a scalpel while conducting an autopsy on a woman who had died from childbed fever, developed all the main symptoms of this disease and died within the usual several days. Semmelweiss had the background to know that a small cut in itself could not produce such an effect. The whole situation gave him the means to see, therefore, that there must be something that could be transferred from one human body to another whenever, because of some break in the surface membranes of the external or internal organs, some entry of material might occur which otherwise would be prevented.

As this example illustrates, these favorable "circumstances" often have to include some special background or preparation of the observer. The instructive juxtaposition of external conditions is not likely to be sufficient in itself. Flemming's discovery of penicillin, for example, did not depend merely on the fact that some spores of mold had happened to fall on some bacterial cultures with which he was working and that, in consequence, a clear area could be seen around each bit of mold—a clear area in which the pathogenic bacteria he was studying had not been able to grow. In addition, he was helped by the fact that he had been working for years trying to discover some better antiseptic. He was assigned to this task through all four years of the First World War. He had been able to make no progress on his assignment, but he had built up the apperceptive mass, as we might still say, that enabled him to take advantage of the fact that some of his bacterial cultures had been improperly prepared.

3. Maybe it is not too much to claim if we say that some persons, out of their backgrounds of experience, build up a proclivity for seeking for such relatively impalpable factors. This does not have to mean that they do not appreciate relatively palpable factors as well. But some persons can have been impressed with the evidence that on one matter after another, both within practical everyday life and with technical scientific work, the experience of mankind has given many demonstrations that many factors and relationships that are "too slight or subtle to be grasped easily by the mind" are more important practically and more significant scientifically than many other factors and relationships which can be recognized relatively easily. The history of science is laden with demonstrations of this point.

The development of impalpabilistic conceptions of emotion in prescientific thinking.—As evidence that impalpabilistic concepts about emotional processes can be developed and used in prescientific thinking, and even in societies with relatively simple cultures, I would like to quote three examples described in Erik Erikson's *Childhood and Society*. It may seem that I am giving undue space to these quotations, but they are significant paradigms for the conception of emotional processes which will be developed in the final section of this paper, and hence they are important in this discussion.

Erikson first quotes Ruth Benedict as having given the following report from a fellow anthropologist:

> Dr. Ruth Underhill tells me of sitting with a group of Papago elders in Arizona when the man of the house turned to his little three-year-old granddaughter and asked her to close the door. The door was heavy and hard to shut. The child tried, but it did not move. Several times the grandfather repeated: "Yes, close the door." No one jumped to the child's assistance. No one took the responsibility away from her. On the other hand there was no impatience, for after all the child was small. They sat gravely waiting until the child succeeded and her

grandfather gravely thanked her. It was assumed that the task would not be asked of her unless she could perform it, and having been asked, the responsibility was hers alone just as if she were a grown woman [1950, p. 208, quoting from Benedict, 1938].

Commenting on this description, Erikson says:

The essential point of such child training is that the child is from infancy continuously conditioned to responsible social participation, while at the same time the tasks that are expected of it are adapted to its capacity.

Then, after speaking of our own practices of regarding children as persons for whom responsible social contributions lie merely in the future, Erikson adds this example regarding another American Indian group:

The gravity of a Cheyenne Indian family ceremoniously making a feast out of a little boy's first snowbird is far removed from our behavior. At birth the little boy was presented with a toy bow and arrow, and from the time he could run about, serviceable bows and arrows suited to his stature were specially made for him by the man of the family. Animals and birds were brought to his awareness in a graded series beginning with those most easily taken, and as he brought in his first of each species his family duly made a feast of it, accepting his contribution as gravely as the buffalo his father brought. When he finally killed a buffalo, it was only the final step of his childhood conditioning, not a new adult role with which his childhood experience had been at variance [1950, p. 209].

From his own studies with the Sioux Indians of South Dakota, Erikson adds a third example:

Upon one occasion I laughed, as I thought, with and not at a little boy who told his mother and me that he could catch a wild rabbit on foot and with his bare hands. I was made to feel that I had made a social blunder. Such daydreams are not "play." They are the preparation for skills which, in turn, assure the development of the hunter or cowboy identity [1950, p. 126].

Comparable examples could be found at least within the practice of particular families in modern western culture, even if our modal customs and presuppositions are different. If such examples deal with emotional functioning, the interpretations of emotion that are implicit in them are certainly strikingly different from the palpabilistic conceptions we have reviewed in previous sections of this paper. In those palpabilistic conceptions, emotions have been interpreted as strong, tempestuous processes that tend to interfere with what the person "ought to do," as processes distinguished by unusual visceral states, and so on. In contrast, if we might say that the primitive tribes described by Erikson were dealing with emotional phenomena in these instances portrayed, the conception that is illustrated is a conception of emotional processes as including constructive emotional processes which a society ought deliberately to cultivate to provide a firm basis for the adult life of the individual.

The development of impalpabilistic conceptions of emotion within scientific psychology.—As we have seen, there have been strong tendencies for both clinical and experimental psychologists to continue the preceding popular tradition that emotions are primarily strong disruptive processes, heavily or solely visceral, and so on. But, this has not been the whole story. On the contrary, if we are to have an adequate grasp of the historical background for our present discussions of emotion, we must also recognize that, just as some of prescientific thinking included some concepts about very subtle factors, so also have some comparable developments and emphases been seen among technical psychological workers as well. Our survey should recognize at least the following developments:

First, the orthodox Freudians made a very significant contribution with their evidence that emotional processes can operate unconsciously even when they are very strong in their motivating effects.

Second, particularly among non-Freudian and neo-Freudian psychotherapists, there have been a number of workers who have emphasized the existence and influence of constructive emotional factors. Jung's concept that the "unconscious" is basically constructive rather than pathogenic is such a case. So also was Adler's shift, after the First World War, to an emphasis on social interest as more fundamental than inferiority feelings (Ansbacher &

Ansbacher, 1964). Other instances of emphasis on such constructive emotional factors come from Harry Stack Sullivan (1964), Erich Fromm (1939), Carl Rogers (1961, 1963), A. H. Maslow (1954), and Walter Bonime (1962). Even within the orthodox Freudian group itself, the view is more and more being developed that, in addition to the forces of the id, there are other essentially constructive forces inherent in the ego.

Third, Kurt Lewin, from the early 1920's, was developing theoretical and experimental concepts for dealing with motivational problems outside the traditional approaches to motivation as a matter of bodily drives that predominated among animal psychologists (Cartwright, 1959).

Fourth, among the neo-Hullians, the thinking about emotions has changed considerably because of the demonstrations by Neal Miller (1948, 1959) that fear might operate as an "acquired drive" which would help in the establishment of effective instrumental habits.

Fifth, especially by ethologists in biology, there has been rich work demonstrating that the emotional motives that can operate as drives are not always "acquired drives," but sometimes are innate or genetically determined drives. In imprinting, for example, learning occurs which reduces, not some "acquired drive of fear," but an innate drive aroused through the absence of certain factors of stimulation in the environment. In many other ways as well, the biologists have shown that the concept of "instincts" need not be a "blanket explanation that blocks research" unless scientists carelessly make it such.

Sixth, the concepts developed by Henry A. Murray's group regarding needs for achievement, affiliation, and so on, have done much to broaden the conception of constructive emotional factors in human life (Atkinson, 1964).

Seventh, various comparative psychologists have provided strong evidence of the existence and influence of "intrinsic motivation" or exploratory drives in animals. Thus, in one of the first Nebraska Symposia on Motivation, Nissen urged such points as the following:

. . . anyone who has observed mammalian behavior, and for that matter behavior of so-called lower animals also, will realize how great a proportion of activity is devoted exclusively to keeping in touch with the environment, finding out what's going on, keeping informed, getting acquainted with a strange environment or with changes and new objects in a familiar one. Such behavior is particularly conspicuous in young individuals, to whom almost everything is still new [1954, p. 299].

Both by his experimental observations and by his forceful summarizing discussions, Harlow (1953) has had an outstanding influence in the same direction. The careful field studies of baboons by Washburn and DeVore (1961), chimpanzees (Köhler, 1925, Appendix; Kortlandt, 1962), and other primates have been important in the same direction.

Eighth, various lines of research with human beings have developed analogous concepts—concepts of human beings as needing some variety of stimulation (Fiske & Maddi, 1961), as motivated by materials that involve some uncertainty and variety rather than relatively repetitious stimulation (Barron, 1963; Berlyne, 1960; Munsinger & Kessen, 1964), as motivated by cognitive dissonance or cognitive imbalance (Festinger, 1958, 1961), and as motivated particularly by a drive for competence or "effectance" (White, 1959).

Ninth, Harlow's work on the emotional reactions and emotional development of infant monkeys (Harlow, 1962; Harlow & Harlow, 1962) has given an entirely different perspective on the old hypothesis that affection for the parents came primarily from the hunger-satisfying role of the mother.

Tenth, a more general factor, back of all else, has been the great development of concepts of self-regulating or cybernetic systems in physiology, in industry, in military devices, and in various phases of psychology outside motivation. When McDougall (1932) was speaking about the "goal-directedness" of behavior, it was hard for psychologists to keep from shying away because of some feeling that his views necessarily were animistic and teleological, even though McDougall explicitly stated that he did not imply any determination of behavior by future events. At the present time, however, in this age of automation in industry and of guided missiles, there is a quite different conceptual background from which to work. We have come to realize more and more that any system which is as complex as the higher organisms, and which has to deal so flexibly with different situations, cannot be constructed economically without being built to cybernetic specifications.

SOME PRINCIPLES OF SCIENTIFIC THOUGHT THAT MIGHT HELP US DEVELOP THE THEORETICAL IMPLICATIONS OF ALL THIS MATERIAL

From any survey such as the above, it seems obvious that there has been a great deal of ferment within the field of emotion. A good deal of the thinking may be merely some technical elaboration of the old rationalistic "emotion is bad" view that became so dominant in most of everyday thought. But some other work has developed evidence and modes of thought that provide drastically different food for thought. We are now confronted, therefore, with the question of whether we can organize the available knowledge into some more useful and convincing conception of emotional processes. It may be that the psychology of emotion never will find the means to get beyond the heterogeneity of views—one is almost tempted to say "chaos"—that now prevails. But as Kuhn (1962) has pointed out, such seeming confusion is often the condition that can aid in the development of significant new scientific generalizations. So our immediate task is one of trying to make some contribution in that direction.

In a situation like this, it is appropriate for us to ask whether there are any rules of work that might be helpful to us. In the discussion of the preceding paper, Howard Kendler mentioned one such principle which his grandmother had given him when he was a boy. "Don't work too hard," she counseled him, "just be a genius!" Dr. Kendler expressed his skepticism about that rule. In fact, I myself feel somewhat skeptical about the usefulness of any abstract rules or principles about scientific thinking, because there are many considerations that suggest that the capacity for careful scientific thinking depends much more on motivation and on some skills at thinking that can be developed only with considerable practice in reasoning and arguing with other persons who previously have developed such skills. However, it still may be true that theoretical discussions could be clarified if we recognized a few basic features which seem to prevail in careful scientific thinking. So let us briefly sketch these, and then we shall turn to the substantive question of the nature of emotional processes.

We shall first mention several principles on which there should be fairly ready agreement. One of these is a proposition which Conant has emphasized in his little volume, *On Understanding Science* (1947)—to wit, that *the basic distinction between a science and a technology is the more highly abstract character of scientific thinking.* This greater abstractness is not a matter, of course, of lack of concern with concrete cases and empirical data. It *is* a concern with developing highly generalized concepts that can be used in efforts to predict and control, or to understand, exceedingly broad ranges of phenomena. Consequently, it is an interest also in the highly abstract terms which must be employed in any such highly generalized principles.

The reason for interest in such highly abstract principles is partly the economy that comes from them. It is also their heuristic value—their usefulness in opening up specially instructive objects for research that would not have been considered if the research problem had been conceptualized merely in terms of some smaller body of phenomena.

The basis of classifying things together under the highly abstract terms used in any science is, of course, not an arbitrary basis. It cannot rest too much on established usage or authority. To serve the purposes of scientific work, *the material that is grouped together under any abstract term must possess important functional similarities.* They must obey the same laws. Hence, the territory covered by any scientific term must always be subject to modification as new empirical knowledge is gained. Therefore, the question of the proper meaning for any scientific term is always an empirical question, basically. It is a question that must be decided on the basis of what things possess some fundamental similarities even though, superficially, they may look quite different.

If old terms (like "emotion" and "emotional") *continue to be used, there must be some historical continuity with older usages.* However, the continuity should be a continuity only in the sense that at least a considerable number (and perhaps a substantial majority) of the instances formerly classified under that term should still be included under it. But what is demonstrated in all fields is that developments of knowledge typically mean that some of the old cases have to be excluded as time goes on, various other examples (and perhaps huge ranges of them) have to be included, and some basic changes of definition (or statements of criterial properties) have to be made. The old concept and definition of "mammals," for instance, ruled out any animals that were able to fly, that lived exclusively in the water and were fish-shaped, or that laid eggs, but our present knowledge of anatomy, physiology, and phylogenetic relationships led to a changed concept that includes dolphins, bats, and the duck-billed platypus.

Beyond these several principles, there are several others which have particular relevance to our present discussion. The first of these is the proposition that *the appropriate classificatory or taxonomic structure for any science is a complex hierarchical structure,* but also that *such hierarchical logical organizations are more difficult for people to develop and use than the practice of dealing with each successive situation in terms of dichotomous or contrasting categories.* Perhaps the term "hierarchical" is not the best term to use here, because all that is meant is that some categories need to be much more inclusive than other categories. In other words, there would be sub-sets within a category, each sub-set might have sub-sub-sets, and so on.

The need for such hierarchical organization comes from the fact that the aim of any science is not merely to achieve highly abstract principles, but also to get abstract principles from which, if possible, fairly exact predictions can be made in relatively specific types of cases. To secure the greatest possible economy and heuristic value of scientific knowledge regarding properties which exist over huge ranges of instances, it is worthwhile, for example, to have some extremely inclusive classes. The modern work on the DNA constitution of genes, for example, permits

more rapid progress on problems of human heredity as a consequence of empirical evidence that, in this matter, man belongs
in the same class with viruses and plants. On some other issues,
however, the properties that are to be studied are those that
are limited to vertebrates, or more narrowly to mammals, or
more narrowly to animals that have highly developed brains,
and so on.

The custom of dealing in such hierarchical classifications
apparently does not come easily to us, at least on complex matters. This is shown even on simple matters by children. Asked in
what way a ball and an orange are alike, a six-year-old is likely
to insist that they are not alike—"you play with a ball and you
eat an orange." On much more complicated materials, all of us
show this same proclivity to think in terms of mutually exclusive
classes rather than in terms of hierarchical conceptual systems.
But it is the latter which has to be developed in any science
if there is to be a, maximally helpful organization of the available empirical knowledge of that scientific field.

A further proposition possibly applies more to psychology
than to many other fields. This is the proposition that *the abstract
concepts in psychology frequently need to refer to continua, or
to dimensions, rather than to sharply separated sub-classes.* We
may refer to separate sub-classes for reasons of convenience, just
as we refer in everyday life to "blondes" and "brunettes." But
we must never forget, in such cases, that we are using such terms
merely as a rough means of description for certain limited
purposes.

The final proposition regarding rules of scientific thinking
is one which applies particularly to psychology. It is the proposition that, although it frequently may be helpful to make use
of relevant physiological knowledge, *we should never decide complex problems in psychology by appealing to physiological knowledge unless the latter really is adequately established and unless
it really has the implications that we are inclined to attribute
to it.*

This point has been urged with special cogency in the concluding chapter of John Atkinson's recent book on motivation

(1964). A main difficulty with our chief contemporary theories about motivation, he notes, is that they have depended on presuppositions that they ought never to have taken for granted. Says Atkinson:

> Grossly inadequate neurophysiological preconceptions have implicitly been given priority over behavioral observations in the attempt to develop a workable conceptual scheme. Only recently has it become apparent how fundamentally inadequate they are and the extent to which they have influenced the mode of thought. . . . an antiquated neurophysiological conception has provided the underlying premise of the mainstream of thought about motivation for many years [1964, pp. 305, 314].

Such are the intellectual tools with which we should equip ourselves, I believe we have reason to say. Now the question is "What can we do with them?"

THE TAXONOMIC RELATIONSHIP BETWEEN EMOTIONS AND MOTIVES

So far in this paper, we have surveyed the different main conceptions of emotion that have been developed, but we have not attempted any critical evaluation of them. It is important for us now, however, to organize what we have surveyed, to subject it to a critical examination, and to see whether we can make some constructive contributions to this whole matter.

As we begin, it would be good for us to indicate where we intend to preserve some historical continuity with the past. To do this, we need to ask for some concrete examples that might be pointed to as generally agreed-on examples of emotion. Whatever model or conception of emotion we decide to use should stake out a territory that would include at least a good portion of such traditionally recognized examples.

A designation of such examples is not too difficult. At least the following types of process or response would be accepted, both in everyday life and in most psychological theories, as definitely acceptable examples of emotion, provided each is understood as having reference to the stronger forms of each process. The examples would be such things as fear, anger, grief, discouragement, depression, embarrassment, shame, disgust, guilt, lonesomeness, joy, affection, and pride.

However, when we mention psychological phenomena like these, what are we pointing to? What are the identifying properties of these examples of emotion? On that question, the disagreements appear.

For instance, if different psychologists had observed the early trials in the experiment by Solomon, Kamin, and Wynne, they would have agreed that the dogs seemed to be showing signs of strong fear. When the dogs actually were receiving electric shocks from the floor, most psychologists would probably have said that the reactions then were primarily a product of a physiologically based motive or drive of pain. And when the dogs showed other reactions, such as their struggles to avoid being put back into the same apparatus on the second day, most psychologists would not have hesitated to say, "Yes, there was fear there, all right."

But in such commonly accepted reference cases or paradigms, what is the "emotion of fear" that is referred to? That is, what are the criteria that different psychologists use when they make the two inferences that are involved in such a statement—first, the inference that the organism engaged in an emotional process, and second, that the organism engaged in an emotional process of fear rather than of anger or grief or joy?

The Five Main Models of Emotion That Have Been Developed

In their answer to this question, psychologists have developed five different main conceptions, or models, as follows: (1) Emotions are conscious experiences, distinguished from each other and from nonemotional experiences by certain subjective properties. In considering another organism, we have to try to infer his conscious emotional experience from the stimulus situation, from his behavior, and so on. But these are merely indirect criteria, and each of us knows how to interpret them only by reference to his own subjective experiences in analogous situations. (2) Emotions are certain special physiological states or processes dependent on the autonomic part of the nervous system and perhaps also on some special centers or sub-systems within the hypothalamus or the limbic system. The defining properties of any emotion are either such nervous processes, where we can record them directly, or, of course, the peripheral visceral effects and the like which we can more feasibly observe under most circumstances. (3) Emotions are distinguishable from other psychological processes by the disruptive effects that they produce. (4) Emotions are distinguished from other processes, not so much on the basis of any interference with adaptive efforts, but on the basis that they are the results of lack of means of adequate adaptation to the situation. (5) Emotional processes are distinguished from each other, and from other types of processes, on the basis of motivational effects which they exert—that is, on the basis of effects which they exert that are analogous to the effects exerted by traditionally recognized motives or drives.

Disadvantages of the First Four Models

All of the first four models have some partial validity as descriptions of such paradigmatic emotional processes as were mentioned above. There are some valid observations from which each of these four models has been developed, but none of them seems sufficiently satisfactory. Let us examine the reasons for this in each case.

The concept of emotions as subjectively distinguishable conscious experiences.—In view of the fact that this model seems seriously deficient to me, perhaps it would be well for me to make clear that I firmly believe that a considerable portion (though perhaps not a majority) of emotional processes are conscious. Furthermore, I firmly believe that people can discriminate to a considerable extent, on a subjective basis, what emotional process is occurring within themselves. Beyond that, I also share the view of many psychologists that conscious experience is something that psychologists should be concerned with, use as a source of hypotheses, and so on.

Nevertheless, I believe there are reasons why this first model proves unsatisfactory as the fundamental one. For one thing, it is important that research on emotional processes should include infants and small children as subjects, and not merely adults. It is important that it should include research with subhuman subjects. Even if for no other reason, our fundamental criteria for emotional processes must be objective.

Furthermore, there are instances where objective criteria seem to indicate the presence of processes which, on most scores, are functionally equivalent to conscious emotional processes but which the individual himself cannot recognize subjectively. I can remember a couple of occasions, myself, when I would not have known how angry I was if I had not found my voice shaking.

However, the most fundamental difficulty is that, even when there are discriminable subjective effects by means of which each of us can tell, to some extent, when he is afraid or angry or lonesome or whatever, no one has found the means of describing such subjective qualities so that he could communicate his knowledge to others by this means. Instead, the person has to describe the situation that evoked his emotional reaction, or he has to describe the thought content that it tended to produce, or he has to describe the behavior it tended to make him engage in. Thus, consider the first two lines of a poem by Upton Sinclair which tried to express his protest against the First World War:

> *Soft as a man with a dead child speaks,*
> *Hard as a man in handcuffs, held where he cannot move.*

Or consider the answer that a young Negro gave, with averted face, when he was interviewed recently by a news commentator and asked how he had felt when he dropped out of school and found that he couldn't get a job anywhere. His answer was: "I felt like I was throwed away." Such descriptions do communicate information about our emotional processes. But they don't do it through descriptions of subjective qualities, except by such indirect means that we are driven back to the question "How did the individual's culture ever communicate to him the meaning of emotional terms like fear, pity, discouragement, and the like?" It seems that the answer must be that the social environment of the child was assuming and using another basic model as a means of knowing when to inform the child that he (or some other person) was afraid, angry, or lonesome. It was not a model which fundamentally was identifying emotional processes by subjective criteria. There had to be a fundamental reliance on other criteria.

Emotions as special visceral states or special subcortical processes.—Many psychologists would echo the criticisms just expressed regarding the first model, but they would believe the case is much better regarding the second one. The way we identify emotions, they say, is by noting special physiological effects, such as those governed by the autonomic part of the nervous system. But is this really true?

First of all, when there are technical studies of motivational centers or sub-systems within the hypothalamus or the limbic system, what are the criteria by means of which it is determined that one subcortical system is concerned with anger, another with sexual excitement, and so on? It seems quite safe to say that we have no neurophysiological criteria by means of which we can make such distinctions. Our criteria in such studies have to be either the behavioral effects or the subjective reports which are elicited by electrical stimulations of different centers. This does not mean that such neurophysiological work is unprofitable or unimportant, but it does mean that the research workers in such cases have to be using some other more fundamental model about emotional and other motivational processes.

The same observation applies to claims that we can use autonomically produced responses as our criteria of emotions. There is nothing about dilated pupils or about sudden perspiration that intrinsically gave evidence that these responses to some extent were indicative of fear. Such autonomic effects came to be known only because of the fact that they were, to some extent, correlated with more fundamentally useful criteria of emotional reactions. As a matter of fact, at the 1964 APA meeting, one of the main research workers in this field, M. A. Wenger, reported that, to his considerable disappointment, the research on autonomic effects, even with refined physiological measures, was making it more and more doubtful that different emotional reactions could be distinguished from one another by such means. So, even though we have a fondness for objective criteria in psychology, we are having to conclude that the particular sort of criteria proposed by this second model cannot meet our fundamental needs. After all, it doesn't do much good to have a model which can't help you to judge whether a person is badly frightened or has been outside too long in a dark, cold night or is sick with the flu.

Emotions as disrupting or disorganizing processes.—As we have said, there have been strong tendencies in psychology to divide emotions and the traditionally recognized motives into two sharply contrasting classes. Motives have rather commonly been regarded as processes that not only arouse and sustain activity, but organize it or direct it. Motives have been interpreted as processes that tend to make the organism do what is realistically needed in the environmental situation, partly because only what is realistically needed is likely to yield rewards. Emotions, on the other hand, have often been described as processes that tend merely to disrupt or disorganize the organism's adaptive efforts.

This third model, however, runs into appreciable difficulties. For one thing, it provides no means for distinguishing between very strong "motives" and very strong "emotions," because both types of process are very disruptive of interests or activities that are irrelevant to the motive or emotion aroused. Both of them can be very disruptive even of highly relevant behavior tendencies. Both of them create handicaps when some difficult problem solving is called for. But, on the other hand, both types of intense process can operate as very effective organizing and directing factors in some situations where some relatively simple and well-mastered form of activity is called for which requires intense muscular activity.

For another thing, the third model is suspect because its portrait of "motives" is drawn from a consideration of the full range of different strengths of such motives as hunger, thirst, and pain, while the portrait of "emotions" is drawn only from a consideration of very intense emotions. This use of merely very strong instances of some influence is not a typical procedure in scientific work. We do not define electricity only in terms of the properties of lightning, nor the properties of air movements in terms of the effects of tornadoes. There is more heuristic value in grouping together, for fundamental discussions, all of the different strengths in which any given type of phenomenon may be found. The more intense forms of the phenomenon may be those that attract attention first, but the milder forms are commonly those that are more practicable objects for experimental investigation.

Furthermore, the third model runs into the difficulty that it gives no efficient means for distinguishing between one type of emotional process and another. No advocate of this model has attempted to present evidence that there are different kinds of disruption that come from extreme fear as contrasted with extreme rage or extreme emotions of other sorts, and yet its advocates continue to refer to such different emotions. Implicitly, therefore, they are assuming some other model to be more basic, just as did the advocates of the first two models.

Emotions as products of lack of adequate means of adjustment.—This is the model that has been preferred by P. T. Young (1961), S. H. Bartley (1958), and Jean-Paul Sartre (1962). There is a certain degree of truth in it, of course. There are situations in which, when the organism learns to cope skillfully with the situation, it does thus deal with the situation and thereby prevents the situation from developing into such a further state that a much stronger form of the same emotion would be aroused (Solomon & Wynne, 1954). But the same fact is true of the traditionally based motives. Under normal circumstances, a person or an animal never gets intensely hungry or thirsty. He or it takes steps to serve such motives before they reach more than a rather mild strength. In the same way, after the dogs of Solomon, Kamin, and Wynne had learned that they could avoid the shock by quickly jumping over the barrier, they became quite willing to enter the apparatus each day without any forcing, and their overt behavior (in many respects) seemed to indicate that they were no longer afraid. But they continued to jump, even more invariably and promptly than would have been the case with hunger motivation and with food rewards. It seems, then, that the fourth model is only a specification of one of the conditions under which an emotional process will tend to become intensified. It is therefore not a satisfactory general conception of emotional processes.

Another difficulty with this model is the same one mentioned with the preceding examples: it gives no means of distinguishing between one emotional process and another, and yet the proponents of the model continue to talk about different emotions as though they were distinguishable.

There are, then, special objections to each of these first four possible models of emotion. But, as we have seen, another charge can be made against all of them: they all seem to presuppose some other, more basic means of determining whether some emotional process is occurring and of identifying, in such a case, which emotional process is taking place from the whole gamut of those that are possible. What we need to ask, therefore, is what this more fundamental model may be.

The Nature and Basis of the Motivational Theory of Emotion

Even in prescientific thought, as we have seen, there has been some use of a fifth model of emotional processes which is quite at variance with all of the four models which we have just discussed. Such was the case with the customs of the three Indian groups described in the quotations from Erikson. For example, as he said, Cheyenne Indian families used to follow the practice of making an impressive little feast when a son first killed a wild animal and on each succeeding occasion when he killed a more difficult type of game. In so doing, one might say, these Cheyenne Indians were acting on the conception that the workaday life of an adult hunter depends not only on bodily drives of hunger and the like but also on acquired drives or learned motives of pride, self-confidence, and enjoyment of social recognition. This may have not been a conception that this Indian group could have formulated, at least in abstract terms, but there does seem to be a conception involved in such customs which is drastically different from thinking of emotional processes primarily as subjective experiences, as special visceral reactions, as disturbing or disruptive processes, or as consequences of lack of means of coping with environmental situations. Basically, it seems that this particular sort of custom rested on an underlying *motivational* interpretation of emotional reactions.

Does such a motivational interpretation of emotion give us a satisfactory model for understanding emotional processes as an object for technical psychological study? For example, would such a model, unlike the four reviewed above, call our attention explicitly to the criteria that we actually use in judging whether some emotional process is occurring and in judging, more specifically, what type of emotional process is occurring?

To answer such questions, we need to turn back to a previous question: "How, actually, do we decide that an organism is motivated by one of the traditionally recognized types of motive?"

The criteria of motives in general.—Sometimes we speak as though psychologists identified the traditionally recognized motives on the basis of the physiological requirements or "needs" of the body. But this is, of course, not the case. An organism is in deadly danger if it remains in an environment which contains an excess of carbon monoxide or a serious deficiency of oxygen. But, presumably because neither of these situations tended to exist during evolutionary history, no motivational mechanisms were developed for putting the organism under pressure to deal behaviorally with such situations. Similarly, there are no hungers for some indispensable mineral elements and vitamins that ordinarily are provided by normal diets. So the existence of some bodily requirement is not something from which a corresponding motive may be inferred.

Furthermore, even where there are motives that serve real needs of the body, our means of learning about these have been behavioral rather than physiological. For example, it has been known for a half-century and more that pigs will grow better if they are allowed to eat on a cafeteria basis rather than being given some "scientifically balanced diet." The same principle was indicated by the frequently cited experiment of Clara Davis with human infants (1928). The identification of the physiological mechanisms of such qualitative food hungers has involved great

difficulties, but the existence of such motives is demonstrable by behavioral effects. Indeed, even our fundamental knowledge of ordinary hunger and thirst has had to come from psychological observations. We now know that the earlier physiological "explanations" were seriously in error (Rosenzweig, 1962; Deutsch, 1960).

Very well, then. If, fundamentally, we cannot identify physiologically based motives from the organism's physiological needs or by identifying the physiological mechanisms of such motives, how do we infer that an animal is hungry or thirsty or sleepy or sexually motivated, and how do we make inferences about the strength of any such motive?

The answer is that, fundamentally, we infer the traditionally recognized motives by their behavioral effects. This holds true even when we use a "deprivation period" or some other property of the stimulus situation to judge how an organism will be motivated. Any such clues are useful only because of prior observations of the behavioral effects that occur under such stimulus conditions. Otherwise, for example, we would hardly know that a neurosurgeon can slice into the brain without producing pain. Nor would we know how often an animal will be motivated to eat, when it would prefer to sleep, and so on.

What are the psychological effects from which we make our inferences about motives? The answer seems to be that in any given case we use one or more of the following types of effects:

1. Active motives tend to modify sensory perceptions, particularly in the direction of making relevant things stand out focally.

2. Active motives tend also to determine the content of thought processes, even when there is no relevant stimulation which would normally arouse such thoughts.

3. In situations where the organism does not have some means of satisfying an active motive, the motive tends to produce exploratory activity which may lead to the learning of new ways of dealing with the situation. The active motive will facilitate this learning by other means, too, such as the longer perseveration of nervous processes and the consequent translation of this per-

severative activity into enduring structural changes within the brain (Glickman, 1961; Deutsch, 1962).

4. Active motives govern the utilization of previously developed innate mechanisms or habits.

5. Active motives tend to govern the choices between positive goals. They sometimes produce a searching for positive goal-objects not physically present.

6. Active motives tend to make the organism accept penalties or perform work in order either to reach a positive goal or to escape from some situation where negative motivational effects are being aroused.

In general, these six types of effects provide an extension or supplementation of the reflex homeostatic mechanisms of the body. Motives are processes that tend to produce some relatively more complex means of dealing with situations to supplement the simpler means that the reflex mechanisms provide. Because of such motives, for instance, a person does not merely shiver when he is cold, but tends to use his more complex neural mechanisms to find means of protection from the cold, if such can be found. A person does not merely perspire profusely when he gets hot. He also tends to find means whereby he will be protected from the heat. Motives, in other words, lead to a use of the more complex behavioral mechanisms that are found particularly in the more complex species. They have this influence as factors that persist and that tend to dominate the functioning of the organism until the motive is served and either satiated or reduced to less strength than some competing motive.

The six types of effects which we have outlined could be illustrated from many different research studies with animals. With human subjects, the most systematic study has been that reported by Ancel Keys and his associates (1950). This was a study of a group of 32 conscientious objectors who volunteered to serve as subjects in an experimental study of the effects of semi-starvation. The study was conducted at the University of Minnesota late in the Second World War. After a preliminary testing period with a normal diet of about 3,500 calories a day, the men lived for six months on a diet of about 1,600 calories, which brought an average weight loss of 24 per cent during the six-month period. In total starvation, hunger eventually disappears, but with this semistarvation regimen, there was no lessening of the desire for food as the study progressed. The evidence for this was not just a matter of subjective reports, however, but also a matter of many different specific effects. Let me cull out a sample of the observations summarized in the condensed report by Franklin, Schiele, Brozek, and Keys (1948):

Food in all of its ramifications became the principal topic of the subjects' conversations, reading, and day dreams. More dreams about food were reported as the stress continued. When subjects read books and attended movies, they were deeply impressed by the frequency with which food and eating were mentioned [p. 32].

. . . to maximize the pleasure of eating, there was much planning done by the men as to how they would handle their day's allotment of food . . . All food was consumed to the last crumb. The men were cultured and refined, yet they routinely licked their dishes in order to obtain every vestige of food. They quickly became intolerant of food waste and were visibly upset when they noticed others discarding food [p. 31].

In fact, even during the post-deprivation phase of the study, when food intake was not restricted,

licking of plates and neglect of table manners persisted. Attempts to avoid wasting even a particle continued in the face of unlimited supplies of immediately available food [p. 38].

At the table some hovered closely over their trays with their arms placed so as to protect their ration. . . . the subjects increased the bulk of their food by "souping." For example, a man would drink the fluid from his soup, then fill the bowl with hot water, salt it heavily, drink the fluid off again, and repeat this process before eating the solid part of the soup [p. 31].

Cook books, menus, and information bulletins on food production became intensely interesting reading matter to many of the subjects. . . . Some men went so far as to re-plan their lives according to their newly-acquired respect for food [p. 32].

But

their earlier interest in having a voice in the making of policies and rules for the conduct of the non-scientific aspects of the experiment dwindled. . . . It became "too much trouble" or "too tiring" to have to contend with other people. . . . The educational program, designed to prepare the men for foreign relief work and followed at the start with enthusiasm, in time quietly but decisively collapsed [pp. 34–35].

When we use effects like these to infer the kind and strength of motivation of a person, we of course are not denying the value, for certain purposes, of the considerations which provided the basis for the first four models of emotion we reviewed above. Those same four models also apply, to some extent, to such physiologically based motives as hunger. So the hypothesis that motives are identified through their effects on behavior, thinking, and perception does not deny the propositions that the traditionally recognized motives often operate as conscious processes and that the person can recognize on subjective grounds that he is hungry rather than thirsty or whatever. The concept does not deny that physiologically based motives often have important autonomic effects—as, strikingly, in the case of the sex motive and in cases of pain. The concept does not deny that motives often have disorganizing effects on some aspects of the person's life, and maybe even quite generally, if the motive becomes very intense. The concept does not deny that the development of a motive into a strong state often occurs because the organism lacks adequate means of adaptation to its environmental resources. In fact, a place is made for each of these considerations where they apply. But these special considerations are seen merely as more particular problems or more particular dimensions within the body of phenomena that are grouped together basically on the basis of the primarily behavioral effects we have outlined and illustrated above.

Applicability of the same criteria to emotional processes.— Now the important point in all this for our present discussion of emotional processes is the fact that we actually use these same basic criteria as our means of inferring that an emotional process is occurring and as our means of inferring *what type* of emotional process is occurring. Even those psychologists and neurophysiologists who prefer to think of emotions as functions of special sub-systems within the limbic system or the hypothalamus still depend basically on these behavioral effects as their means of saying that such and such neural tissue is concerned with one sort of emotion rather than another, or with some emotional process rather than with some bodily drive. These effects are the ones which clinical workers have to depend on when they judge that a person has a great deal of hostility, say, or a great craving for security and dependence. These effects are the means which, fundamentally, we have to depend on in everyday life in judging the emotional processes in other persons. Despite all of our talk about emotional processes as disruptive, as merely visceral reactions, etc., the criteria by means of which we infer emotional processes of different sorts are the same basic criteria by means of which we infer, in some other cases, that a physiologically based motive is operating. In both cases, we are identifying or inferring such processes on the basis of evidence that there must be some process within the organism which not merely arouses but also organizes and directs the psychological functioning of the organism.

The conclusion that seems indicated, therefore, is that emotions are motives. They may be distinguishable in some important ways from other processes which also belong with the total class of motives, but they possess such important functional similarities to the traditionally recognized motives that they belong with them in some more inclusive category.

The distinction between emotional and physiologically based motives.—If there is some basis for distinguishing between emotional motives and the more traditionally recognized motives, what is this distinction? A number of the S-R psychologists, including Kendler in his *Basic Psychology* (1963), seem essentially to be proposing that the distinction is one between "acquired drives" or "learned or secondary drives," on the one hand, and "physiological or primary drives," on the other. Fear and rage, for example, are discussed by Kendler as instances of learned drives; hunger, thirst, and sex drives as examples of physiological drives.

This is hardly a satisfactory division, however. Drug addiction, for example, is to some extent an "acquired drive," and yet it is still dependent on physiochemical processes. On the other hand, the aggressive reaction that is aroused in a mother hen when she sees a cat prowling near her brood of chicks can hardly be understood as an acquired or learned drive. Nor can we describe as "learned" the fear in young ducklings which provides the motivational basis for imprinting. Yet alongside the classical experiment of Neal Miller (1948) on the role of fear as an acquired drive which can help in the development of new responses, an experiment by Howard Hoffman equally deserves to become classic as a demonstration that innately aroused fear can serve as the motivational basis for learning. In work which I had an opportunity to observe last year at Pennsylvania State University, Hoffman has made intensive studies of the behavior of ducklings in a situation where, in good Skinnerian tradition, they would be rewarded for pecking at a translucent key. However, the reinforcement establishing and maintaining this operant response was not any reward of a physiological drive, nor was it, as in Miller's experiment, a chance to escape from an area where they previously had been shocked. The reward was merely this: when the duckling tapped on the translucent key, the illumination would shift to the other side of a one-way-vision screen so that the duckling could see, in the adjoining compartment, a little electric car with a white plastic milk bottle on it move slowly back and forth. In this situation, the small ducklings showed great restlessness (as recorded, for example, by distress calls) until they learned to produce this effect, and they would return faithfully to the key after each stopping of the train and blocking out of their vision of it at the end of each 5-second exposure. But the origins of this fearfulness, thus assuaged, are as innate as are the origins of hunger or thirst.

As a rough statement, therefore, even though most emotional motives have some dependence, at least, on past learning, we cannot draw the distinction between emotional motives and other motives on the basis of "learned *versus* non-learned." The distinction seems to be more on the following lines: Emotional motives are processes that depend on cues which, in many respects, are like those required for traditional perceptual or cognitive processes. They are processes that can be touched off even by very slight or subtle external stimulations, or which occur even because of the *absence* of some needed stimulation. The physiologically based motives, on the other hand, are heavily dependent either on special chemical conditions within the body or on unusually strong peripheral stimulation.

Emotional and physiologically based motives as parts of a continuum.—The statement of this distinction, however, compels us to make the further observation that there is no sharp dichotomy between emotional motives and physiologically based motives. Consider the sex motive. We commonly treat it as a physiologically based motive. But as Beach (1951) has said, some species of fish will not mate unless the aquarium has some water plants growing in it and some rocks around; some ducks will not mate unless the surface of at least a small expanse of water is nearby in their boudoir; and some birds become sexually aroused only when elaborate courtship rituals are performed. In fact, a recent article on the ringdove (Lehrman, 1964) gives evidence that the development of the ovaries and oviduct in the female occurs only when the female has a chance to watch a male dove who, because not castrated, *acts* like a male—and this even when he is on the other side of a pane of glass and there is only visual contact between them.

The motive of pain shows the same sorts of influence. As W. K. Livingston and Ronald Melzack (Melzack, 1961) have emphasized, the pain that a person experiences is not very predictable from the intensity of stimulation from burns or wounds or electric shocks. Soldiers who have severe wounds that incapacitate them for further military service often decline the sedatives or opiates which they would plead for if the same sorts of tissue injury had occurred under other circumstances. George Klein (1958) emphasizes the same phenomenon from the research of his associates and himself on thirst.

In other words, the forces which operate as the "physiological motives" of hunger, thirst, pain, sex, fatigue, and so on are processes somewhat dependent on the "psychological situation." Such dependence is not characteristic solely of the emotional motives, and marks the fact that physiological motives are part of a continuum with the more clearly emotional motives. The more we learn about each of these types of process, the more we learn that we are dealing with a continuum, rather than with a dichotomy or with two classes possessing merely contrasting properties.

Let me give one further example to indicate something about the range of coverage that is intended for the term "emotional motive" and for its synonym, "emotional process." Suppose that a scientist is busy hour after hour, year after year, doing experimental work, tabulating results, or writing up reports. Such persistent goal-directed behavior must be said to be motivated. Motivated by what? Not by bodily drives, despite the impression that cynics sometimes get that legislatures believe scientists would work better if they were somewhat hungry or cold or physically uncomfortable. By what motives, then? Suppose that, in answering this question, we stick to the criteria that we have outlined above. That is, suppose we stick to the propositions that emotional processes or emotional motives are what we have to infer when (a) there are behavioral effects analogous to those that come from physiologically based motives, and (b) the inferred processes are apparently complex processes aroused by relatively subtle cues rather than processes dependent on special biochemical states or unusually strong peripheral stimulations. If we stick to these propositions, we then must say that the sustained hard work of the scientist is the product of emotional forces or emotional motives within him during all that work. In this interpretation, then, we are back with the Cheyenne Indians or the Papagos or the Sioux, because we are saying that the development of the solid, socially valuable parts of the individual's life is a matter of the development of emotional habits and not a matter of minimizing the emotional components in human lives. Some emotional motives, of course, are destructive of individual and social values, and the means should be found of lessening the prevalence and influence of these. But the great attention paid in older times to the more dramatic and attention-commanding emotions, like fear and anger, should not prevent us now from appreciating the emotional processes that were too impalpable to get much notice in older times.

The Special Significance of Emotional Motives in the Higher Species

Evolution has led to the development of more complex animals. The biological survival of these animals came to depend, more and more, on the means whereby these animals could make more complex and efficient use of their environments. Such use was facilitated especially by three main assets: the excellent distance receptors of these higher species, their extraordinary perceptual capacities, and their great learning capacity. These were the biological assets, for example, that enabled such animals to detect enemies at great distances from almost infinitesimally faint cues and often on the basis of cues that were significant only by virtue of the past learning of the particular organism.

But if these three resources were to be maximally advantageous, they needed to be related to motives that could be aroused, not through some bodily state or some strong peripheral stimulation, but as subtle perceptual reactions to stimulus situations. If, for example, the unusual potentialities for learning were to be exploited, the animals had to be strongly motivated to engage in exploratory activity, play, imitation, and so on merely for the sake of intrinsic satisfactions in such activities and not because of their service of bodily drives or through some derivation from the bodily drives. Furthermore, these higher species needed to possess a type of motive that could be tremendously modified by learning so that different individuals could be motivationally adapted to quite different special conditions. And all of this is what apparently did happen with the higher species, as we are coming increasingly to realize from such research as that (reviewed earlier in this paper) by Washburn and DeVore, Kortlandt, Harlow, Berlyne, White, Piaget, and so on.

In other words, it is no blunder of evolution that the higher animals, such as chimpanzees and gorillas and human beings— or even dogs and coyotes and antelopes—are such highly emotional creatures. Rather than being outside the pale of biologically adaptive motivation, the emotional processes are the chief sort of motivation that we need to learn to understand, recognize, and deliberately emphasize if we are to develop a useful scientific and practical understanding of these higher forms. Furthermore, the kinds of emotional motives that we must learn to recognize are not merely the dramatic negative forms which were first recognized by older cultures, but the more subtle and modest, and perhaps more complex, positive emotional motives that carry the burden of motivating most of our behavior as members of modern society.

EMOTIONAL MOTIVES AS PERCEPTUAL OR COGNITIVE PROCESSES

The Almost Universal Conception of Emotional Processes as Lower-Level Processes

One of the observations we made earlier is that people generally find it easier to think, not in terms of hierarchical conceptual systems, but in terms of contrasting categories and in terms of the contrasting properties that seem to justify such dichotomies. They apparently find it more difficult to recognize that, in some more or less heterogeneous field, there are differences on some scores and yet similarities on others. We have suggested that this difficulty with hierarchical conceptual systems played a role in the development of the modes of thought which portrayed "motives" and "emotions" in strongly antithetical terms, emphasizing the organizing and directing roles of motives, but also emphasizing disruptive influences of emotions. We have also suggested, however, that a more careful logical analysis of all that we know about emotions and about the traditionally recognized motives suggests that emotional processes need to be seen as a part of a larger continuum of motivational processes that ranges from the most clearly physiologically based motives to an opposite pole of the most clearly emotional motives.

In the remainder of this paper, we turn to another matter on which both everyday thought and most of technical psychological thought have similarly tended to create a dichotomy and to describe the properties of the two classes of psychological phenomena in terms of two sharply contrasting pictures.

In this dichotomizing that we now need to examine, emotional processes and the traditionally recognized motives have been put together into a single category. In the thinking of most psychologists, however, this single category has not been one defined on the basis of motivational properties, as the preceding discussion has suggested. Instead, the dichotomy which has been assumed is a dichotomy which has put emotional and physiologically based motives into one group and has assumed another *nonoverlapping* group which would include all perceptual, cognitive, intellectual, representational, or information-processing processes.

When bodily drives and emotional processes have been thought of in this context, what has been the common property which they were seen as possessing in contrast with "cognitive" processes? The answer, I think, is that the almost universal assumption has been that emotional and other motivational processes are processes of a lower level, neurologically and psychologically speaking, than cognitive processes. Emotional and other motivational processes have been treated as processes that appeared at a lower level of evolutionary development, that are less distinctively human functions, and that are less dependent on the parts of the nervous system which reach their highest development in human beings. They have been treated as processes that, accordingly, are more characteristic of small children than of adults, that are more important in the life of primitive peoples than in highly developed cultures, and so on.

In short, as contrasted with perceptual or cognitive processes, which have been seen as "cortical processes," the emotional processes and traditionally recognized motives have been thought of as "subcortical" or even as basically visceral in nature. This conception found rather extreme expression in the following statement by R. S. Woodworth when he was discussing emotion in his general psychology text: "If the brainy life of relation dominates the organism at the moment, the emotional response is minimized. But if the situation gets out of hand, the emotion appropriate to the situation surges up" (1940, p. 418).

This dichotomizing, however, does not always include such

uncomplimentary evaluations of emotional processes. Thus, a number of quite important recent treatises on motivation have interpreted emotional processes as sharing, with bodily drives, some important constructive influences. I am referring here to the books on motivation by Bindra (1959), Judson Brown (1961), Duffy (1962), and Cofer and Appley (1964), as well as to articles by Hebb (1955), Lindsley (1957), Spence (1958), and Malmo (1959). According to these authors, our most important clues to the role of emotions and bodily drives have come from the research of the last fifteen years or so on the reticular activating systems and on the motivational sub-systems within the limbic system in the brain. The general hypothesis which these authors develop is that emotions and bodily drives, in addition to producing some specific autonomic effects like salivating and increased heartbeat, also have a more directly psychological effect. The latter is their influence in producing a higher arousal level of cortical activity through the diffuse or nonspecific neural discharges from these subcortical systems up into the cerebral cortex.

In other words, this theory challenges the common older view that motives "arouse, sustain, and direct activity." It proposes, instead, that emotions and bodily drives do not "direct," but have merely the simpler role of alerting, arousing, energizing, or invigorating the part of the brain which has long been regarded as the focus of cognitive processes of one sort or another.

Some psychologists have questioned this whole conception of motives as being processes of a lower level than cognitive processes. But it still seems safe to say that, in one form or another, it remains the almost universal assumption.

Origins of This Conception of Motives as Lower-Level Processes

There are various sources of this view that emotions and bodily drives are lower-level processes as compared with cognitive processes. One of these is the fact that emotional motives, and, even more strikingly, other forms of motivation, appear at lower phylogenetic levels than cognitive processes except those of the simplest sorts. A second origin is the arousal theory just referred to. Another origin lies in the types of process that have been most heavily investigated in cognitive research, particularly in research by perceptual psychologists. A fourth source is probably to be found in some rather common assumptions which were formerly made regarding the nature of neural processes. Each of these sets of premises may be in need of revision. But let us first see what they are and then come back to the task of critical evaluation.

The relative antiquity of motivation, phylogenetically.—In some respects, motivational phenomena are basic biological phenomena. They appear in strong, fundamental terms very early in the evolutionary development of animals and perhaps prevail to some extent down through the whole range of animal life. It is probably safe to say, for example, that hunger is a significant motive in flies, bedbugs, earthworms, starfish, squids, fish, toads, chickens, mice, rats, monkeys, and humans. The bisexual means of reproduction exists in almost all animal forms, and sexual motivation in some simpler or more complex sense probably parallels this. Motivation from excessive warmth probably goes very far down. Phylogenetically, therefore, there seems to be little doubt that motivation is a more primitive biological function, at least in its earlier forms, than those processes that we frequently refer to as "cognitive processes."

It hardly seems appropriate to hypothesize that emotional motives go down as far, phylogenetically, as the bodily drives. As has been suggested above, emotional processes needed to come on the scene with the development of more adequate distance receptors and with the development of greater capacity for perceptual activities and learning, so that the organism could be motivated with reference to subtle cues from the environment. These biological developments have occurred in birds, however, even though there is little yet by way of cortical development of the brain. As can be seen even with reference to chickens, there are important evidences of aggressive reactions and fear (as in social conflicts and the formation of social hierarchies within any flock). At least in hens there are expressions of parental motivation, and many other birds show such motivation in both the females and the males.

We might well expect, therefore, that some central nervous mechanisms would have been developed to serve such motives fairly early in the whole evolutionary process. Furthermore, we might well expect that these neural mechanisms would persist in the "older" parts of the brains of the most highly evolved animals. The basic developments should be the same, presumably, as with the reflex centers for breathing, temperature control, sleep, and excretory responses—to wit, such reflex centers would remain in the older portions of the nervous system rather than being replaced by new structures in the cortical parts of the brains of rats, wolves, or primates.

The transient character of the processes studied by perceptual psychologists.—The conception of motives as lower-level processes has therefore tended to be suggested by the phylogenetic antiquity of motives. The same conception of a fundamental antithesis between motivational and cognitive processes is also implicit in the types of cognitive processes selected for investigation by experimental psychologists. To illustrate this point, let us consider a number of features of the psychology of perception. On each point, we can note the difference between the emphasis and usage in the perceptual field and the emphasis and usage in the motivational field. Some main points that we can recognize are the following:

1. Over much of the history of psychology, perceptions have been defined exclusively as conscious processes. Clinical studies, on the other hand, have convinced psychologists rather generally that motives may operate either consciously or unconsciously.

2. Perceptions have been studied largely with adult human subjects, using subjective reports, rather than with some wider range of subjects and rather than by objective means of study. The field of motivation, on the contrary, has taken much interest in animals and children and has assumed the need for primarily objective methods of investigation, at least on many motivational problems.

3. The particular psychological processes investigated in perceptual research have been processes of very brief duration and of very restricted influence within the whole life of the organism. Perceptual research has involved, for instance, experiences of apparent movement, form constancy, reorganizations of reversible figures, and figure-ground organization. Motivational psychology, in contrast, has been concerned with long-continuing processes that play major roles in the rest of the life of the organism.

4. Perceptual experiments usually have not dealt with temporally extended stimulation. This limitation has not prevailed in all perceptual research, of course, because there have been studies of the perception of speech, rhythms, and music. However, practical considerations often shape the way that perception is explained and discussed, and temporally extended perceptions tend not to be emphasized in textbooks or journals and tend to receive an unduly small portion of research attention merely because they are harder to use than perceptions of static visual stimuli. Motives, on the other hand, particularly emotional motives, are commonly related to temporally extended stimulations.

5. The processes studied in perceptual laboratories typically have been motivationally neutral processes, typically lacking even any minor affective or emotional qualities, whether judged subjectively or behaviorally.

6. Perceptual processes commonly have been studied as though they were end products rather than as processes that would tend to translate themselves into further phases of the psychological functioning of the organism. It is not that perceptual psychologists would argue against any suggestion that perceptual processes have such further relationships, but, for practical reasons, perceptual psychologists have dealt with a truncated portion of the full response process. Motives, on the contrary, of course need to be studied in terms of their influences on further functioning of the organism.

7. Perceptual processes commonly have not been studied as processes that play a cybernetic role with reference to overt behavior. There have been some exceptions, as in work on "tracking"

and on the perceptual guidance of speaking and singing, but most perceptual work has not been along such lines. Motivational phenomena, on the other hand, are basically cybernetic.

8. Most perceptual research has paid little attention to phenomena of positive feedback within perceptual processes, even though there are reasons for believing this is an important consideration in perception. In contrast, emotional processes, and also some physiologically based motives, require a major use of this concept.

9. Most perceptual research has not been phrased in terms of perceptions as processes involved in interactions with the objective environment. The "transactional psychologists" (Kilpatrick, 1961) have urged a study of perception in such terms, but their proposals have not been widely utilized. Motives, on the other hand, especially emotional motives, clearly need to be considered in relation to such organism-environment interactions.

The background assumption that the brain operates only by quick processes.—Near the start of his chapter on "Perception and Related Areas" in Koch's series, Attneave speaks of the difficulties of giving any formal definition of perception. However, he says, "there is in practice remarkably little disagreement among psychologists about which studies belong in this area and which do not. On the crudest and most superficial level: perception has to do with the input side of the organism, with certain short-term consequences (*how* short is difficult to specify) of variations in stimulating conditions" (1962, p. 620).

This separating off of short-term consequences as constituting the domain of perception has probably been a result, in part, of the tendency to emphasize relatively palpable factors and relationships in the earlier stages of experimental psychology. It probably also has been a result, in part, of some underlying conceptions about the nature of neural processes. Until relatively recently, chiefly because of knowledge of the speed of conduction of nervous impulses within peripheral nerve trunks and because of lack of knowledge of many features of brain anatomy and physiology, it seemed reasonable to infer that the brain could not be the locus of any long-sustained processes.

In contrast, however, bodily drives and emotions seemed obviously to be long-sustained processes. Thirst, for example, can intensify over days. Emotional moods of grief or depression or the like can endure similarly for long periods. Consequently, it seemed obvious that motives were processes of "lower" parts of the body rather than processes of the brain. It seemed obvious, furthermore, that they were fundamentally different in character from perceptual processes because of the seemingly legitimate assumption that perceptual processes are merely short-term consequences of stimulus situations.

Perhaps there are still other sources that might be found for the sharp antithesis that developed between the conception of emotional processes and the conception of perceptual and other cognitive processes. But even if we restrict our consideration to the three sets of factors mentioned above, it is easy to sympathize with this antithesis. There certainly are some properties that distinguish between motivational processes and perceptual processes as these two types of processes are ordinarily exemplified and interpreted. It is not surprising that, on this very complex matter, psychologists have tended to come to the same conclusion that the small child reaches on his much simpler question when he says: "An orange and a ball just *aren't* alike—you can eat an orange and . . . ."

Our Need to Re-examine These Background Assumptions

Even though it is fairly understandable that motives (including emotional motives) and cognitive processes should thus be conceived in quite contrasting terms, it still is not so clear that this dichotomizing of motives and cognitive processes along the line of lower-level and higher-level processes is a legitimate conceptualization that we want to continue to use. This conception may be one where we need to go back and re-examine the generally relied-on presuppositions. It may be one where such a re-examination would suggest a drastic reorganizing of our thinking. So let us see what we can find when we re-examine the various preceding points in turn.

What we find when we re-examine the argument from phylo-

genetic antiquity.—As we have seen, one of the reasons for viewing motives as merely subcortical processes, rather than cortical processes, has been the fact that motives, especially of the physiologically based types, run back so very far in the evolution of animal life. This consideration, taken in conjunction with the principle that phylogenetically older types of function tend to be cared for by the "older" portions of the central nervous system of the vertebrates, does tend to suggest that motives, then, are such lower-level processes, neurologically speaking.

But we must not use these biological considerations in a naïve way. Take the concept that "old functions" will still be cared for in the highest animals by "older parts of the brain." When we assume that any phylogenetically old function will be cared for "merely," or even that it will be cared for "primarily," by the older parts of the brain, we are taking a principle which is valuable as a rough proposition and debasing it by overstating it. For, actually, there are plenty of examples of processes which are phylogenetically older than the cerebral cortex but which, in the higher vertebrates, have been transferred over to the cerebral cortex as the crucial governing part of the brain. Take an extreme example first. The sense of touch is perhaps the oldest of the senses. It can be demonstrated with coelenterates like the sea anemone. It even operates in the sponge, which lacks even a nerve-net type of nervous system. But this terrific antiquity of the sense of touch does not mean that tactual discriminations in, say, human beings are accomplished solely by subcortical neural mechanisms. The same holds true for the olfactory sense, for visual sensitivity, and so on. It is merely some of the simpler aspects of such sensory functioning which remain restricted (and then only "restricted primarily") to the subcortical centers. There are reflex mechanisms, for example, which govern the size of the pupil. There are reflex mechanisms which, with increasingly loud sounds, reduce the pressures from very loud noises by turning, at somewhat of an angle, the little bone which transmits sound vibrations to the liquid of the cochlea and thereby reduce the pressures from very loud noises. Such reflex activity normally is cared for by subcortical mechanisms. But human beings also can be trained to use warning signals to make this completely unconscious response on a learned basis, as in the case of tank crews trained to respond thus to a click given through earphones just before the guns of the tank are discharged.

In tactual, auditory, visual, and other perceptual fields, it is of course well known that the perceptual processes depend in very significant ways on mechanisms outside the cerebral cortex. In fact, research is turning up surprising information about how complex these extracortical mechanisms are. In vision, for example, the development of means of recording activity within single cells in the retina, in the transmission channels, and in the visual cortex is unfolding some amazing pictures of the elaborateness and significance of peripheral and peripherally related mechanisms of vision.

However, whether in vision of in other sensory fields, there is nothing in this whole body of research that means that perceptions are not cortical processes in some primary and most crucial senses. On the contrary, the newer research is spelling out, frequently, the means by which cortical processes operate to control subcortical and peripheral mechanisms. Thus, in her important review on "Reticular Mechanisms and Behavior" (1959), Ina Samuels has summarized the following points regarding the connections between the cerebral cortex and the reticular system:

> The importance of these cortical connections can scarcely be overemphasized, for they provide a means whereby the cortex can control the activating mechanisms of the brain stem and thus influence its own level of arousal (French & Hernández-Peón, 1955). . . . The efficacy of cortical processes in inducing wakefulness has been confirmed by studies in which threshold electrical stimulation of areas with projections to the reticular formation aroused a sleeping animal and produced cortical desynchronization just as effectively as an intense peripheral sensory stimulus (Segundo, Arana, & French, 1955). Of even greater import to behavior is the role of cortical projections in providing a mediating mechanism whereby learned, meaningful stimuli may influence the organism's activity in the waking state. That this influence is a powerful one is evident even in the behavior of relatively "ungifted" animals. Thus, the appearance of a human being may come to elicit a far more consistent and intense arousal from the rabbit than strong sensory

stimuli such as loud noises and bright lights (Gangloff & Monnier, 1956) [Samuels, 1959, p. 15].

In this whole matter, one of the most important concepts is that of *encephalization*—the concept that "higher centers, as they increase in size and complexity, come to take over functions originally invested in lower centers, and synchronously higher centers tend to lose their generalized functions, becoming more diversified and specialized" (Osgood, 1953, pp. 476–477). This encephalization does not mean that *all* of the functions of phylogenetically older centers are taken over by the phylogenetically later structures as these develop. In fact, sometimes the ultimate power is left with the lower centers, so that, even though the cortical mechanisms can inhibit or accelerate some "reflex processes," they can do this only within some limits. A person, for example, cannot inhibit his breathing or urinating indefinitely, even though he can indefinitely refuse to swallow food. Even in the case of breathing, however, which ordinarily is taken care of automatically by lower brain centers, provision has been made whereby the need for breathing can affect the complex psychological mechanisms of the organism so that some complex behavioral means may be employed to serve this biological need, and not merely reflex movements be used.

The general concept that seems justified regarding the evolution of the vertebrate brain seems, therefore, to be along the following lines: The simpler means of serving any basic biological function continue to be cared for at lower neurological levels, much as in a complex business organization, where the responsibility for dealing with increasingly smaller details is delegated to lower and lower echelons. Part of the responsibility of the lower echelons, however, is also the responsibility of summarizing and selecting information for transmission to the higher echelons. The president of a concern must not be overwhelmed with details that other levels in his organization should have been able either to deal with or to summarize for him. But, on the other hand, the ultimate authority to make decisions and to exert pressure on almost any matter is reserved for the higher levels of organization. Furthermore, these highest levels must also have the means of requesting more detailed information on many matters, so that they can review on occasion what might otherwise ordinarily be outside their range of interest.

Within the organism, what this means is that some of the biologically oldest processes must be represented in cortical activity. Even though touch is a very old process, the organism still needs to be able to know, through its finer cortical processes, what it is touching. It needs to be able to answer the questions "What am I seeing?" or "What am I wanting to do?" or "Which of several possible objectives would be more worth choosing?" Consequently, even though some superficial considerations tend to suggest that motivation must be a lower-level process rather than a cortical process, the phylogenetic antiquity of motivation does not justify this conclusion. This antiquity does give us some reason to expect that some motivational processes, at least, would have some subcortical mechanisms contributing to them and used by them. And this is of course what is found, not only with regard to hunger, sex, and some other physiologically based motives, but also with regard to some emotional motives. But the phylogenetic antiquity of motivation does not mean that the main responsibility for most motives remains with the subcortical centers in any physiologically intact higher vertebrate, any more than the phylogenetic antiquity of vision means that visual perceptions are not cortical processes.

What we find when we re-examine the arousal theory of motivation.—As was mentioned earlier, much interest has been taken in recent years in what is variously referred to as an arousal theory, activation theory, or invigoration theory of bodily drives and of emotions. The conception that motives are lower-level processes, both neurologically and psychologically speaking, certainly is implicit in many features of these theories. Thus, this implication appears in the fact that the main contribution of motives which is emphasized is a general arousing or energizing effect resulting from the diffuse neural discharges to the cerebral cortex that come from the reticular activating systems in the lower portions of the brain.

The conception of motives as lower-level processes also appears in various negative statements such as the following. Judson Brown asserts:

> . . . one might assume that drive can function both as an activator and a director. . . . Unfortunately this solution seems unsatisfactory, since the directive function it ascribes to drive is precisely the same function traditionally reserved for cognitions or associative tendencies. . . . If both drive and habit are to be included in our theories, then the two should affect behavior in different ways; otherwise only one construct seems to be required. . . . A second solution . . . promises to be more useful. . . . On this view, which is tentatively adopted throughout the remainder of this book, the construct denoted by the words drive or motivation . . . is assumed to have no function as a behavior guide or director [1961, pp. 58–59].

Similarly, Cofer and Appley state: "We think it is evident from this discussion that motivation does not need to be invoked to account for the directional property of behavior or for the fact that behavior occurs" (1964, p. 826).

In these same two books, and in other discussions of the arousal theory, the main criteria mentioned as measures of the presence and strength of any drive are such relatively simple physiological indices as general muscular tonus, GSR, wakefulness, and desynchronization of brain waves. There is little discussion of possible means of distinguishing different drives except by their different origins. All drives (as such) are, as a matter of fact, assumed to energize, indiscriminately, whatever innate mechanisms or habit mechanisms are being tentatively aroused by the immediate stimulus situation. In fact, Brown argues that the practice of speaking of "drives" is inappropriate and "confusing if, as we have argued, it is desirable to limit the function of a drive to that of an activator or motivator. If this latter position is adopted, drive can never be directed toward any specific goal, nor can it selectively activate one type of associative tendency to the exclusion of others, since this would indirectly involve a directive function. . . . But if this is the case, then we no longer have different drives, as behavior determinants, but only *different sources of drives*" (1961, p. 60, italics Brown's).

However, although there are such respects in which the presentation of the arousal theory suggests that motives are lower-level processes, strikingly different in properties from cognitive processes and habits, a full examination of the arousal theories and of the evidence cited in support of them leads to no such conclusion at all.

First of all, we may note that *although the arousal theorists do not emphasize these facts, they admit that behavior does have directional properties and that this directional character of behavior can be predicted only when we know about the motivation of the organism at the moment as well as about the peripheral stimuli and about the habits of the organism.* Thus, although Cofer and Appley were saying that "motivation does not need to be invoked to account for the directional property of behavior," they also say: "It is clear that behavior often has a directional character" (1964, pp. 825–826). Furthermore, and more crucial to our present problem, they summarize a whole series of experiments, starting with the initial study by Hull (1933), which have demonstrated that rats and other animals can learn to make one response in a given apparatus when hungry and a different response when thirsty, even when, as in an experiment by Kendler (1946), the rats were simultaneously hungry and thirsty in all their training trials (Cofer & Appley, 1964, pp. 265–266). It is true that Brown does not mention such experiments in his 1961 book, but when he presented his arousal theory of motivation in the first Nebraska Symposium on Motivation in 1953, he referred to the experiments on hunger-thirst alternations by Hull (1933) and Leeper (1935a) as showing that rats can learn to take one route when hungry, another route when thirsty.

Perhaps it is worthwhile to mention some specific data to indicate how definite this "differential motivational control of the utilization of habits," as I termed the phenomenon, can be under easily discriminated external stimulus conditions. In part of my study, 9 rats were trained on a 3-arm elevated maze with food in one end-box, water in a second end-box, and nothing in the third. After they mastered this problem in 6 days, with 5 trials or less a day, they were required to learn another set of locations in another 6 days and then a third set of locations in a final 6-day period. On the fifth and sixth days of these three training periods, there were 54 initial runs. Each rat was hungry on one of the two final days in each training arrangement, thirsty on the other day. Out of these 54 choices, a person could have predicted 53 of them correctly if he had known how the rats were motivated. He could not have predicted the behavior effectively if he had known only the habits of the rats and the external situation in which they were placed (Leeper, 1935a, pp. 23–28).

Such directional properties are important. One of the most important things we are interested in predicting is the direction that activity will take. By comparison, the various changes that go with different degrees of arousal are relatively incidental. It seems likely that the arousal theorists would agree with this statement. They have chosen to consider almost solely the arousal function when they discuss motivation, but they are making no assertion that the arousal level is as important, except in extreme conditions, as the directional properties of activity. This leaves us with a puzzle. If the direction of behavior is important and if knowledge about motivation does need to be included if we are to predict the direction of behavior, why do the arousal theorists give so very little attention to the fact that directionality is partly a function of the organism's motivation?

The answer is indicated by statements such as the following: "If motivation does direct behavior, this can occur only through the stimuli which motivational states provide—the stimuli to which such states sensitize the organism, the incentive objects to which they orient it, or the activation of innate or habit structures. . . . the *directional* component of behavior is determined by innate or habit factors brought into play by situational stimuli in combination with arousal" (Cofer & Appley, 1964, pp. 826, 837). "The behavior-directing function is performed . . . by the hypothetical associative tendencies, whether learned or instinctive, functioning in combination with both internal and external stimuli. . . . Whichever reaction tendency is dominant at the moment is catalyzed into overt action by drive" (Brown, 1961, p. 61). That is, drives like hunger, thirst, or fear have two roles: they energize, and they provide drive stimuli which, together with other stimuli, decide which habits will be transformed for the time being into "excitatory potential," "reaction potential," or tendency to respond. Through this latter role, drives do indeed help to determine the direction of activity, but in this latter role, they are operating only indirectly. Motives, *as such*, merely energize or invigorate.

In view of the fact that such great importance is attached to the idea that motives contribute to the directing of behavior only through drive stimuli which they produce, we naturally become curious to learn how to identify such "drive stimuli" operationally so that we can use them as variables from which we can make predictions about the directional properties of activity. What we learn, however, is that such "drive stimuli" are defined merely in "functional terms." There is no necessary implication that they act on receptor cells. They might be chemical states within the brain; they might be cortical processes that stimulate other cortical processes; or they might have some other nature. All that is implied in saying that there are "drive stimuli" is that there is *something* which exists as a consequence or aspect of drives and which produces a response.

None of such discussions, to the best of my knowledge, has used the method of "converging operations" described by Garner, Hake, and Eriksen (1956) and Neal Miller (1959) as the necessary basis for inferring any such intervening variable. Accordingly, all that we are left with is the proposition that motivating conditions (1) have an arousal effect, of an indiscriminate sort, on cortical mechanisms and (2), by means of some unspecified and unidentifiable intervening variables called "drive stimuli," help to determine the directional properties of behavior.

Therefore, it is hard to see that the arousal theorists make any assertion which is fundamentally different from the view which existed previously that motives both arouse *and* direct activity. They have added some verbiage regarding what it is that motives do and do not do *as such,* and on this score they should be referred to the paper by Kendler which I mentioned in the opening paragraph of this paper. Furthermore, they have chosen to focus most of their attention on the general arousal effects that come from motives, and this can be viewed as a matter of taste. But in terms of what we can predict from those intervening variables that we refer to as motives, they have not changed our situation.

As a matter of fact, when we look more closely at emotional motives, in particular, we find that there is even less justification than might have appeared at first for Brown's demand that we assume there is merely drive (singular) and not some diversity of drives. For, when we look more closely, we find, for example, that there is not just some single drive of "fear," but different fears in different cases. The process which produces the various "motivational effects of fear" is, in one case, a fear of losing one's job. In another case it is fear of embarrassment and ridicule. In other cases it is fear of injury, fear of loss of sense of self, or fear of some particular sort of emotional experience. And the directional qualities of behavior that come from such fears are specific to the particular kind of fear and not simply to fear in general.

An interesting expression of this point is found in a recent article by R. A. Cloward and R. Ontell which discusses the problems in current attempts to provide job training for unemployed youth from slum areas. Such work, they say, has been founded on the premise that such youth are "unmotivated." But, Cloward and Ontell suggest, the trouble seems to lie in the partly realistic grasp which these young people have regarding the nature of the current world. As they say, "a young person who has no feeling that he can master the jobs available in the modern world is not likely to exhibit many of the psychological and social traits the absence of which we mistakenly call poor motivation.... Today's slum youth encounter difficulties in the marketplace not so much because they are unmotivated but because they are intimidated ... because they are not equal to the world that confronts them, and they know it. And it is the knowledge that is devastating" (1965, p. 7). One might conclude that Cloward and Ontell are saying that these slum youth are held back by fear. But, if so, it is not simply "fear," nor even just "fear of failure," but a fear of some very specific consequences in a particular social situation. The same sort of thing holds true of other emotions, too.

What we find when we re-examine the psychology of perception.—When we look more closely at the arousal theory of motives, as we tried to do in the preceding section, we seem forced to say that motives do actually help to direct behavior rather than have merely some general arousing or invigorating influence. Furthermore, it seems that emotions are relatively specific in character rather than something as vague as the usual names of "emotions" suggest. Fear is fear of something. Anger is anger about something. And so on. Hence, if cognitive processes are marked by fairly definite character, too, and if cognitive processes do direct behavior, as Judson Brown says, one begins to wonder whether motives belong within some larger category of processes that we might speak of as a category of cognitive or perceptual processes. Brown argued that one of these terms would be redundant if both motives and cognitive processes operate to direct behavior. This is merely another instance, however, of disregard for the possibility of hierarchical relationships within conceptual systems. Brown was merely arguing as though, if we say that all vertebrates have backbones and all mammals have backbones, we ought to eliminate one of these terms or the other. Motives, analogously, may have status as a sub-class within a larger category of cognitive processes or perceptual processes.

Before we attempt to deal with this question, however, we should go back and re-examine the traditional conceptions of perceptual processes. Earlier, we outlined the reasons for saying that the traditional concepts and examples from perceptual laboratories tended to encourage the idea that motivational and cognitive processes are radically different from one another. However, we also realize that research in any area of science tends to start with relatively palpable material—with phenomena where the independent and dependent variables are relatively tangible, relatively close temporally, and relatively invariable in their relationships. But with continued work, the material that gets emphasized originally tends to prove inadequate, and the opportunistic considerations which dominated the early choice of research problems and the early theoretical interpretations become less important than some other factors and relationships which originally were "too slight or subtle to be grasped easily by the mind." And in the case of perceptual psychology, it may be that some changes have been occurring which would suggest some more important conceptual relationship between motivational processes and perceptual processes. As instances of such changes, the following points come to mind:

1. Probably the majority of psychologists would no longer accept the old view that perceptual processes should be studied solely or even primarily by introspective reports. Instead, there is interest in using objective behavioral methods as well so that there can be studies of perceptual phenomena in animals, small children, feeble-minded subjects, and so on.

2. Even among psychologists who reject the behavioristic interpretation, the tendency is diminishing to assume that perceptual processes ought to be thought of as always having a conscious character. There are apparently many processes which are not conscious, but which are important in governing behavior and which are functionally equivalent in most respects to conscious perceptual processes. The belief is growing, therefore, that such processes should be grouped with conscious perceptions as part of a continuum running from unconscious perceptions to an opposite pole of very clearly conscious perceptions. The same stimulus attributes, for example, are probably involved in judging the direction of a sound, regardless of whether the individual consciously perceives the sound with its directional character or whether the individual unconsciously uses this directional quality as the basis for some aspect of his behavior.

3. Increasingly, perceptual research, instead of dealing merely with static visual material, is dealing with temporarily extended material such as speech (Lashley, 1951; Broadbent, 1958). As Lashley said, it is hard to construct any plausible hypotheses about how the nervous system can deal with such material, but perceptual psychologists are increasingly insisting that their area of investigation ought not to be restricted to what they can explain neurologically.

4. Increasingly, it is being emphasized that perceptual processes are not end products but are parts of the full stream of the response process to any given stimulation. Indeed, beyond that, they are processes that exert a cybernetic control over motor movements (Smith & Smith, 1962). They are an integral part of interactional processes with the environment. Hence, psychologists are increasingly saying that we need a purposive conception of perceptual activity or cognitive activity, much as Kendler is saying with his proposition that S-R psychologists need to do more work on long units of activity, such as Muenzinger described as "start to end-phase units," and much as Miller, Galanter, and Pribram (1960) speak of with reference to their TOTE units.

5. Increasingly, we are realizing that perceptual processes, even of the simplest sorts, are not to be understood simply as processes set in operation within the cerebral cortex by the arrival there of afferent material. Instead, from work on the brain-stem reticular formation, we now are left with a fundamentally different picture of the brain processes involved in perception. We now know that the ordinary activity of the cortex requires the diffuse invigorating discharges from the reticular system to give a sufficient arousal level for perceptual activities to occur within the cerebral cortex. It is not merely strongly motivated behavior which requires the nonspecific discharges from the subcortical systems, but even relatively weak and motivationally neutral perceptual processes also depend on conditions of activation that require such subcortical contributions.

6. This newer knowledge of the neurological mechanisms of perception is revealing that the phenomenon of positive feedback is very important in the development of perceptual processes (Köhler, 1958; Maruyama, 1963). It is not merely the simple physical properties of stimulation which decide how much of a diffuse cortical discharge there will be from the reticular system. When the perceptual processes of an organism identify some peripheral stimulation as significant, this leads to the use of several special means whereby the neural input from that stimulation is "made more of" and other potential afferent material is kept from interfering (Bruner, 1957b). Not only is there a "gat-

ing" effect on peripheral mechanisms and lower synaptic connections, but also there are dominant relationships of the cerebral cortex to the reticular activating system. As was mentioned earlier, a much more steady and intense discharge from the reticular activating system of a rabbit can be aroused by the sight of a human being than by loud noises or bright lights. The work in neurology, therefore, demonstrates the means of a phenomenon which is a commonplace in everyday knowledge—to wit, that some of the most intense perceptual activity can be initiated by very slight cues, commonly cues that are significant only because of some complex past learning of the organism.

What makes this cortical control possible has been vividly described by Hebb. According to current neurological conceptions, he said, it still seems clear that sensory functions depend on "the great projection systems . . . the direct sensory routes, the quick efficient transmitters of information." But, in addition, there is a second pathway through the reticular activating system, a pathway which "is slow and inefficient; the excitation, as it were, trickles through a tangled thicket of fibers and synapses, there is a mixing up of messages, and the scrambled messages are delivered indiscriminately to wide cortical areas. In short, they are messages no longer. They serve, instead, to tone up the cortex with a background supporting action that is completely necessary if the messages proper are to have their effect" (1955, p. 249). Still further, Hebb continues, "there is one problem in particular that I would urge should not be forgotten. This is the cortical feedback to the arousal system." This is an effect clearly illustrated, he suggests, in some observations on fears in infant chimpanzees by Hebb and Riesen (1943). Such is the case, Hebb says, "when the baby chimpanzee, who knows and welcomes attendant *A* and attendant *B*, is terrified when he sees *A* wearing *B*'s coat. The role of learning is inescapable in such a case" (1955, p. 252).

These comments about cortical control of the reticular system are not intended as statements that the cortex can engage in such controlling discharges to the reticular system when the cortex is deprived of all diffuse activating discharges from below. They are intended as a proposition, however, that, provided the cortex has the usual minor level of activation that runs all through our waking hours, the cortical processes then have sufficient power, in themselves, to send nerve impulses down to the reticular system and stir it into a major positive feedback to those same cortical processes, further intensifying them and helping to sustain them over some much longer time. The reticular system, in other words, is to a great extent the servant of the cortical processes rather than their master. Were this not the case, our lives would be dominated by stimuli in proportion to their physical intensity, and this becomes less and less the case as we have reference to animals higher and higher on the phylogenetic scale.

7. As the work in perception has proceeded, the evidence has become more and more substantial that perceptual processes depend both on innate neural mechanisms and on learning. Furthermore, the modifications of perceptions by learning are coming to be seen clearly as of two sorts. A few psychologists, such as James Gibson (1959; Gibson & Gibson, 1955), have argued that all perceptual learning is merely of one sort, namely, the development of finer differentiations within perceptual processes that already can occur in a rougher form under the influence of environmental stimulations and innately given perceptual mechanisms. There are, of course, such cases. For example, people can learn to follow separate voices within a quartet or, as Gibson says, can learn to make exceedingly fine discriminations between different wines. However, there seem to be strong reasons for saying that there is a second sort of perceptual learning—one that leads to a development of meanings or anticipatory mechanisms. These are the perceptual habits that make it possible for the person to represent *beforehand* what will come next in some stimulus situation. Thus, the person who is an expert in differentiating the tastes of different wines also anticipates beforehand, when he knows that he is about to taste a wine of a certain type, what the taste of that wine will be. When a person listens to a piece of music, he does not merely structure the sounds that are now coming to him, but "sets himself beforehand" for what will come next at each point. Similarly, Solomon's dogs came to perceive their shuttlebox apparatus not only as a situation in which

they would get a shock from the floor if they tarried before jumping when each warning signal was given, but also as a situation in which they could invariably escape the shock if they jumped quickly.

A major reason for regarding these anticipatory processes as perceptual processes is that, in at least most cases, they are reflections of earlier sensory-perceptual experiences of sequential sorts. Their neural mechanisms, whatever their details may be, are presumably the deposits from such earlier sequential perceptual processes and differ from the neural mechanisms used earlier only in that they can permit a running off of the same perceptual process on a redintegrative basis—with less external support than was required originally. This is particularly illustrated in what Osgood (1957) has spoken of as the "predictive relations" or "predictive integrations" which occur so frequently in perceptions. Various unfavorable or impoverished stimulus conditions can be used to demonstrate these. Thus, the latter portions of sentences can be presented against a background of noise, can be presented with very low levels of sensory stimulation, or can be presented with very brief tachistoscopic exposures. Under these conditions, recognition scores on the latter parts of the sentence are definitely higher than they would have been without the clear presentation of the first part of the sentence, even though the first part of the sentence still did not have any possibility of being used as a strict means of prediction of the remainder. Thus, when the person is enabled to read the words "The farmer slowly and methodically," this permits him to perceive effectively any of the various completions of the sentence that might legitimately follow after this, even under conditions in which the latter part of the sentence could not have been read without the preamble to it. As Osgood says, much more of our perceptual life depends on such predictive integrations than we would appreciate from merely our common-sense knowledge.

This concept of anticipatory processes has its analogue in S-R theory in the idea of fractional antedating goal responses (r_g's). The difference between the two views is primarily related to different conceptions of the degree to which brain processes can be complex and long sustained. The antedating processes that S-R theory hypothesizes have been proposed as typically peripheral responses, such as abbreviated chewing or swallowing movements. If the anticipatory processes were merely of such a nature, they could not account for much of what needs to be explained. The evidence for this statement lies not merely in animal experiments, such as those of Tinklepaugh (1928, 1932) and Crespi (1942, 1944), but also in very clear human experience. We do not order food on the basis of what chewing movements the food would require, nor do we order liquids on the basis of what swallowing movements would be involved, but on the basis of sensory effects that can be anticipated. Nor do we select a phonograph record to play on the basis of what listening postures it would evoke. We sometimes make incipient movements and incipient glandular responses, of course, to some preliminary signals, but such peripheral responses are merely a very crude manifestation of the much more complex and subtle anticipatory processes that occur as reflections of the earlier *perceptual* processes which the same type of stimulus situation had involved in the past.

8. Both with regard to differentiation effects and with regard to anticipatory effects in perception, psychologists have been emphasizing more and more frequently at least some very important similarities between concepts and relatively simpler perceptual processes. One example of this is the stress that Bruner (1957a, 1957b, 1964) has been putting on the principle that perceptual processes are categorizing processes or hypotheses about the stimulation that is being received. Some statements by other perceptual psychologists have gone even further in suggesting that the fields of concept formation and concept use at least overlap the field of perception to a high degree. Thus, Attneave says, "a great deal of the research and theorizing that has been done in the area known as 'concept formation' is of such unmistakable relevance to 'perception' that it might be reclassified under the latter without objection" (1962, p. 642). Joe Adams, in a paper on "Concepts as Operators" (1953), suggests as a basic proposition that concepts are "used to structure perception" (p. 242).

Furthermore, a great deal of impetus toward this type of thinking is coming from work in which, for various reasons, efforts are being made to simulate psychological processes by means of electronic computers. It becomes very clear in such work that the requisite means for identifying or recognizing stimulations cannot be stored efficiently as concrete storage items for all of the particular stimulus constellations that might be met. Sufficient economy in storage can be achieved only through the use of generalized programs which can bring common outcomes out of any of a diversity of concrete stimulus presentations. With such work, it becomes difficult to see the distinction between conceptual learning and perceptual learning.

On a whole series of scores, then, psychologists have been developing ideas about perceptual processes which have been making very great changes from the traditional conceptions of perception. When we think at the present time, therefore, about the taxonomic relationships between motivational processes and perceptual processes, we can hardly expect to do a good job if we take into account merely the available knowledge with regard to motives. We must also deal in terms of some new conceptions of the nature of perceptual functioning.

What we find when we re-examine the assumption that the brain operates only by quick processes.—As we noted earlier, there have been strong tendencies to mold psychological interpretations along lines consistent with now disproved concepts about the structure and functioning of the nervous system. Thus, the older conceptions of the nervous system included these beliefs: (1) The brain is merely a transmission device from receptors to effectors and is inactive except as activated by peripheral stimulations. (2) Since nerve impulses travel in the long peripheral axones in an all-or-none fashion and since nerve impulses travel at a considerable speed, brain processes are probably merely short-term processes and would possess some long-sustained character only as some continuing external factors would feed continuing stimulation into the brain.

This picture might well have looked dubious in view of the vastly greater investment in purely central neurones than in neurones that connect the central nervous system with the receptors and effectors. For each afferent neurone in human beings, there are almost 6,000 central neurones, and there are about 40,000 central neurones for each peripheral efferent neurone. But such facts were not in themselves sufficient to counterbalance the influences that tended to suggest that the brain was merely a device for quick guidance of nerve impulses from receptors to effectors.

In recent decades, however, the modern techniques of research on the brain have revolutionized our conceptions of the brain (as, see Livingston, 1962). We now know that the brain is spontaneously active in some ways, even aside from the fact that the peripheral receptors add perpetually to that activity by spontaneous discharges of their own. We know that the main tissues of the brain do not act on a quick all-or-none basis, but that this is a property only of axones. We know that there are tremendously complex interconnections between different parts of the brain and that, through these, there exist the means for very complex influences between different parts of the brain and for long-sustained activities whose specific character would not depend on any current afferent material.

In terms of what is now known, therefore, there seem to be good reasons for saying that the brain presumably is quite capable of the sorts of long-sustained representations which seem suggested by more directly psychological observations. We can see increased reasons for interest in the remarkable paper which Woodworth published in 1937 on "Situation-and-Goal Set." We might put the matter like this: if higher organisms are to get the maximum biological advantage out of their excellent distance receptors and their great learning and perceptual capacities, they need to be able to take momentary information and keep it dominant within their bodies as long-continued and rather specific brain processes. For example, after an animal has perceived a dangerous predator in its environs, it is highly adaptive for the possible victim to be able to maintain this perception or representation of its situation even though the predator immediately conceals itself and moves toward its intended prey under cover of some intervening rise of ground, as coyotes and many other predators do. The predators, on their side of the war of biological resources, have had to push their potentialities for representing their prey during periods in which the prey could not be directly sensed. Out of such circumstances would come the conserving of those genetic variations that produced animals more able to engage in such long-sustained nervous processes. The acme of such capacity is reached in the primates and particularly in man.

An Alternative to the Conception of Motives as Lower-Level Processes and Representational Processes as Higher-Level Processes

In the remainder of this paper, an attempt will be made to extend the various lines of thought which have been considered above. Particularly, an attempt will be made to use this material to develop a more satisfactory conception of the nature and role of emotional processes or emotional motives. The intended ideas, however, are only a part of a more general conception of motivation, and part of the discussion will go on in terms of physiologically based motives. I will begin the discussion with a relatively minor matter of terminology. This first point is not indispensable, but I believe it can facilitate our later discussions.

Some reasons for viewing all representational processes as perceptions.—Traditionally, perceptions were thought of as quite different in character from complex thoughts or complex representational processes, especially when the latter were concerned with objects or events not directly affecting the individual through some sort of external stimulation. Complex representational processes were interpreted as resting on a basis of deductive or other complicated relational activities. Perceptions were interpreted as relatively quite simple utilizations of direct sensory material.

Many psychologists have continued to assume that perceptions ought to be defined as relatively simple processes or relatively more primitive processes, and various possible means for some sharp distinction between perceptions and more complex representations have been proposed. One such means which has been proposed is that perceptions are those processes that rest solely on autochthonous factors (stimulus characteristics and innate neural mechanisms). But the influences of learning on perceptual organization are so pervasive, and so impossible to distinguish except through very difficult developmental studies, that any attempt to distinguish perceptual processes as those that rest either entirely or mainly on autochthonous factors proves impossible to use for most purposes. Another proposal has been that perceptions are those representational processes in which, when learning is involved, the learning is merely some sort that leads to a finer differentiation of the features of present sensory stimulation, and not some anticipatory kind of learning that would enrich the perceptions or give redintegrative qualities to them. But this distinction also proves impossible to use. As we have seen earlier in speaking about Osgood's concept of "predictive integrations," a person can hear or see material under unfavorable conditions through the help of certain redundancies or probabilistic features of the material. The person uses anticipatory habits to achieve perceptual processes which seem subjectively to him to be merely products of the immediate external stimulation.

Another proposed distinction has been that "perception has a certain *immediacy,* whereas rational processes require appreciable time" (Attneave, 1962, p. 644). However, as Attneave says, this proposed division doesn't hold up well. Some traditional perceptual effects, such as the shifts in binocular rivalry or shifts with reversible figures, require considerable time; and, on the other hand, when two scientists are talking and thinking about some very abstruse experimental study, there is an immediacy of meaning with regard to most of the referents of their thought and speech.

As a matter of fact, the research on perception and thought has been showing that many properties formerly regarded as restricted to complex thought processes are operative also in much of what was formerly thought of as merely simple perceptions. And, vice versa, many important principles originally worked out with reference to traditional perceptual examples are proving to be illuminating with reference to more complex representational processes as well.

In the light of all this, two courses seem open. One of these is that which Attneave has favored, as in the following statements at the end of his section on perceptual and cognitive mechanisms: "With calculated vagueness we may, as suggested earlier, associate 'perception' with lower levels, and 'cognition' with higher levels of a hierarchical representational system. An alternative usage . . . is to call the whole representational system 'cognitive,' and to refer to that portion of the system which is active in the representation of the present sensory input as 'perceptual' " (pp. 644–645). The other possible course of action would be to grant that, truly enough, there are differences of degree of complexity, differences of degree of present sensory support, and so on, among different representational processes, but to suggest, nevertheless, that some such term as "sensory perceptions" might be used for the more traditional materials and that the unmodified term "perception" (or "perceive," "perceptual process," etc.) ought to be used to cover the whole domain of representational processes. We need some term to cover the whole domain, and the term "representation" actually would not be easily understood in simpler examples. There are perhaps equal difficulties, however, in getting adjusted to a more comprehensive meaning for the term "perception." Hence, the main argument for a broad usage is the value of some term which would suggest emphatically that a series of propositions which have been established with reference to the more traditional phenomena of sensory perception also hold true for much more complex processes.

Probably I ought to illustrate what I mean by this, using two paradigms which have been quite important in my own thinking. Thus, if you have not met her previously, I would like to introduce you to a young lady who has interested me for so long that I sometimes wonder what would have happened to my scientific thinking if I had not met her and her mother when I did. I refer to Figure 1. A main effect found with the right-hand part of this figure is the well-known fact that whichever perceptual

Fig. 1. A single-phase drawing (*left*) and a composite drawing illustrating several points about perceptual processes (Leeper, 1935b).

organization is first achieved with reference to it tends to obstruct the development of the other possible organization which, originally, would have been almost equally likely to occur. A second paradigm carries this principle much further. In any region where a person originally gets a faulty sense of direction and uses this for a short time before learning what the directions properly are, there are generally great difficulties in changing the sense of direction except by some highly self-conscious and awkward process. Thus, many people who come to Eugene, Oregon, become disoriented by 90 degrees because the railroad and one of the main highways go through the town along an east-west axis, whereas the newcomer knows that the main axis of this highway and of the railroad is a north-south axis from San Francisco to Portland and Seattle. For years and even decades afterwards, when such people see the sun setting over the Coast Range west of town, they have the feeling that the sun is setting in the north. In this case, since the relevant evidence is so tangible and easily assembled, they can also build up a second perceptual mechanism which they can use momentarily, but the first perceptual habit proves almost entirely resistant to any ordinary means of attempting to achieve some second perceptual organization which will operate immediately and naturally.

This same obstructive influence of a first organization is seen on much more complex representational matters, and constitutes one of the main factors that make peaceful international relations difficult. Because of different backgrounds of training, the peoples of different countries see the same objective social events in drastically different ways. Or, within a given country, it proves almost impossible, sometimes, for one race or class to apprehend how the other race or class would experience certain facts that they all know about. It is for reasons like this, therefore, that I feel quite at home with the usage that is developing among many social psychologists when they speak about the perception of social roles, perceptions of other racial or national groups, and perceptions of one country's relationship to another country.

Since I want to emphasize these perceptual principles as principles that hold for all sorts of representational processes, I shall use the term "perception" in this broad sense in the rest of this paper. However, I am willing to grant that this is a quite debatable terminological detail. And if any of you, when I say "perceive," prefer to mutter to yourself "represent," and "representational processes" every time I say "perceptual processes," this will cause me no appreciable distress. In fact, I probably feel sufficiently apologetic about the proposal that I will betray this by occasionally speaking of "perceptual or representational" processes rather than following the simpler usage I have suggested.

The hypothesis that, with perceptions thus understood, motives are perceptual processes.—The central hypothesis of this paper may now be explained through the following three propositions:

Proposition 1. In the course of evolution, there were great advantages to animals in their becoming capable of engaging constantly in such perceptual processes as have been discussed above. It was useful to animals to be able to respond to situations by perceptual processes in which crucial features of the situation were made to stand out, even though related to relatively weak stimulus inputs, and in which other stimulation from the environment was inhibited or neglected. It was biologically advantageous for animals to become able to perceive such stimulus situations, furthermore, not merely in terms of organizations reflecting actually present physical stimulations of receptors, but also in terms of anticipations of further perceptual effects that would occur if such and such things were done. There would be advantages, as well, if such perceptual processes could then be used flexibly to guide overt behavior cybernetically to adapt the overt responses precisely and flexibly to particular environmental features. Such properties in perceptual processes would have all of the advantages which radar-guided or self-guided missiles possess as compared with the older fixed-route anti-aircraft shells that were used formerly.

Proposition 2. There are great biological advantages in the fact that such perceptual processes can operate as very quick affairs in most cases. Predator-prey conflicts often are decided by relative quickness of response, and it should have been expected, therefore, that if evolutionary development could have produced the neural mechanisms for extremely complex and yet also extremely quick perceptual processes, these would have been favored in the course of evolutionary development.

Proposition 3. For such perceptual processes to have their maximum biological value, however, it was necessary for them to exert the various effects on activity which we listed earlier as our criteria of motives. Thus, there would have been advantages if the quick perceptual processes could, in some cases, make the organism willing to forego some present satisfaction or endure some temporary penalty to escape some impending danger. There would have been advantages if the quick perceptual processes could have governed the choices between possible positive goals, or if they could have governed the further perceptual activity, or if they could have evoked immediately certain habits developed in the past, and so on. On the other hand, it would have been seriously disadvantageous if the organism would first have had to engage in a perceptual process, *then* have this arouse some slower-moving visceral or subcortical process and have this be reported back to the cortex before the organism could have the several kinds of effects which motives possess. There would simply be too much biological disadvantage in such a mechanism for it to be established as the mechanism of motivation if, instead, the other development could have occurred—of having the quick perceptual processes serve both as information-processing or information-encoding processes and as motivational processes. In other words, to put the chief point of all this in a very blunt statement, it would have been highly advantageous if, in the course of evolution, some processes could have been developed which were both perceptual and motivational.

To say all this is not equivalent to saying that we should expect that all perceptual processes are motivational processes, any more than our previous discussions have been equivalent to saying that all perceptual processes are unconscious processes, or that they all are sensory-perceptual processes, or that they all are veridical processes rather than illusory processes, or that they all are learned rather than innate. What is being proposed is that the perceptual domain is a large and complex domain and that it needs to be described in terms of a number of more or less orthogonal or independent dimensions. And, just imme- diately, what is being proposed is that one of the dimensions or continua that exist among different perceptual or representa- tional processes is a dimension of motivational quality. Some perceptual processes are motivationally neutral, at least for all practical purposes. But a motivational quality or property is inherent in other perceptual processes—sometimes of only minor importance, but sometimes of such major importance that we tend to pay attention merely to this motivational quality and forget the other properties which even such motivationally intense perceptions share with the motivationally neutral perceptions like those aroused by looking at almost any of the traditional textbook examples of perceptual organization.

In fact, if bodily drives and emotional processes were always such perceptual or representational processes, this could help explain how each of these types of motive could help account for goal-directed behavior. We are already familiar with the idea that perceptual processes can serve as a means of guiding specific movements of the body, such as those required to keep a pointer on a moving line or to reach out and pick up a small object. We know that a controlling process of a rather precise sort is required for such actions. In much the same way, except for the fact that the guidance frequently deals with much more complex matters, we can see that the guidance of activity toward some motivational goal also requires some process that can take account of the particular activities of the organism and their developing relationship to the particular environmental situation. Such guidance usually could not be accomplished except by processes that are determined partly by details of present stimulation, partly by habit, partly by present mental set, partly by physiological condition, partly by present state of satiation, and so on. Perceptual processes are processes which are thus determined, and anything simpler than them could not account for the finely shaded effects by means of which we infer that one person is motivated in one way, another in a second way, etc., within the same external situation.

The relation of such perceptual-motivational processes to subcortical and visceral processes.—What we have said in the previous section is that there would be great biological advantages for the higher animals if they could be capable of complex perceptual or representational processes which could get under way very quickly, yet operate directly and immediately as motives. We might also have added that there would be great biological advantages if such perceptual-motivational processes could be long-sustained processes where this was needed, continuing with a minimum of dependence upon directly relevant external stimulation.

Now the problem that we face is: "Is this what motives actually are? Or, as has been assumed almost universally, are motives processes of a lower level, neurologically and psychologically speaking, as compared with perceptual or representational processes?"

It is probable that one of the reasons that motives have generally been regarded as lower-level processes is the following unmistakable fact: In many different kinds of motivation, there are indeed involvements of lower brain centers and even involvements of visceral organs in a degree far more marked than in the case of motivationally neutral perceptions. Thus, in thirst there is an actual shortage of water through the tissues. In pain there actually are some unusually strong stimulations of peripheral receptors. In sexual motivation there are extensive autonomic effects. In many different emotional reactions there are various unusual visceral reactions.

On the neurological side, too, there frequently are distinctive involvements of subcortical centers within the brain. There apparently are special limbic systems that are involved in hunger, in sexual motivation, in anger, and perhaps in some other motivational reactions. Furthermore, in the case of such bodily drives as hunger and fatigue, it seems that the arousal of such limbic motivation systems can occur directly, as through chemical factors in the bloodstream.

Granting all this, the question still remains, however, as to whether bodily drives and emotions are such lower-level processes within the viscera and within the lower parts of the brain, or whether these lower-level processes are merely accessory to perceptual-motivational cortical processes.

When we consider this question at the present time, we have a fresh perspective on it because of the relatively new knowledge about the relations between ordinary perceptual processes and the reticular system. As we have considered earlier, we know at present that even the simplest of perceptual processes are dependent partly on the maintenance of some degree of cortical arousal by nonspecific discharges to the cortex from the reticular system. Furthermore, we know that apparently one means by which the cortical processes maintain themselves for longer periods of time and even intensify themselves is by sending neural discharges down to the reticular system to stir it into more powerful activity than would have occurred there merely on the basis of the afferent neural material reaching the reticular system.

However, these involvements of the reticular system in perceptual functioning do not mean that the reticular system directly controls the main motor activity of the organism. Nor does it mean that the reticular system is the main determinant of what environmental matters should be the subject of unusually strong perceptual activity. Frequently the matters that call for main perceptual activity are signaled by relatively weak physical stimulations from the environment. What has been needed in the course of evolution has been the development of neural mechanisms that could take such relatively weak stimulations and transform them, by one means and another, into the dominant brain processes. What has been needed has been the development of neural mechanisms that would free the organism from being dominated by stimuli in proportion to their physical intensities. And, apparently, the cortical tissues, as the most elaborately developed part of the brain in the higher vertebrates, have the capacity for soft-pedaling some reticular activities which otherwise would be quite arousing and the capacity for intensifying the reticular activity in other situations where the reticular system, on its own responsibility, would have done very little.

But the key point remains this: *When the reticular system engages in diffuse discharges to the cortex, either because cortical processes aroused such reticular activity or because afferent material aroused it, these reticular discharges influence the behavior of the organism only through the changes that they help induce and maintain in the perceptual processes.*

The same basic principle seems a reasonable one with reference to bodily drives and emotional processes. Let us think first of the physiologically based motives (bodily drives). The distinctive thing about them is that there are either strong peripheral stimulations (as in toothache and pain from electric shock) or else other "lower than cortical" mechanisms that give rise to them and to a great degree determine their strength. This is what distinguishes the physiologically based motives from emotional motives. But even though there are these somatic contributions of different sorts, their mode of operation within the main life of the organism is only by the same means that stronger afferent arousals of the reticular activating system affect the main life of the organism. In other words, the somatic origins of the physiologically based motives exert their psychological effects only through the cortical activities or perceptual-motivational processes that they help to produce. And, as was said earlier, this whole mechanism is of such a character that various other influences help to determine the strength of the physiologically based motives. The pain that a person feels and that tends to affect his behavior is determined by rather subtle psychological factors as well as by simple peripheral stimulations. The hunger, thirst, or sexual motivation that is aroused is governed by more than merely somatic factors, and may be either intensified or lessened by such other factors. As George Klein expressed the conclusion that he and his associates reached, after long struggles to make sense out of their experimental data on the effects of thirst with human subjects, "thirst, like the so-called 'higher needs,' is evidently very much a cognitive event linked in some way to somatic deficit, though not necessarily requiring such deficit for arousal, but always implicating intentions and conceptualizations as well as a range of consummatory objects. The processes 'pushed' somehow determine the 'push' itself" (1958, pp. 90–91).

Take next the case of the emotional motives. The property which most distinguishes them is their great dependence on constellations of stimulations or situations that are significant to the organism only because of complex discriminatory or perceptual mechanisms that either exist innately (as in the case of the fear and restlessness which helps lead to imprinting) or exist because of previous learning. In a situation which is emotionally arousing for the given organism, the perceptual process that is aroused can have immediate motivational effects, as in the case of Solomon's dogs. In addition, the perceptual process can lead to strong arousal of the reticular activating system and other subcortical centers. Through this activating of subcortical systems, the perceptual-emotional process can produce widespread autonomic effects. These, in turn, along with the reticular contributions, can help to sustain the emotional process in a strong form for a longer time than it might otherwise have operated. They also help to prepare the body for some of the behavior that may be required in the environmental situation. But, even so, the case is analogous to the case of the physiologically based motives. *The subcortical processes and occasional widespread visceral effects influence the thinking and decisions of the individual only through their contributions to the cortical processes of the organism. These cortical processes—these perceptual or representational processes—are the motivational processes of the organism.* These are the processes that we experience subjectively as emotions within ourselves, and these are the processes that are pointed to by the behavioral effects that we use as our means of inferring emotional motives in ourselves or in other organisms.

Some possible criticisms and answers.—One objection that might be raised to a perceptual interpretation of motivation is that if motives are perceptions, we have no need of two categories because the properties of each category would be the same. This is, as a matter of fact, somewhat the objection I have felt to the "reformulation of the perception-motivation dichotomy" by Julian Hochberg and Henry Gleitman (1949). They were suggesting that the factors that operate in so-called "cases of motivation" are merely the same factors that operate all through the field of perceptual phenomena. The present proposal is not the same as that. I have been emphasizing the idea that there are a number of properties of motivational processes which are the same as properties of other motivationally neutral perceptual processes, and I have been urging that these are very important properties. But I have also been suggesting that there are some properties which distinguish some perceptual processes, so that, within the total perceptual domain, we need to recognize a continuum from motivationally neutral perceptions to motivationally very powerful perceptual processes. Those properties are the ones which we have long recognized as the properties of motives, such as the tendencies to determine the content of thought and of perceptual activities, the tendency to govern choices between different possible goals, the tendency to produce long-perseverative effects that can yield enduring habit residues from the perceptual processes that have occurred, and so on. I believe it is true that in this paper I have devoted less space to these effects than I should have. But, at any rate, there seems no reason for saying that a perceptual theory of motivation makes no distinctions between perceptual-motivational processes and other perceptual processes.

Another note of skepticism which might be sounded is that emotions frequently make the person do things which are very unreasonable, or at least he believes they are unreasonable. The implication of this criticism would be that perceptual or cognitive processes, on the other hand, are always realistic and sensible processes. Any such conception, however, misjudges the nature of emotional processes and misjudges the nature of motivationally neutral perceptions. For, on the one hand, emotional motives can have very healthy influences in the individual's adaptive activity. Thus, if we really had powerful emotional interests in eliminating poverty, slums, and racial injustices, many of our perceptions as American people would be shaped into forms unlike those they commonly have, but these modifications probably would be in the direction of more valid perceptions than we now entertain. And, on the other hand, we must not assume that motivationally neutral perceptions are always veridical. When the moon looks larger on the horizon, this does not mean that it actually is. When a small child walks at night through a grove of trees, he sees the moon as moving with him, and can hardly be argued out of this. When the small child sees water poured from a low, broad glass container into a tall thin one, he believes, as Piaget has demonstrated, that the amount of water has been increased. So whether ordinary perceptions are veridical or not depends partly on the degree to which the individual has developed the requisite skills or requisite perceptual habits that the situation requires. Furthermore, even adults can establish perceptual habits which they know are quite irrational and yet which they cannot change. I have already mentioned this with reference to geographical disorientations in Eugene. Let me cite another case which this particular audience ought to trust, because the individual involved is a native Nebraskan and was an honors graduate of the University of Nebraska. I refer to my very sensible and intelligent colleague, Dr. Norman Sundberg. When he went to the University of Minnesota to do his graduate work, some circumstance or other caused him to get the territory around the campus twisted around by about 75 degrees. Later he lived in a spot several miles from the campus, in a place where he got the directions straightened out in relation to the sun and the North Star and all the other clear facts of life which native Nebraskans learn to trust so much. But each day, over about four years, when he would drive back and forth between his home and the campus, he would find that he could not hang on to this sensible geographical orientation that he was able to maintain in the rest of Minnesota, but had this little island pull around in defiance of all the clear evidence of what his perception of that area should have been.

A third criticism might be that emotions sometimes change suddenly, as when a person "falls in love." The implication would be that other perceptual processes never show such sudden changes. However, no psychologist would maintain such a view who has worked much in the field of concept formation, problem-solving thinking, or even just with difficult incomplete figures such as those in Figure 2. In some situations, perceptual changes are gradual and cumulative, as in research on figural aftereffects (see Crosland, Taylor, & Newsom, 1929, for the fullest data on individual cases). In other cases, sudden reorganizations occur. Sometimes these sudden reorganizations merely change one motivationally neutral perception into another motivationally neutral perception, as with the drawings in Figure 2. In other cases, they transform one motivationally powerful perception into a different perception, but one which is still a motivationally powerful perception ("I used to be angry with him; now I just feel sorry for him."). In still other cases, a motivationally neutral perception may be transformed into a motivationally powerful perception, or the reverse. In any of these cases, however, we are dealing with perceptual processes and reorganizations or transformations of them and not with any motives which are not simultaneously perceptual as well as motivational in character.

(From Street)

(From Street)

FIG. 2. Some relatively difficult incomplete figures illustrative of materials where a perceptual reorganization may be hard to achieve but easy to retain and use, once achieved (Leeper, 1935b).

Previous Statements of a Perceptual Theory of Motivation

In this paper, I have not yet spoken about other presentations of essentially the same conception which I have sought to develop here, but there are such earlier statements. Thus, in addition to some psychologists who have proposed such concepts in incidental statements, the following psychologists have dealt with the problem at some length. In his address on "Some Cognitive Aspects of Motivation" as president of Division I of the APA, William Prentice explored various implications of the idea that "what we call motives are really a particular kind of perceptual or cognitive event" (1961, p. 503). Donald Taylor, in the 1960 Nebraska Symposium on Motivation, said that his research had led him to an "information-processing model of motivation." In such a model of human motivation, he said, "the study of human values is of primary importance" and "values are one kind of concept" (1960, pp. 66–67). (Taylor's term "concept" is, of course, different from the term "perceptual process," which I have preferred, but the difference is slight. It consists partly of the fact that Taylor was referring to the enduring predispositions or habits as "motives," whereas I have been speaking of motives only in the sense of the active use of such habits. The difference, aside from this, lies only in the fact that I have preferred the term "perceptual" as more inclusive than the term "concept.")

In his address as president of the APA in 1959, Wolfgang Köhler devoted about a third of his discussion to problems of motivation, focusing especially on the suggestion which he summarized by saying that motives are not "scalars (that is, facts which have a magnitude but no direction)," but "vectors (which have both an intensity and a direction)" (1959, p. 733).

The most complex hypothesis regarding motivation is that which George Klein has developed, stimulated particularly by an experimental study he conducted (1954) in which differences of performance on a number of tasks were studied in human subjects selected as having certain strong differences of general cognitive style. The subjects were tested under a condition of thirst. Klein summarizes the conception of motivation which he finally developed out of this study as follows:

It seems . . . parsimonious . . . to . . . think of drive as a construct which refers, on the one hand, to the "relating" processes—the meanings —around which selective behavior and memories are organized, and in terms of which goal sets, anticipations, and expectations develop, and, on the other hand, to those processes which accommodate this relational activity to reality. . . . The first characteristic of drive is that it involves a goal set, a requirement for object qualities appropriate to it. Drives bring the organism into readiness for certain things, certain meanings. The relational core of a drive is, therefore, conceptual activity. . . . the second aspect of drive structure [is reflected in the fact that] . . . the activity of drive consists not simply of arousal or even of readying the organism for particular goals. It includes specific ways of dealing with the environment; it involves accommodative structures. Since cognitive attitudes describe a person's typical accommodative patterns in confronting reality, they are thus best conceived as integral aspects of his drive structure [1958, pp. 92–94].

Still earlier, David Krech (1949, 1950a, 1950b, 1951), in his usual impassioned style, had reasoned that it is unrealistic to conceive of psychological phenomena in terms of separate processes of perception, motivation, and learning. Instead, he urged, we ought merely to conceive of "Dynamic Systems." These, he said, are so definitely organic unities that no single aspect of such a system can be changed without changing the other aspects as well—we have been dealing in myths in believing that we could vary some one of these aspects while keeping the other aspects constant. Though proposing a less drastic statement on this point, E. C. Tolman (1932, 1948) had been suggesting some perceptual factors in motivation in his view that motivation is partly a matter of reward expectations and punishment expectations. Kurt Lewin similarly had been discussing many problems of motivation in terms of factors in the organism's "psychological environment" (see the discussions of his work by Cartwright, 1959, and by Heider, 1960). In my own previous writing, my original paper on a motivational theory of emotion (1948) was extended to some extent into the perceptual-motivational theory which has been elaborated in the present paper (see Leeper and Madison, 1959, pp. 190–223; Leeper, 1963a, pp. 418–434; Leeper, 1963b).

One odd fact about these various earlier discussions of a perceptual or conceptual interpretation of motivation is that their authors have made practically no references to the related ideas of the other papers. This is the more surprising in view of the fact that most of this group are more or less closely related to one another both personally and as regards their general theoretical outlooks and interests. It seems, therefore, as though each of these persons had to grope to the concept on his own, even though possibly helped in ways that he did not recognize by his predecessors or colleagues. I make this suggestion with somewhat more confidence because I remember that, in my own case, when I first read Krech's papers on "Dynamic Systems," they did not make much sense for me, despite my high regard for most of Krech's work and strong sympathy for most of his ideas. It was only later, after having come belatedly to somewhat similar ideas on my own account (as I thought), that I recognized their significant relation to what he had said. And, peculiarly, it took me a long time to recognize that Lewin's ideas might be thought of as a perceptual theory of motivation.

Maybe this sort of thing will continue to be the case. If a perceptual theory of motivation is to become more common, perhaps each psychologist will have to figure it out for himself. But this is time consuming, and it would be more helpful if energy and time could be invested in some more elaborate theoretical and empirical development of this kind of interpretation. Consequently, in this paper, I have tried to spell out the logic of a perceptual theory of emotional processes in some clearer and fuller form than previous papers have done. And, I believe, if the present paper makes some contribution to the development of the motivational interpretation of emotion, this contribution cannot lie on the side of suggesting that we need to think of motives in perceptual terms. That contribution has already been made by other psychologists. If there is any contribution in the present paper, it will have been merely to indicate somewhat more fully the nature of this perceptual theory of motivation and the nature of the larger conceptual structure in which it would most naturally find a place.

The Advantages of a Perceptual-Motivational Theory of Emotion

The suggestion that comes from a number of sources, therefore, is, first of all, that emotions are motives, and then, second, that emotional processes, along with all other motives, are perceptual or representational processes. The suggestion that comes is that emotions and other motives do not exist or operate in any less complex sense than this.

When a proposal like this is made, the immediate comment, of course, needs to be: "So what! Is this proposal merely a change of terminology, or does it have really important implications both within psychology and within the larger world of practical life?"

In this final section, let us try to answer this question.

Research Implications of a Perceptual-Motivational
Theory of Emotion

Even if psychologists took seriously only the concept that emotional processes are motives (in a full sense of arousing and directing processes, rather than merely arousal processes), there would be some very considerable consequences that would come as a result. These might be summarized by saying that if psychologists took this concept seriously, there would be work which would lead to a fundamentally different sort of chapter to deal with emotion in general-psychology texts. The present preoccupation with the physiological mechanisms of emotional activity would shift to a primary concern with the behavioral or psychological relationships of emotional processes. Some material on physiological mechanisms would remain, but it would be accessory. The main emphasis would shift to questions like these: (1) What emotional motives occur innately in different species to what stimulus situations? (2) How are emotional habits developed from such innate origins? (3) What are the effects of emotional motives on the life of the organism? (4) What are the means of identifying, and to some extent measuring, the emotional habits of the individual and also the more particular emotional processes that come partly in consequence of those emotional habits?

If we took the further step of conceiving of emotional processes as perceptual or representational processes rather than as processes of a lower-level character, this would have some other very considerable implications. For, fortunately, there has been a huge amount of research dealing with motivationally neutral perceptual processes. This research would not illuminate all of the properties that emotions and other motives have; otherwise there would be no reason for saying that motives are merely a part of a larger continuum of perceptual processes. But there are many important hypotheses that are suggested by research with motivationally neutral perceptual or representational processes. All such hypotheses ought to be checked and explored further in the more difficult field of motivationally strong perceptual processes. Such should be the case, for instance, with the following principles:

1. The brain apparently operates by dynamically organized functional units or chunks, and learning is more fundamentally a matter of enlarging or changing these functional units of brain activity than it is any matter of learning of any peripheral responses, essential though these are for the expression of such functional units. If emotional processes are perceptual processes, presumably the learning of emotional habits is also to be understood in such terms.

2. Perceptual processes are abstractive or selective with reference to the myriad possibilties that most life situations offer. They are hypotheses, as it were, and either conceptual or concept-like. Emotional processes should also have this character.

3. Even in situations where alternative perceptual organizations are almost equally balanced, whatever perceptual organization occurs first tends to obstruct the development of any other organization which, under other circumstances, would have occurred.

4. Perceptual processes often develop by a process of positive feedback. This is not always a nuisance or a maladaptive process; on the contrary, it is essential to highly sensitive functioning. If emotional processes are perceptual processes, they should show this same process in their operation.

5. In some examples of perception, such as with reversible figures like the Rubin vase or that shown in Figure 1, the achievement of a second possible organization seems not to destroy the neural mechanisms for the prior organization, but

leaves the individual with two coexisting and yet incompatible habits, between which the individual will tend to alternate. If the individual is to use merely one of these consistently, as with reorganized perceptions of the drawings in Figure 2, that one organization has to be given some special advantages of greater simplicity or quality of organization, has to be incorporated into a powerful larger system of habits, or somehow has to be made predominant. Emotional habits very probably are the same.

6. Perceptual processes develop states of satiation with long-continued use—states of satiation that tend to produce perceptual reorganizations even with the same context of habits and of external stimulation. Emotions should show the same.

7. In addition, perceptual processes depend on complex factors of set, cognitive style, temporary physiological state, and peculiarities of the particular stimulus situation. Emotions should show these same complex determinants.

8. At least in some cases, perceptual or representational processes tend to be dominated by some background presuppositions or commitments of the person, and some perceptual organizations can hardly be changed, more than momentarily at least, until such background commitments are changed. Emotions the same.

9. Perceptual mechanisms continue to get developed and elaborated all through the life of the individual. If emotions are perceptual processes, they must similarly be subject to infinitely varied sorts of modification under different cultural and individual circumstances.

10. Even though perceptual habits are hard to change in some cases, as in the case of directional-orientation habits, it seems that all perceptual habits can be modified by learning and that sometimes such modifications can occur suddenly and dramatically. If emotional habits are perceptual habits, these same possibilities should exist for them, and we should set ourselves to the task of locating the factors that decide whether the situation will be of one sort or the other and how, in either case, one can work to make the desired changes as efficiently as possible.

These suggestions do not exhaust, of course, the implications of a perceptual interpretation of emotional processes. But they may indicate, I hope, that it really would make a great deal of difference in psychological theory and psychological research if we came to think of emotions, not as primarily disruptive processes and not as primarily visceral or subcortical processes, but as main motivating processes that have the detailed, complex character that we have learned to infer from work on other perceptual or representational processes.

Implications for Practical Life

In our modern society, as I suggested early in this paper, we have very strong tendencies to emphasize the tangible values that we can produce through our highly developed technology. We have very strong tendencies to emphasize the factual knowledge and intellectual skills that are required in that technology and in scientific work and in all the rest of our complex modern life. In this modern world, we have not made much place for emotional processes. We have not seen them as a motivational basis that must be developed if, for example, any given student is to become a deeply committed scientist or dramatist or political leader. Instead, we have tended to view the emotional aspects of life either, at worst, as a tragic source of distortions or, at best, as a relatively trivial source of some color and esthetic glow to life.

But when we have dealt with life in the terms that such a palpabilistic view of emotions would favor, we have developed a modern society in which there is so much dissatisfaction, hostility, boredom, and insecurity that the whole social and personal structure of our lives is tending to disintegrate. When the social costs of the more easily recognized emotional factors are so great, it is not surprising that we tend to perpetuate the old rationalistic view of emotional processes. It is not surprising that we emphasize the ills that emotional processes can produce and fail to recognize the constructive possibilities in the emotional constitution which is so important in all of the higher vertebrates, particularly in the higher primates and man.

However, there are many other matters in human history where knowledge and skill tended to develop first with reference to relatively palpable factors and relationships. Our blindness to the subtler and more complex aspects of emotional motivation is merely another instance of what we have done in many other areas before. But it also is true that in those other areas there was finally an awakening to the significance of relatively impalpable factors as well. Perhaps this can also happen with reference to the emotional phase of life. Perhaps this will be another case where the factors that are "too slight or subtle to be grasped easily by the mind" will prove to be much more significant, practically as well as scientifically, than those other factors that were more easily recognized first.

REFERENCES

Adams, J. Concepts as operators. *Psychol. Rev.*, 1953, **60**, 241–251.

Ansbacher, H. L., & Ansbacher, Rowena R. (Eds.) *Superiority and social interest: a collection of later writings of Alfred Adler.* Evanston, Ill.: Northwestern Univ. Press, 1964.

Atkinson, J. W. *An introduction to motivation.* Princeton, N. J.: Van Nostrand, 1964.

Attneave, F. Perception and related areas. In S. Koch (Ed.), *Psychology: a study of a science.* Vol. 4. New York: McGraw-Hill, 1962. Pp. 619–659.

Barron, F. *Creativity and psychological health.* Princeton, N. J.: Van Nostrand, 1963.

Bartley, S. H. Emotion and the evaluative feature of all behavior. *Psychol. Rec.*, 1958, **8**, 39–41.

Beach, F. A. Instinctive behavior: reproductive activities. In S. S. Stevens (Ed.), *Handbook of experimental psychology.* New York: Wiley, 1951. Pp. 387–434.

Berlyne, D. E. *Conflict, arousal, and curiosity.* New York: McGraw-Hill, 1960.

Bindra, D. Organization in emotional and motivated behavior. *Canad. J. Psychol.*, 1955, **9**, 161–167.

Bindra, D. *Motivation: a systematic reinterpretation.* New York: Ronald Press, 1959.

Bonime, W. *The clinical use of dreams.* New York: Basic Books, 1962.

Broadbent, D. E. *Perception and communication.* New York: Pergamon Press, 1958.

Brown, J. S. Problems presented by the concept of acquired drives. In J. S. Brown *et al., Current theory and research in motivation: a symposium.* Lincoln: Univ. of Nebraska Press, 1953. Pp. 1–21.

Brown, J. S. *The motivation of behavior.* New York: McGraw-Hill, 1961.

Bruner, J. S. On going beyond the information given. In J. S. Bruner *et al.,*

Contemporary approaches to cognition: the Colorado symposium. Cambridge: Harvard Univ. Press, 1957. Pp. 41–69. (a)

Bruner, J. S. On perceptual readiness. *Psychol. Rev.*, 1957, **64**, 123–152. (b)

Bruner, J. S. The course of cognitive growth. *Amer. Psychologist*, 1964, **19**, 1–15.

Bruner, J. S., & Potter, Mary C. Interference in visual recognition. *Science*, 1964, **144**, 424–425.

Cartwright, D. Lewinian theory as a contemporary systematic framework. In S. Koch (Ed.), *Psychology: a study of a science.* Vol. 2. New York: McGraw-Hill, 1959. Pp. 7–91.

Cloward, R. A., & Ontell, R. Our illusions about training. *Amer. Child*, 1965, **47**, 6–10.

Cofer, C. N., & Appley, M. H. *Motivation: theory and research.* New York: Wiley, 1964.

Conant, J. B. *On understanding science.* New Haven: Yale Univ. Press, 1947.

Crespi, L. Quantitative variation of incentive and performance in the white rat. *Amer. J. Psychol.*, 1942, **55**, 467–517.

Crespi, L. Amount of reinforcement and level of performance. *Psychol. Rev.*, 1944, **51**, 341–357.

Crosland, H. R., Taylor, H. R., & Newsom, S. J. Practice and improvability in the Müller-Lyer illusion in relation to intelligence. *J. gen. Psychol.*, 1929, **2**, 290–306.

Davis, Clara M. Self-selection of diet by newly weaned infants. *Amer. J. Dis. Child.*, 1928, **36**, 651–679.

Deutsch, J. A. *The structural basis of behavior.* Chicago: Univ. of Chicago Press, 1960.

Deutsch, J. A. Higher nervous function: the physiological bases of memory. *Annu. Rev. Physiol.*, 1962, **24**, 259–286.

Douglas, Anna G. A tachistoscopic study of the order of emergence in the process of perception. *Psychol. Monogr.*, 1947, **61** (Whole No. 287).

Duffy, Elizabeth. An explanation of "emotional" phenomena without the use of the concept "emotion." *J. gen. Psychol.*, 1941, **25**, 283–293.

Duffy, Elizabeth. *Activation and behavior.* New York: Wiley, 1962.

Erikson, E. H. *Childhood and society.* New York: Norton, 1950.

Festinger, L. The motivating effect of cognitive dissonance. In G. Lindzey (Ed.), *Assessment of human motives.* New York: Rinehart, 1958. Pp. 87–118.

Festinger, L. The psychological effects of insufficient rewards. *Amer. Psychologist*, 1961, **16**, 1–11.

Fiske, D. W., & Maddi, S. (Eds.) *Functions of varied experience.* Homewood, Ill.: Dorsey Press, 1961.

Fraisse, P. Les émotions. In P. Fraisse & J. Piaget (Eds.), *Traité de Psychologie Expérimentale.* Vol. 5. *Motivation, émotion, et personnalité.* Paris: Presses Universitaires de France, 1963. Pp. 83–153.

Franklin, J. C., Schiele, B. C., Brozek, J., & Keys, A. Observations on human behavior in experimental semistarvation and rehabilitation. *J. clin. Psychol.*, 1948, 4, 28–45.

Fromm, E. Selfishness and self-love. *Psychiatry*, 1939, **2**, 507–523.

Garner, W. R., Hake, H. W., & Eriksen, C. W. Operationism and the concept of perception. *Psychol. Rev.*, 1956, 63, 149–159.

Gibson, J. J. Perception as a function of stimulation. In S. Koch (Ed.), *Psychology: a study of a science.* Vol. 1. New York: McGraw-Hill, 1959. Pp. 456–501.

Gibson, J. J., & Gibson, Eleanor J. Perceptual learning: differentiation or enrichment. *Psychol. Rev.*, 1955, 62, 32–41.

Glickman, S. E. Perseverative neural processes and consolidation of the memory traces. *Psychol. Bull.*, 1961, 58, 218–233.

Harlow, H. F. Mice, monkeys, men and motives. *Psychol. Rev.*, 1953, **60**, 23–32.

Harlow, H. F. The heterosexual affectional system in monkeys. *Amer. Psychologist*, 1962, **17**, 1–9.

Harlow, H. F., & Harlow, Margaret K. Social deprivation in monkeys. *Scient. Amer.*, 1962, **207** (5), 136–146.

Hebb, D. O. Drive and the C. N. S. (conceptual nervous system). *Psychol. Rev.*, 1955, **62**, 243–254.

Hebb, D. O., & Riesen, A. H. The genesis of irrational fears. *Bull. Canad. psychol. Ass.*, 1943, 3, 49–50.

Heider, F. The Gestalt theory of motivation. In M. R. Jones (Ed.), *Nebraska symposium on motivation: 1960.* Lincoln: Univ. of Nebraska Press, 1960. Pp. 145–172.

Hochberg, J. E., & Gleitman, H. Towards a reformulation of the perception-motivation dichotomy. *J. Pers.*, 1949, 18, 180–191.

Hull, C. L. Differential habituation to internal stimuli in the albino rat. *J. comp. Psychol.*, 1933, **16**, 255–273.

Kendler, H. H. The influence of simultaneous hunger and thirst drives upon the learning of two opposed spatial responses of the white rat. *J. exp. Psychol.*, 1946, **36**, 212–220.

Kendler, H. H. "What is learned?"—A theoretical blind alley. *Trans. N. Y. Acad. Sci.*, 1950, Ser. II, 13, 73–77.

Kendler, H. H. *Basic psychology.* New York: Appleton-Century-Crofts, 1963.

Kendler, H. H. Motivation and behavior. In D. Levine (Ed.), *Nebraska symposium on motivation: 1965.* Lincoln: Univ. of Nebraska Press, 1965. Pp. 1–23.

Keys, A., Brozek, J., Henschel, A., Mickelsen, O., & Taylor, H. L. *The biology of human starvation.* Minneapolis: Univ. of Minnesota Press, 1950. 2 vols.

Kilpatrick, F. P. (Ed.) *Explorations in transactional psychology.* New York: New York Univ. Press, 1961.

Klein, G. S. Need and regulation. In M. R. Jones (Ed.), *Nebraska symposium on motivation: 1954.* Lincoln: Univ. of Nebraska Press, 1954. Pp. 224–274.

Klein, G. S. Cognitive control and motivation. In G. Lindzey (Ed.), *Assessment of human motives.* New York: Rinehart, 1958. Pp. 87–118.

Köhler, W. *The mentality of apes.* London: Routledge & Kegan Paul, 1925.

Köhler, W. The obsessions of normal people. In S. Goudsmidt *et al., Frontiers of knowledge.* Waltham, Mass.: Brandeis Univ., 1958. Pp. 14–23.

Köhler, W. Gestalt psychology today. *Amer. Psychologist,* 1959, **14**, 727–734.

Kortlandt, A. Chimpanzees in the wild. *Scient. Amer.,* 1962, **206** (5), 128–138.

Krech, D. Notes toward a psychological theory. *J. Pers.,* 1949, **18**, 66–87.

Krech, D. Dynamic systems, psychological fields, and hypothetical constructs. *Psychol. Rev.,* 1950, **57**, 283–290. (a)

Krech, D. Dynamic systems as open neurological systems. *Psychol. Rev.,* 1950, **57**, 345–361. (b)

Krech, D. Cognition and motivation in psychological theory. In W. Dennis *et al., Current trends in psychological theory.* Pittsburgh: Univ. of Pittsburgh Press, 1951. Pp. 111–139.

Kuhn, T. S. *The structure of scientific revolutions.* Chicago: Univ. of Chicago Press, 1962.

Lashley, K. S. The problem of serial order in behavior. In L. A. Jeffress (Ed.), *Cerebral mechanisms in behavior: the Hixon symposium.* New York: Wiley, 1951. Pp. 112–136.

Leeper, R. W. The role of motivation in learning: a study of the phenomena of differential motivational control of the utilization of habits. *J. genet. Psychol.,* 1935, **46**, 3–40. (a)

Leeper, R. W. A study of a neglected portion of the field of learning—the development of sensory organization. *J. genet. Psychol.,* 1935, **46**, 41–75. (b)

Leeper, R. W. A motivational theory of emotion to replace "emotion as disorganized response." *Psychol. Rev.,* 1948, **55**, 5–21.

Leeper, R. W. Learning and the fields of perception, motivation, and personality. In S. Koch (Ed.), *Psychology: a study of a science.* Vol. 5. New York: McGraw-Hill, 1963. Pp. 365–487. (a)

Leeper, R. W. The motivational theory of emotion. In C. L. Stacey & M. F. DeMartino (Eds.), *Understanding human motivation.* (2nd ed.) Cleveland: Howard Allen, 1963. Pp. 657–666. (b)

Leeper, R. W., & Madison, P. *Toward understanding human personalities.* New York: Appleton-Century-Crofts, 1959.

Lehrman, D. S. The reproductive behavior of ringdoves. *Scient. Amer.,* 1964, **211** (5), 48–54.

Lindsley, D. Psychophysiology and motivation. In M. R. Jones (Ed.), *Nebraska symposium on motivation: 1957.* Lincoln: Univ. of Nebraska Press, 1957. Pp. 44–105.

Livingston, R. B. How man looks at his own brain: an adventure shared by psychology and neurophysiology. In S. Koch (Ed.), *Psychology: a study of a science.* Vol. 4. New York: McGraw-Hill, 1962. Pp. 51–99.

McDougall, W. *The energies of men.* New York: Scribner's, 1932.

Malmo, R. B. Activation: a neuropsychological dimension. *Psychol. Rev.*, 1959, **66**, 367–386.

Mandler, G. Emotion. In R. Brown *et al.*, *New directions in psychology*. New York: Holt, Rinehart, & Winston, 1962. Pp. 267–343.

Maruyama, M. The second cybernetics: deviation amplifying mutual causal processes. *Amer. Scientist*, 1963, **51**, 164–179.

Maslow, A. H. *Motivation and personality*. New York: Harper, 1954.

Melzack, R. The perception of pain. *Scient. Amer.*, 1961, 204, (2), 41–49.

Miller, G. A., Galanter, E., & Pribram, K. H. *Plans and the structure of behavior*. New York: Holt, 1960.

Miller, N. E. Studies of fear as an acquirable drive: I. Fear as motivation and fear-reduction as reinforcement in the learning of new responses. *J. exp. Psychol.*, 1948, **38**, 89–101.

Miller, N. E. Liberalization of basic S-R concepts: extensions to conflict behavior, motivation, and social learning. In S. Koch (Ed.), *Psychology: a study of a science*. Vol. 2. New York: McGraw-Hill, 1959. Pp. 196–292.

Munsinger, H., & Kessen, W. Uncertainty, structure, and preference. *Psychol. Monogr.*, 1964, **78** (Whole No. 586).

Murray, E. J. *Motivation and emotion*. Englewood Cliffs, N. J.: Prentice-Hall, 1964.

Nissen, H. W. The nature of the drive as innate determinant of behavioral organization. In M. R. Jones (Ed.), *Nebraska symposium on motivation: 1954*. Lincoln: Univ. of Nebraska Press, 1954. Pp. 281–321.

Osgood, C. E. *Method and theory in experimental psychology*. New York: Oxford Univ. Press, 1953.

Osgood, C. E. A behavioristic analysis of perception and language as cognitive phenomena. In J. S. Bruner *et al.*, *Contemporary approaches to cognition: the Colorado symposium*. Cambridge: Harvard Univ. Press, 1957. Pp. 75–118.

Prentice, W. C. H. Some cognitive aspects of motivation. *Amer. Psychologist*, 1961, 16, 503–511.

Rogers, C. R. *On becoming a person*. Boston: Houghton Mifflin, 1961.

Rogers, C. R. Actualizing tendency in relation to "motives" and to consciousness. In M. R. Jones (Ed.), *Nebraska symposium on motivation: 1963*. Lincoln: Univ. of Nebraska Press, 1963. Pp. 1–24.

Rosenzweig, M. R. The mechanisms of hunger and thirst. In L. Postman (Ed.), *Psychology in the making*. New York: Knopf, 1962. Pp. 73–143.

Samuels, Ina. Reticular mechanisms and behavior. *Psychol. Bull.*, 1959, **56**, 1–25.

Sartre, Jean-Paul. *Sketch for a theory of the emotions*. London: Methuen, 1962.

Smith, K. U., & Smith, W. M. *Perception and motion: an analysis of space-structured behavior*. Philadelphia: Saunders, 1962.

Solomon, R. L., Kamin, L. J., & Wynne, L. C. Traumatic avoidance learning:

the outcomes of several extinction procedures with dogs. *J. abnorm. soc. Psychol.*, 1953, 48, 291–302.

Solomon, R. L., & Wynne, L. C. Traumatic avoidance learning: acquisition in normal dogs. *Psychol. Monogr.*, 1953, 67 (Whole No. 354).

Solomon, R. L., & Wynne, L. C. Traumatic avoidance learning: the principles of anxiety conservation and partial irreversibility. *Psychol. Rev.*, 1954, 61, 353–385.

Spence, K. W. A theory of emotionally based drive (*D*) and its relation to performance in simple learning situations. *Amer. Psychologist*, 1958, 13, 131–141.

Sullivan, H. S. *The collected works of Harry Stack Sullivan.* New York: Norton, 1964. 2 vols.

Taylor, D. W. Toward an information-processing theory of motivation. In M. R. Jones (Ed.), *Nebraska symposium on motivation: 1960.* Lincoln: Univ. of Nebraska Press, 1960. Pp. 51–79.

Tinklepaugh, O. L. An experimental study of representative factors in monkeys. *J. comp. Psychol.*, 1928, 8, 197–236.

Tinklepaugh, O. L. Multiple delayed reactions with chimpanzees and monkeys. *J. comp. Psychol.*, 1932, 13, 207–243.

Tolman, E. C. *Purposive behavior in animals and men.* New York: Century, 1932.

Tolman, E. C. Cognitive maps in rats and men. *Psychol. Rev.*, 1948, 55, 189–208.

Washburn, S. L., & DeVore, I. The social life of baboons. *Scient. Amer.*, 1961, 204 (6), 62–71.

White, R. W. Motivation reconsidered: the concept of competence. *Psychol. Rev.*, 1959, 66, 297–333.

Woodworth, R. S. Situation-and-goal set. *Amer. J. Psychol.*, 1937, 50, 130–140.

Woodworth, R. S. *Psychology.* (4th ed.) New York: Holt, 1940.

Young, P. T. *Motivation and emotion.* New York: Wiley, 1961.

Reinforcement Theory[1]

DAVID PREMACK[2]

University of Missouri

Along with imposing various constraints upon the subject in order to study reinforcement, we have been conducting other studies in which the subject is as little constrained as possible. What the rat does when unconstrained may be looked upon as the operating characteristics of the species; in time, the principles of reinforcement may prove to be illuminated by, if not derivable from, a proper understanding of the operating characteristics. Accordingly, we will start with a brief account of the unconstrained rat and then turn to the animal that is constrained in the various ways which a study of reinforcement demands.

FREE RESPONDING AS A BASE STATE: OPERATING CHARACTERISTICS

To obtain a comprehensive account of the operating characteristics, we perform what might be called an anti-experiment: vary nothing and see what the animal varies. That is, place the organism in as undemanding and invariant an environment as possible and observe the manner in which the animal varies despite the invariance of the environment. Environments come close to leaving the animal alone when they drop three standard constraints: contingencies, deprivation, and gradients. If there are no gradients of temperature, light, or noise, any activity cycles found can be attributed to the animal. Similarly, if stimuli such as food and water are continuously available, rather than

[1] The research reported here was aided by grants from the National Science Foundation, the National Institute of Mental Health, and the University of Missouri Graduate Research Council. I am indebted to Walter Kintsch for criticism and helpful comments.

[2] Present address: University of California, Santa Barbara.

123

being constrained, on the one hand, by a deprivation schedule or, on the other, by an instrumental response requirement, then any variation in the animal's responding to these stimuli can be ascribed to the animal.

Four rats were maintained for 150 days in an environment approximating the one described.[3] The animals were housed individually in standard-size cages, each of which provided an activity wheel, a food source, and a drinkometer. Continual illumination was used, along with the usual controls for ambient sound and temperature. Throughout the 150 days of observation, the animals had continuous access to food, water, and wheel, except for brief periods of daily maintenance.

The results may be best summarized by starting with the smaller units of behavior and working toward the larger. A fair amount has been written about the invariance of the lick rate: when rats lick, they lick about 7 times/sec. (Stellar & Hill, 1952). We have found 18-day-old rats, licking for the first time, to lick 7 times/sec. (Schaeffer & Premack, 1961). But it is less widely considered that an apparently comparable invariance is found in other behaviors; indeed, it would be surprising if the invariance were confined to licking. Other behaviors do not offer as convenient a topographic unit as the lick, but it is not strictly necessary to measure recurrence anatomically in order to establish that certain movements of the animal may occur at constant rates. For example, rats appear to eat standard 45-mg. Noyes pellets in about 6.5 sec. As in the case of the lick, this appears to be independent of deprivation: ad lib fed and starved rats both consume the pellet in about 6.5 sec. Similar constancies appear to obtain for running. Skinner (1933) observed some years ago that in a properly balanced wheel, the rat's paws contacted the running surface a constant number of times/sec. The intervening years have not dimmed these constancies; rats complete most 360-degree turns in our wheels in about 1 sec. (Premack & Schaeffer, 1962). If locomotion differs from eat and drink, it is in occurring in more than one form. But each form appears to be nearly invariant: locomotion may thus be a family of con-

[3] R. W. Schaeffer collected these data, assisted by G. Collier and myself.

stant-speed gaits. Grooming, too, appears to consist of a small set of stereotyped motor sequences, each with a fixed rate of occurrence. Finally, the copulatory movements of the male rat may be subject to a comparable stereotypy. Although only a few of these cases are based on measurement, and others—grooming and copulation—on impression alone, it is not too great an inductive leap to wonder if, in the rat, all recurrent behaviors do not occur at constant momentary rates.

Dethier (1964) has aptly dubbed an apparently similar state of affairs in certain insects the "little motor theory of motivation." We may view the fetal rat as moving down an assembly line, receiving first a motor from one bin, a little later on a motor from another bin, the bins marked "eat," "drink," "run," etc. Each motor has only one operating speed, and this speed is the same for all motors in the same bin. That is, at the level of the "little movements," there are not even individual differences. Seven licks per second is not an average figure, but a constant from rat to rat.

Individual differences are found up a level, not in the speed at which the motor operates, but in the durations for which the motors operate once they have started. The story appears to be much the same for eat, drink, and run, and so may be told for all of them in terms of any one of them. For example, the rat eats (or drinks or runs) throughout the day in a series of bursts—periods in which the behavior is essentially unbroken.[4] Dura-

---

[4] Bursts were originally defined as the ingestion of a 45-mg. pellet, a tongue lap, or 90 degrees of wheel revolution separated from any other like instance by at least 8 sec. To examine the possibility that definition of burst might affect the outcome of subsequent correlational analyses, certain of the analyses were repeated using different burst definitions. Bursts were redefined as like instances separated by as little as 0.1 sec. and by as much as 32 sec.; for this appreciable range, burst definition had no essential effect upon the conclusions reported here. A condition which may have more effect upon the present conclusions is that the data be for animals that are thoroughly adapted (and perhaps kept in constant light rather than constant dark). We find rats to drop their activity cycles after several weeks of such maintenance, and thenceforth to distribute their eat, drink, and run more or less randomly throughout the day. This may or may not be essential for the conclusions reported here; in any case, our animals tended to be stationary. As regards specifically eating, more recent data based upon bulk food obtained at the end of a "tunnel" confirm the present data based upon pellets obtained by a bar press.

tions of the individual bursts are definitely not constant, but vary over a considerable range. However, the average of the distribution of burst durations for any behavior is reasonably stable for the individual rat from day to day. Also, the three behaviors tend to order on the basis of the average burst duration, eat being the longest and run the shortest. Thus, for any one behavior it is possible to tell one rat from another by the average duration of the burst—how long the "little motor" operates once it has started—and for any one rat tell one behavior from another on the same basis. Some indication of the range of the distributions and stability of their means and variances is provided in Table 1.

TABLE 1
MEANS AND VARIANCES OF BURST LENGTH FOR EACH BEHAVIOR
PER SIX-HOUR PERIOD

		Period I	Period II	Period III	Period IV
		Drink			
S1	Mean	4.4	4.3	5.4	5.0
	Variance	7.5	7.3	9.6	6.2
S2	Mean	10.8	8.0	12.8	10.2
	Variance	36.4	38.8	26.2	37.1
S3	Mean	7.0	5.7	7.7	4.3
	Variance	18.9	4.0	16.1	21.1
S4	Mean	5.9	6.5	9.0	8.4
	Variance	12.4	19.3	18.6	21.0
		Eat			
S1	Mean	12.0	11.1	10.0	9.2
	Variance	87.7	76.3	61.4	68.6
S2	Mean	10.6	10.7	12.9	10.7
	Variance	130.0	106.0	119.3	88.1
S3	Mean	21.0	15.0	20.7	16.9
	Variance	140.3	146.2	205.1	137.0
S4	Mean	4.6	3.7	4.2	3.9
	Variance	27.4	19.3	22.5	25.4
		Run			
S1	Mean	4.3	4.0	4.2	3.7
	Variance	18.7	13.9	15.9	15.5
S2	Mean	3.4	4.1	3.6	4.2
	Variance	7.2	23.8	7.0	9.0
S3	Mean	3.7	3.8	4.8	4.8
	Variance	19.7	14.4	25.9	23.5
S4	Mean	3.8	4.1	4.8	3.5
	Variance	25.4	23.7	30.9	15.2

Is it possible to account for the variation in duration of the individual bursts? Since the individual bursts vary widely in duration, it would seem reasonable that factors could be found which would account for this variation. The rat sometimes engages in a burst of eating that lasts for five or six minutes, while on other occasions it may eat a "meal" that lasts only a matter of seconds. How long it waits between bursts also varies considerably. It would seem reasonable to suppose that if a current "meal" were greater than average, the rat would wait longer than average before eating again and/or would eat a "meal" smaller than average.

Again the answer is very similar for all three behaviors and thus may be told in terms of any one of them. All seemingly reasonable suppositions as to what may control burst duration turn out to be unfounded; at least we have been unable to collect evidence in support of them. For example, auto-correlations on adjacent pairs of like bursts are typically of the order of about .04. This is borne out by the Von Neuman ratio, which is 2 for independent events and for which we obtain 1.96, 1.97, and 1.95 for the relation between durations of successive pairs of eat, drink, and run, respectively (Kintsch & Premack, 1965). Likewise, the correlation between duration of the individual burst and duration of the preceding nonresponding interval of like kind—for example, "meal" and preceding noneating interval—is of the order of about .20. The only correlations we have found of any magnitude are those between duration of the burst and total duration of like responding in the preceding 15 min. However, these largest of all correlations leave approximately 87 to 98 per cent of the variance in burst duration unaccounted for.

There would thus appear to be an appreciable random component in the duration of the individual bursts. This conclusion is so far based on negative evidence; it will remain so until we are able to go beyond suggesting a random process and can specify what kind of random process. (It is exactly at this point that the need for massive data is felt.) In the meantime, there remains the fact that, given that the animal has started to respond—the motor has begun to operate—we are unable to find any factors that provide appreciable help in predicting when it will stop. This state of affairs would appear to be incompatible with standard reactive inhibition-type models, for rest and amount of responding are not playing their assumed roles. One condition which this state of affairs does support is the propriety of using response duration as an estimate of response probability. The relevance of this last implication will become evident when we turn to reinforcement, and we will leave its development for that time.

Although durations of the individual bursts are unpredictable, the average of the distribution of burst durations can be manipulated in the standard deterministic fashion. For example, by increasing the sucrose content of the food, we can shorten the average duration of bursts of eating, but without affecting the unpredictability of the duration of the individual bursts. Doubtless other parameters can be found that will affect the average of the process without simultaneously affecting predictability of individual events. Probably what is most surprising here, by (risky) analogy to physics, is that the unpredictability is for macroscopic events—the behavior of the whole organism. A comparable unpredictability for neural events would be more easily accepted.

What behavior state the rat enters into is in marked contrast to how long it stays there, for the data reveal strong dependencies between current burst and kind of immediately preceding burst. Thus, whether the rat runs, eats, or drinks depends upon what it did previously. Additional though weaker dependencies are found for two-preceding and three-preceding bursts. What motor operates thus depends upon which ones recently operated. Kind of burst will not predict duration, however, any more than duration will predict duration. Thus, while a drink is more likely to follow a run than would occur were the two classes independent, there is nonetheless no correlation between duration of the preceding run and duration of the drink that follows. Furthermore, the number of drinks following long runs is about the same as the number that follow short runs. Thus, kind of burst will predict only kind, while duration will predict neither duration nor kind.

To summarize *tentatively* the operating characteristics of the rat:

1. The motor sequences that comprise the recurrent behaviors occur at fixed rates.

2. Duration of the individual bursts, that is, when an animal will stop a given behavior, is to a large extent unpredictable.

3. The behavior the rat enters is dependent upon the behaviors it previously entered.

4. Much of the unconstrained increase in any behavior is produced by shortening the pauses between successive bursts, that is, by entering the state more often (Premack & Schaeffer, 1962, 1963).

These are not offered as an account of the rat's response system, but as tentative descriptions representing the present state of our knowledge. We are now in a position to turn to reinforcement, having at least some idea of the natural response tendencies of the animal before we operate upon them with the constraining procedures of reinforcement.

REINFORCEMENT: INTRODUCTION

The traditional account of reinforcement provides a nice introduction to the present one, for the latter is a simple transform of the former in the following sense. First, the basic assumptions of the traditional account appear to be empirical propositions with a confirmation status so high that further test is unnecessary; actually, the assumptions were little more than common sense, which is to say, they were never tested. Second, when tested, they proved to be invalid. Thus, all of the major assumptions of the traditional account have essentially the same logical character. They appear to be propositions involving empirical claims, claims so weak as to be essentially trivial. It is only when the propositions are seen to be nonempirical that they become nontrivial.

We may start with the standard definition according to which a reinforcer is any stimulus that, given a certain relation to a response, produces a change in the frequency of that response.

Since presumably it is only philosophers who delight in null classes, tradition hastened to add that, of course, there are such stimuli. From there it seemed only reasonable to add: there are other stimuli that do not have this property. The combination, there are some stimuli that have this property and there are others that do not, will be recognized as a familiar version of the first of the several assumptions that make up the traditional descriptive account (e.g., Skinner, 1938, p. 62).

The second empirical claim is that reinforcers are trans-situational (Meehl, 1950). Inevitably, the discovery that any stimulus is effective will be made with some particular base response; the claim of trans-situationality is that a stimulus effective with one response will be effective with all responses (and thus that the discovery could have been equally well made with any response). The classical example is food; it is said to reinforce all responses.

A third empirical claim is that there are two classes of responses, one that is reinforcing but not reinforceable, another that is reinforcible but not reinforcing. This is less an explicit assertion, though versions of it can be extracted from traditional discussions of goals and drives, than a conclusion that can be reached by examining a sufficient body of experiments. For example, eating and drinking were for many years used only in the role of reinforcer, never as the events that were reinforced; conversely, bar pressing and running were used only as "instrumental activities," never as reinforcers. The segregation here was impressive, there being no instances of crossover between these would-be categories in about forty years of experimentation.

It is important to recognize that the above three assumptions were not viewed as a *theory* of reinforcement, but rather as a first-order, low-level description of the field. Theorists differed as to whether or not reinforcement was coterminous with, say, drive reduction, or whether it was necessary for learning, but they did not differ in their acceptance of the three assumptions.

Are these assumptions, which certainly give the impression of being empirical, actually members of that class in the standard sense of being abstractions from test evidence?

In order for the assertion concerning two classes of stimuli to be an empirical one, the literature must show some body of experiments in which, for any species, some stimuli were shown to change the frequency of a response while other stimuli, given the same temporal relation to the response, failed to produce a change. This kind of functional division of the environment is clearly implied by the classical assumptions, but it is equally clear that no actual division ever took place. That is, it is not possible to list for any species any set of events that have been shown not to be reinforcing. Nor is this omission the result of being hamstrung by the null hypothesis. The tests were not made because the claim of two classes was never seen to be a claim of any empirical consequence. The fact was too trivial to merit test.

The assumption of trans-situationality cannot be met with the same charge of being wholly nonempirical, for food has been shown to reinforce a number of responses. Food has at one time or another reinforced the bar press, running down an alley, the string pull, and pushing a marble into a hole; doubtless others could be added. But the necessity of piecing together these outcomes from different experiments, which normally would be disallowed, shows that the comparisons are post hoc; the issue was so little seen as empirical that probably not even a master's thesis was devoted to it.

The third assumption could not have been tested (except by accident), for we have already observed that it was tacit, failing even to attain to the status of a necessary condition for being tested, viz., to be made explicit. With a few quite recent exceptions, no attempts were made to reinforce eating or, on the other side of the coin, attempts made to reinforce with the bar press. These events were kept in their proper places. It is no surprise, therefore, that when Meehl's Martian arrived in the animal lab, primed to execute an epistemological reconstruction of reinforcement, he somehow managed to get the responses "right," i.e., managed to reinforce running with eating rather than, as a Martian might, the reverse. (Was the Martian earthling? He seemed a little too knowing.)

The core assumptions of the traditional account wear empirical masks which, when they are removed, reveal fairly common-sensical assumptions. The assumptions were not tested; it had already been decided what kinds of events were reinforcing and what kind not. Hence the surprise when lights, sounds, puzzles, etc., proved to be members of the class.

Two choices were given by the "new" reinforcers, either to enlarge the drive category, admit some unforeseen events, and essentially retain the traditional logic of reinforcement, or to drop the standard approach and seek another one.

One reaction to the sudden plethora of reinforcers—lights, sounds, puzzles where a moment ago there had been only food—was to pronounce everything effective, to declare all stimuli rein-forcing. But this blanket denial of the former categorical assumption is not one for which any appreciable evidence was ever collected.

The approach we have taken is to observe that reinforcement involves a *relation*, typically between two responses, one that is being reinforced and another that is responsible for the reinforcement. This leads to the following generalization: of any two responses, the more probable response will reinforce the less probable one. Given the generalization, the view of which it is the core can now be set forth in an orderly manner:

1. Anatomically different responses can be compared directly.

2. For any pair of responses, the more probable one will reinforce the less probable one.

3. An indifference principle holds such that the reinforcement value is determined by response probability independent of parameters used to produce the probability or kind of response that manifests the probability.

4. Reinforcement is a relative property. The most probable response of a set of responses will reinforce all members of the set; the least probable will reinforce no member of the set. However, responses of intermediate probability will reinforce those less probable than themselves but not those more probable than themselves. Intermediate members of the set thus both are and are not reinforcers, depending upon the relative probability of the base response.

5. The reinforcement relation is reversible. If the probability of

occurrence of two responses can be reversed in order, so can the reinforcement relation between the two responses.

The logical status of these five assumptions differs from one
assumption to the next, and they are presented as a group in
the interests of communication rather than for their logical
homogeneity. For example, 2 is the central empirical claim, 1
is presupposed by 2, while 4 and 5 are revealing implications of 2.

For the generalization to be tenable, no more than that, it
must be possible to compare anatomically different responses.
Obviously, it is not possible to talk about the effect that a more
probable response may have upon a less probable one if it is not
first possible to establish the order of their probabilities. Is it
possible to compare anatomically different responses? Tradition
may give the impression that it is not, but if so, the impression is
misleading, for tradition has not decided against the comparison
so much as it has simply never involved itself in issues that
required such comparisons.

RESPONSE METHODOLOGY

Standard response methodology deals only with what may
be called *within-response* comparisons. One and the same response
class is compared under different conditions. Approximately
99 per cent of psychological data would appear to be of this sort.
As a simple example, consider the classical question of whether
rats run more when hungry than when not. Along with more
complex issues, this simple question is answered by a within-
response comparison. With the use of an activity wheel, a run
may be defined as, for example, a 360-degree turn, provided only
that a run is counted by this same unit both when the rat is and
is not hungry. The use of 360 degrees is, of course, quite arbitrary
—359 degrees might be used as well, or even 35 degrees—but the
arbitrariness is not injurious to the comparison, for the only
criterion in the case of within-response comparison is consistency.
That is, whatever the response unit used, it must be the same
for the several conditions of the comparison. The criterion
for *between-response* comparison is, as we shall see, decidedly

stronger, although this is no criticism of standard response procedure, for there is no advantage in making criteria stronger than the performance of a task requires.

A further reason for possibly supposing that comparisons between different responses may not be possible is the sheer number of different measures that are used, along with the evident fact of their incommensurability. For example, volume, number of pellets, licks, degrees of turn, number of bar presses, and speed of running are all in use, and quite legitimately, although they are plainly incommensurable. Which of them are to be used for between-response comparison? They cannot all be equally suitable, and yet we appear to have no rule for deciding among them.

In fact, a rule is easily found, for while the criterion for within-response comparison is merely consistent application of *any* unit, the criterion for between-response comparison is that *all* responses be measured by the *same* unit. This requirement is not special to responses, of course, but is simply the general requirement for the comparison of any set of items. Thus apples and eggs are commensurable in the case of weight because the same measurement procedure can be applied to both. Similarly, diverse responses will be commensurable, provided they can be measured by the same unit.

A little reflection will show that time, response duration, will fulfill the requirement nicely. Given an operational definition of the onset and offset of a behavior, a clock sensitive to the fulfillment of the operational definition will determine the duration for which the organism is in a state of the designated responding. The clock will not tick more rapidly because the rat is copulating rather than merely eating; the unit of measurement will be invariant from one behavior to the next. Moreover, time is extrinsic to all behaviors and thus can be applied universally, in contrast to all anatomical units, such as the lick, which are intrinsic to given motor sequences and can be used to measure only those sequences composed of the unit in question.

Time not only fulfills the requirement of measurement by a common unit, thus permitting comparison of anatomically diverse responses, but it takes priority over traditional response criteria such as common-effect-upon-the-environment or anatomical similarity. In fact, these traditional criteria do not provide sufficient conditions for commensurability, and the attempt so to use them can lead to malpractices. Consider two response classes whose members are either substantially alike anatomically or which have like effects upon the environment but have different average durations. Can the probabilities of the two classes be estimated comparatively from their frequencies? In which case is the organism more apt to be in a state of responding, when it makes 90 1-sec. responses or 10 15-sec. responses? This example alone should make it clear that having a comparable effect upon the environment, such as getting a bar down, is not a sufficient basis for comparing the frequency of two events when the frequency is to be used as an estimate of probability. Comparable average durations of the events in question is at least a necessary condition, and we would argue that it is a sufficient one.

Thus, what permits comparing the frequency (number) of anatomically identical responses is no different from what permits comparison in the case of anatomically disparate reponses: average duration of the response events is the same. This point appears to have escaped the attention of several writers (e.g., Hodos & Valenstein, 1962) who have implicitly accepted either same-effect-upon-environment or anatomical likeness as a sufficient basis for comparing frequencies. The conclusion that in brain stimulation rate will not predict choice would appear to be the result of this malpractice, and probably can be rectified simply by restricting rate comparisons to events of comparable duration.

Moreover, response duration will provide a strict estimate of probability insofar as the distribution of responding is random throughout the considered interval of time (e.g., Parzen, 1960). Here we may recall the previously noted operating characteristics of the rat, the remarkable extent to which burst duration approximates a random process, which was so surprising. It is always gratifying to put surprises to work.

The above analysis would appear to justify the comparison

of anatomically unlike response events and thus would appear to establish the feasibility of testing the generalization. Tests were directed at four implications: relativity, nonuniqueness of consummatory events, reversibility, and indifference.

RELATIVITY

An original test was made with manipulation responses of Cebus monkeys (Premack, 1963a). By using manipulation—lever pressing of one kind or another—as both reinforcing and reinforced responses, the intent was to show that reinforcement could be produced without the use of goal responses. Tradition had divided the animal's repertoire into goal responses and nongoal responses or "instrumental activities" (the counterpart of neutral stimuli). Accordingly, the standard reinforcement paradigm was: make a goal response contingent upon an instrumental activity. Our gambit in this first test was thus to draw only from the nongoal category, and to demonstrate reinforcement notwithstanding, provided only that one nongoal response was more probable than the other.

Four manipulanda were used—a lever, plunger, hinged flap or door, and a horizontally operated lever—each of which could be used potentially both as the reinforcing or the reinforced response. A solenoid-operated lock made it possible to render any item inoperable; thus, the animal could be given any pair of items, with one of them locked and its operation made contingent upon the prior operation of the other member of the pair.

A two-stage test procedure was used. First, estimates were obtained of each animal's probability of operating each item. Second, the items were presented in pairs—one free, one locked—with operation of the locked item contingent upon operation of the free item. For example, the door and plunger might be given together, with the plunger free and the door locked. Release of the lock, and thus the opportunity to operate the door, was contingent upon the prior operation of the plunger.

Repeated measures on the items, presented one at a time with no response restrictions, showed the animals to differ substantially. Of four monkeys tested, one showed reliable differences between three of four items, another showed no reliable differences whatever, while two others were intermediate.

In a second procedure, still aimed at estimating response probabilities rather than testing the generalization, the monkeys were presented with *pairs* of items, again with no response restriction. The main purpose was to determine whether simply pairing the items would disturb the ordinal relations among the individual response probabilities. Inevitably, contingency tests will require pairing items; thus, if merely pairing the items should disturb the rank order of the individual response probabilities, tests of the individual items could not reasonably serve as a basis for predicting reinforcement values. Comparison of the outcome here with that of the previous procedure showed that (1) frequency of responding to any item is apparently always less when the item is paired with another (nonzero) item than when it is presented alone, but (2) the ordinal relations among items are not disturbed simply by the pairing procedure.

Contingencies were next arranged between the pairs of items, using a continuous reinforcement schedule and a rule that required at least one free response between any two contingent ones, thus precluding the hoarding of response possibilities. The six pairs of items (produced by the four manipulanda) generated twelve possible contingency pairs, since in this procedure each item can serve both as a free item on one occasion and as a contingent item on the next occasion. For each pair, a block of four daily contingency sessions were given, followed by a block of four daily extinction sessions, after which the animal was given a new pair of items and the procedure repeated.

The outcome for the four animals differed in a manner generally predictable from their original protocols. Results for Willy, the no-difference animal, were clear cut: rather than showing an increment on any of the five pairs on which he was tested, he declined on all pairs.[5] Willy's overall decrement would

[5] At least for the present set of items, Willy should be unreinforcible; it may be possible, by habituating him for some items and not for others, to establish the difference needed for reinforcement, but then the ceiling would be low indeed. Would a different set make Willy look like Chicko, or are the differences more a function of the organism than the items? An interesting

be expected on the following grounds: With no countering incremental effect of reinforcement, the 24-hr. interitem interval that was used in contingency training should produce a lower rate than the 96-hr. interitem interval that was used to obtain the original estimates of response probability (Premack & Bahwell, 1959). The contrast in the rest intervals used for contingency training and for estimation of response probabilities is pertinent to all the results. All increments will be conservative estimates: any increment produced by the contingencies will occur despite an interval that by itself would be predicted to produce a decrement.

The outcome for the two intermediate monkeys, Bimbo and Gimbel, showed one strong and two weak incremental effects; further, in neither S did any less probable response increase the frequency of any more probable response. But the clearest predictions possible were those for Chicko, who in the first procedure showed three reliably different response probabilities. Indeed, Chicko's protocol made possible three kinds of contingencies: contingent response higher than, less than, and, in one case, about equal to the free response. In brief, the outcome for the three types of contingencies were as follows: (1) contingent response higher than free response produced in all five cases an increment in the free response; (2) contingent less probable than free response produced in all three such cases a decrement in the free response, which is not predicted by the generalization—it says simply that such a case will not produce an increment—but which may be merely the result of the unfavorable intersession

---

individual difference would be the tendency to visit a fixed amount of relative preference among the items of any set. Some organisms may display preference among the items of all sets, while others may show no preferences among the items of any set. Thus Willy's flat profile might obtain generally, for all sets, in which case he should be insusceptible to reinforcement. This would be operationally equivalent to a defective reinforcement mechanism, in another idiom to "the salt has lost its savour," or in still a third idiom to the flat-affect model of Meehl's (1962) several models for schizophrenia. We might thus distinguish between two behavioral views of mental disease. In the traditional one, the reinforcement mechanism is intact but the history of reinforcement is untoward, whereas in another, the mechanism itself is defective, either genetically or as a result of a previously untoward reinforcement history.

interval; and (3) the one case in which the two responses were about equal produced little or no change, increment or decrement.

A last major point of interest in Chicko's data was the evidence concerning the relativity of reinforcement. H was the most probable member of Chicko's response set, P the least, and D intermediate. H reinforced all members of the set; P reinforced none (and instead was itself reinforced by all other members). Considered jointly, the results for H and P appear to substantiate the traditional absolute view: H, which is a reinforcer, reinforces all responses, while P, which is not a reinforcer, reinforces none. This appears to exemplify the "some are, some are not" view, as well as to support the standard trans-situationality assumption—H reinforced not one member of the set but all members. However, the results for D controvert the traditional view; D, which was of intermediate probability, reinforced P but failed to reinforce H. Thus, depending upon the relative probability of the base response, D both was and was not a reinforcer.

Since the present case appears to represent the first direct test of the trans-situationality assumption, the previous success of the assumption may rest upon a failure to have tested it. Indeed, we are now in a better position to contemplate the success of this assumption. The evidence for it is based entirely upon the demonstration that food (in the starved rat) reinforced all challengers—bar press, string pull, roll a marble. But I think we may see that, rather than proving trans-situationality, this more likely demonstrated that for the given parameters eating was simply the most probable member of the set; certainly all the events reinforced are low operant-level events, while eating in the starved rat can attain substantial probabilities. One response in any set would be predicted to be trans-situational: the most probable member of the set. In using eating and a starved rat, tradition worked exclusively with a most probable member. But a general theory of reinforcement cannot be based upon the special properties of the most probable member of the set. Reinforcement is not confined to this member, and the properties of the other members differ from those of the most probable member. For example, they are not trans-situational.

REINFORCEMENT OF EATING AND DRINKING

Two further basic assumptions that go hand in hand are that consummatory responses are reinforcible and that reinforcement is a reversible relation. Food or water is customarily used to reinforce the bar press or running, but it is not asked: Can this relation be reversed? Will the bar press or running reinforce eating or drinking?

Are there intervals of time in which eating or drinking are less probable than certain other responses? If there are, then eating and drinking should be reinforceable. The present assumptions do not, of course, make any predictions of the above kind; they deal only with the effect of one response upon another, and thus can make no predictions until after the individual response probabilities are given.[6]

As to whether or not organisms could be found for which nonconsummatory responses take priority over consummatory, we first considered the need for an advanced organism—something pretty ethereal. The rat did not seem apt to produce so sublime an interval of time. Accordingly, the first test was made with children. Only later did we lift the ban on rats, having found appropriate intervals for them too.

In a first test using children, a pinball machine rewired for continuous operation and a candy dispenser, the two placed side by side, comprised the experimental arrangement (Premack, 1959). Candy consisted of constant-size chocolate bits, delivered one at a time by a conveyer belt into a dish each time the child ate the piece in the dish. Thirty-three children, the entire first-grade class of a public school, served as subjects. Their average age was 6.7 years.

On the first test, both the candy and the pinball machine were

[6] We have not attempted to provide a general characterization, let alone theory, of events that for a given species lead to a high probability of responding, though such a theory could be of substantial value; e.g., it might be used to deduce the present reinforcement generalization. Cf. Pribram (1963) for an intriguing set of suggestions toward such a theory.

available without restriction. Sixty-one per cent of the children made more pinball-machine responses than they ate pieces of candy. (The average duration of the pinball-machine responses was just slightly greater than the visually approximated duration of the ingestion of a piece of candy. Thus the advantage in frequency of pinball responding would convert into an even greater advantage in terms of response duration; since the difference was not great, however, the scores were left in frequency as in the manipulation case.) We thenceforth referred to those who preferred the machine as "manipulators," the others as "eaters."[7]

On the second test, the availability of the candy and the pinball machine were made subject to either of two contingency relations, E-M or M-E. For E-M, each operation of the machine was contingent upon the prior ingestion of a piece of candy, whereas for M-E, each piece of candy was contingent upon the prior operation of the machine. Both the "manipulators" and the "eaters" were randomly divided, and half of each main group tested under E-M and half under M-E. For a manipulator, E-M was the experimental condition, M-E the control; the reverse held for eaters. What characterizes both experimental conditions is that the more probable response is contingent upon the less probable response (manipulators must eat to manipulate; eaters must manipulate to eat). Control conditions make the more probable response freely available, as in the first test, and thus provide a measure of changes in the less probable response that may occur independent of the contingency.

In both cases, making a more probable response contingent upon a less probable one increased the frequency of the latter. Thus, while candy reinforced manipulation in the eaters, operation of the pinball machine reinforced eating for the manipulators. Increments in the control condition were small compared

---

[7] "Manipulator" is somewhat of a misnomer. Only some of those who preferred the machine emphasized the manner in which they shot the ball, shooting first from the hip, then with their back turned, all the while doing a kind of soft-shoe routine and practically never glancing at the ball. Others shot the ball with a minimal gesture, then feasted visually upon each new bank of lights the ball lighted up.

to those for the experimental condition, and the mean differences within both main groups were significant at less than the 1 per cent level.

The results indicate that the consummatory response is not unique in being a reinforcer of other responses but not reinforcible itself. Also, there would seem to be little doubt that with sufficient food deprivation, "manipulators" would become "eaters" and thus the response which had been instrumental could be made reinforcing and vice versa.

REVERSIBILITY OF THE REINFORCEMENT RELATION

Reversibility of the reinforcement relation was shown ultimately with the rat (Premack, 1962). With free access to both food and an activity wheel but access to water for only 1 hr./day, mean total drinking time for a group of six female rats was about 240 sec., while mean total running time in the same period was only about 1 min. On the other hand, with free access to both food and water but access to the wheel for only 1 hr./day, mean total drinking time per hour was now only about 28 sec., while mean total running time in the same period was 329 sec. These are by no means the only parameters that can be used to produce a reversal in the probabilities of drink and run. Combining sucrose concentrations appropriately with force requirements on the wheel will produce the same outcome. So deprivation is hardly the only effective parameter. But whatever parameters are used to reverse the response probabilities, the same prediction follows. It should be possible not only to reinforce drinking with running but also to reverse the reinforcement relation in the same subject simply by changing from one parameter value to another.

The apparatus used to test the predictions consisted of a modified Wahmann activity wheel equipped with a brake and a retractable drinkometer. The rat is placed in the wheel, which itself serves as the test cage. With drinking contingent upon running, the wheel was free but the tube was retracted; a predetermined number of runs brought the tube into the wheel for a predetermined time. Conversely, with running contingent upon drinking, the tube was present at all times but the wheel was locked;

a predetermined number of licks released the brake on the wheel for a predetermined time.

The more interesting case, run contingent upon drink, was tested first. Four female albino rats were given daily 1-hr. conditioning sessions, followed by daily 1-hr. extinction and reconditioning sessions. To augment the output, an FR was used in which each five licks freed the wheel for 10 sec. Throughout this training, food and water were continuously available in the home cage; after the last reconditioning session, water was removed from the home cage, and on the following day, training was begun with the reverse contingency—drinking contingent upon running.

With run contingent upon drink, total drink time was increased in all Ss by a factor of from three to five. For operant-level drinking, with only the tube present, mean total drink time was about 28 sec./hr., with both tube and wheel present about 23 sec./hr., and with run contingent upon drink about 98 sec./hr. The first extinction session further increased mean total drink time to about 175 sec./hr., following which drink returned essentially to its base. The picture was readily completed by changing the parameters so as to make drink more probable than run; then, with drink contingent upon run, the conventional increase in run was easily obtained. In summary, parameters were shown that made run more probable than drink and vice versa, and subsequently, it was possible not only to reinforce drink with run but also to reverse the reinforcement relation in the same subjects merely by changing from one set of parameters to the other.

INDIFFERENCE PRINCIPLE

Each time a response such as run is successfully predicted to reinforce drink or vice versa, a contribution is made to the indifference principle. This principle holds that prediction of reinforcement can be made without regard to the history of the response probability, for the outcome is indifferent to either the parameters used to produce the probability or the responses that manifest it. Successful prediction for such pairs as run and drink would appear to bear this out, for there is hardly any doubt as to their being different neurophysiological systems. Indeed, the interest of the indifference principle accrues from this difference; the principle does not deny the neurophysiological difference, which indeed could not be denied, but asserts that despite the difference, the reinforcement value is predictable from a single scale of response probability. The principle says that the neurophysiological difference does not participate in or mediate the reinforcement value, which is determined solely by the duration for which the animal engages in the behavior.

Sharper tests of the point can be made by a somewhat different procedure. With a third response such as the bar press, which is less probable than both drink or run, the increment produced in the bar press by drink and run can be compared. If identical probabilities of run and drink are made contingent upon the bar press, the indifference principle requires that the increment to the bar press be identical. It further requires that if identical probabilities of drink—produced in one case by deprivation, in another by sucrose concentration, in still another by temperature or any other parameter—are made contingent upon the bar press, then, again, the increment to the bar press must be identical. Likewise, it requires that the same experiment in the case of running—where, in principle, identical probabilities of running can be produced by procedures ranging from oestrus to starvation—must also produce the same outcome, identical increments in the bar press.

Since identical response probabilities are easier described than produced, an approximation to this experiment was performed (Premack, 1963b). A set of response probabilities was produced that included at least one probability of running bounded by probabilities of drinking and at least one probability of drinking bounded by probabilities of running. When subsequently made contingent upon the bar press, the ordered set of run and drink probabilities should produce an identically ordered set of bar-press probabilities.

In Figure 1, bar presses per session are plotted as a function of the associated response probability. The points in the figure

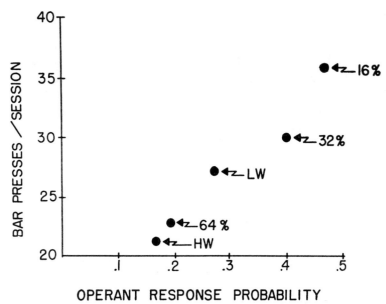

FIG. 1. Mean bar presses per session as a function of the associated operant-level response probability. The abscissa shows proportion of the operant-level session for which the animal responded—duration in seconds for which it ran or drank divided by duration of the session. Points are labeled according to the sucrose concentration (16, 32, and 64 per cent) or force requirement (light, LW; heavy, HW) that was used to control the operant-level response probability (after Premack, 1963b).

are labeled according to the sucrose concentration or force requirement that was used to produce the given drink probability in one case and run probability in the other. The functional relation shown there clearly supports the indifference principle: bar pressing increased monotonically with the associated response probability, and did so whether this was a probability of drink or run. These results were more encouraging than others that might be regarded as more dramatic. The universe hardly guarantees that comparable durations of run and drink will have comparable reinforcement effects; yet they clearly appear to.

The indifference principle is an exceptionally strong assumption, not to be established by any one test. If it should prove to be valid for any large number of parameters, it would perhaps contribute more determinately to a unitary-state concept than any traditional drive notion. Are equal probabilities of eating, produced in one case by food deprivation, in another by sucrose concentration, and in still another by lowered temperature, nonetheless the same in their reinforcement value? An animal may be capable of differentiating states of hunger according to the specific antecedents of the hunger; yet it may not differentiate the reinforcement value of the states on any basis other than the associated probabilities of eating.

AN INCREMENT POSTULATE: THE EFFECT OF THE BASE RESPONSE

If we apply different more probable responses to a common base response, we may expect the increment to be proportional to the probability of the contingent response. A version of this experiment was shown in the application of varying probabilities of run and drink to the bar press; the greater these probabilities, the greater the increment to the bar press.

But consider the converse experiment. Suppose the same reinforcer is applied to base responses that differ in their probability of occurrence. Will the reinforcer bring all the base responses to the same level despite their pre-reinforcement differences? Or will the latter be reflcted in asymptotic reinforced responding?

A first version of this experiment was done with Chicko via manipulation responding. H, the most probable member of Chicko's set, was applied successively to P, D, and L, responses less probable than H but quite different among themselves. H did not overcome the different operant levels of P, D, and L, but, rather, produced asymptotic rates that were proportional to the original operant levels. Thus, the operant levels showed through the reinforcement.

R. W. Schaeffer (in press) performed a more determinate version of this same experiment using groups of rats with drink and run as response materials. The experiment in the rat had been held back by the limited variation in probability of base response that is afforded by the traditional conditioning materials, viz., bar press and eating. But with the reinforcement of drink by

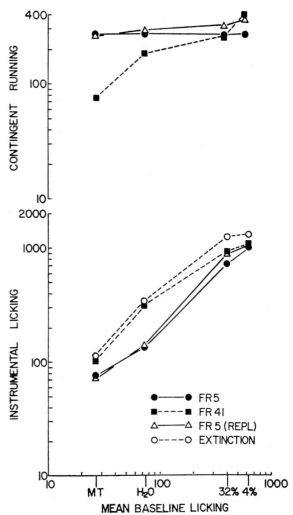

FIG. 2. Mean instrumental licks per session as a function of the mean operant-level licks per session in the operant-level session immediately preceding the contingency (after Schaeffer, in press).

run, Schaeffer was given nearly ideal materials. Run was made more probable than drink (mainly by giving only limited access to the wheel), and the probability of drinking was varied widely over the four groups by tube content ranging from nothing to 32 per cent sucrose. After first establishing clear differences in the operant level of drinking, running was made contingent upon drinking in all four groups. Figure 2, which plots asymptotic licking as a function of the pre-reinforcement level of licking, shows that, as in the case of monkey manipulation, the same reinforcer does not bring base responses of different probabilities to the same level. Rather, the asymptotic response level was proportional to the pre-reinforcement level; once again, the operant level showed through the reinforcement.

A third version of this experiment has recently been performed by Holstein and Hundt (in press), again with rats, but now using brain-stimulation bar pressing and licking. Drinking a 25 per cent sucrose solution reinforced both brain-stimulation bar pressing and plain bar pressing, but for all rats the duration of bar pressing was greater the greater the pre-reinforcement duration.

REINFORCEMENT OF INTRACRANIAL SELF-STIMULATION

The position which eating or drinking once held has now been pretty much usurped by intracranial self-stimulation (ICS); it is the new king of reinforcers. The evidence leaves little doubt that ICS can be made extremely potent—the right combination of brain site and intensity of stimulation—but from the present point of view, intermediate strengths of ICS are of more interest than the maximal strengths. The use of only maximal strengths may lead to the same errors as did the use of only maximal or high strengths of eating. Indeed, this already appears to be the case; ICS-effective sites are described as the neurological substrate of reward, as nice an absolute theory of reinforcement, now in neurological garb, as could be imagined.

Electrical stimulation of the brain, like other kinds of stimulation, whether of taste or kinesthesis, for example, represents yet another means of producing response probabilities. Do response probabilities produced by ICS act like other response probabilities as regards reinforcement? If so, and a response can be found more probable than the ICS-contingent response, then ICS should be subject to reinforcement.

Holstein and Hundt (in press) tested this matter by using drinking as the more probable response. They implanted three male Long Evans rats with bipolar electrodes, each at a different site to determine whether the obtained effect was circumscribed by site. Post-experimental histologies revealed the tip of the electrodes to be in the midbrain tegmentum, preoptic region, and median forebrain bundle, respectively. A constant-current 100-cps sine-wave generator was the stimulus source. Stimulation remained on for the duration of the bar press. Current was manipulated individually for each rat until each produced a moderate, stable response rate during daily session of 15 min. length. These current values were then maintained throughout the remainder of the experiment.

A retractable drinkometer, containing 25 per cent sucrose by weight, was introduced into a standard test cage, three inches to the side of the bar. Animals were given daily 15-min. sessions with the tube present and the ICS bar removed, followed immediately by another 15-min. session with the ICS bar present and the tube removed. The order of the two kinds of sessions was alternated from day to day. For all animals, the asymptotic duration of drinking proved to be greater than that of ICS bar pressing independent of the order of presentation.

A second pre-reinforcement measure was taken, as in the monkey manipulation case, by making the tube and bar concurrently available. Especially recommendatory of this step in the present case is the possibility of a recoil response to the ICS, which would not be recorded simply by a clock registering duration of the bar press. One approach, and nearly the ideal one, would be to arrange to include the recoil in the duration of the response. This did not prove to be necessary here. If recoil were present, it would compete with licking in the concurrent situation where both brain stimulation and tube were available and would reveal itself by an appreciable reduction in the duration of drinking; no such reduction was observed. Rather, the ordinal relationship between the durations of drink and bar press were maintained relative to the individual presentation of the items, and in all cases the duration of drinking exceeded that of ICS bar press by a considerable margin.

A test was made by making access to the tube contingent upon ICS bar pressing. The bar was present at all times, but the tube was retracted and made available only after 10 bar presses. A clear-cut reinforcement effect was shown, the average duration of ICS bar pressing being increased by a factor of at least 2 by the contingency. Further, this increase was extinguished, that is, lost upon removal of the contingency.

A control was run on the unlikely possibility that brain stimulation could, without any change in parameters, reinforce drinking. Since we have attributed the reinforcement of ICS by licking to the relatively greater probability of licking, it would be highly embarrassing if, upon reversing the contingency, ICS should now reinforce licking. The contingency was reversed, and only one lick was required per ICS–bar press opportunity in light of the reported difficulty of generating high FR responding with ICS. No increase in licking was produced (by ICS bar pressing less probable than licking). An experiment in progress examines the effect upon licking of an ICS bar press more probable than licking, but the outcome does not seem especially uncertain.[8]

These first results suggest that response probabilities produced by brain stimulation do not differ from those produced otherwise. When the probability of ICS was greater than that of licking, ICS reinforced licking, but when the probabilities were reversed, licking reinforced ICS. If ICS is ascribed to a reinforcement center, we must now account for the fact that we can reinforce the events of that would-be center, and to do so we must find another center, and so on. Or if we place both events in the same center, we must then admit that events of the reinforcement center can themselves be reinforced as well as rein-

---

[8] This prediction has since been confirmed by S. Holstein. In rats for which ICS was more probable than licking, making ICS contingent upon licking produced an increase in both the frequency and duration of licking. Personal communication, 1965.

force, and then it is doubtful whether we have any longer what tradition contemplates as a reinforcement center. Additionally, we must account for the fact that event A, which reinforced event B on one occasion, can be reinforced by B on another occasion. All of these difficulties can be resolved by ceasing to regard reinforcement as an absolute property, and thus ceasing to suppose that a center exists which supports all reinforcement. A more reasonable anticipation may be a mechanism for sensing the dominance of one event relative to another, along with the predilection of the lesser event to adopt or conform to the properties of the greater event. What have so far been called "reinforcement centers" would more nearly appear to be locations that support dominant, i.e., high-probability, events.

CHOICE

The ordering a subject gives to a set of stimuli can operationally define the basic motivational fact of *preference*. We have already looked at three procedures for measuring preference, and in turning now to choice we consider still another. In the monkey manipulation study, you will recall, a set of items were ordered in three ways: first, by the total duration for which a subject responded to the individual items; second, by which item would reinforce (responding) to which other items; and third, by the increment an item produced in a common base response when made contingent upon that response. Although the monkey data were only partially confirming, we nonetheless assume that the three procedures produce equivalent orderings: if S responds longer to A than to B, then A contingent upon B will reinforce B, but not vice versa; and A contingent upon X will produce a greater increment in X than B contingent upon X. Can choice now be added to this list of assumedly conceptually equivalent procedures? It would seem reasonable to suppose that it could. But this is rather a weak assumption, less interesting than others that could be made. A more important question is whether we can find any formal overlap or commonality between choice and any of these other ordering procedures. If we can, then quantitative relations that have already been established for the case

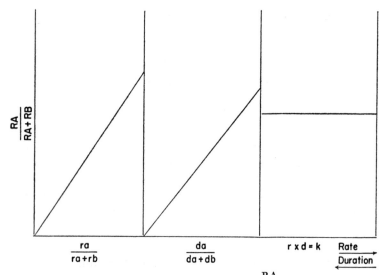

Fig. 3. Relative rate of responding on bar A, $\dfrac{RA}{RA+RB}$, as a function of (1) relative rate of reinforcement, $\dfrac{ra}{ra+rb}$, (2) relative duration of reinforcement, $\dfrac{da}{da+db}$, and (3) relative total duration of reinforcement, r x d. See text for further explanation.

of choice can be extended to the other preference-measuring procedures.

Important data for the free-responding choice situation have been provided by Herrnstein (1961), Reynolds (1963), and Catania (1963a). Using hungry pigeons in a two-key situation with grain available on both keys according to VI schedules, these workers have found the birds to distribute their responding to the two keys in an impressively simple manner. The proportion of the total responses the bird makes on a given key is equal to the proportion of the total reinforcements it receives on that key. This relation is shown in Figure 3, left panel, where relative rate of responding on A, $\dfrac{RA}{RA+RB}$, is plotted as a function of the relative rate of reinforcement on A, $\dfrac{ra}{ra+rb}$.

In Figure 3, middle panel, we have extended this same kind of relationship to another parameter, viz., reinforcement duration, although the actual evidence for this second case is slight (Catania, 1963b). Nevertheless, it seems only moderately risky to consider that if, rather than varying the schedule on the two keys (while equating the magazine duration), the magazine durations were varied (while equating the schedules), one would obtain the outcome shown in Figure 3. Let us make the two cases more explicit. In the first case, duration for which the grain hopper is available following each completion of the instrumental requirement is the same for both keys, while rate of reinforcement is varied; whereas in the second, rate of reinforcement is the same for both keys, while duration of reinforcement is varied. We assume that the two parameters yield identical relations.

If, in fact, rate and duration prove to yield comparable functions, it would be additionally desirable to reduce both cases to the same variable. A variable that would have this effect is simply *total reinforcement time*, i.e., the rate by duration product. This product is necessarily varied by experiments which hold reinforcement duration on the two keys constant while varying rate, no less than by those that hold rate constant while varying duration of the individual reinforcement on the two keys. That is, these two kinds of experiments simply represent two different ways of randomly distributing a block of reinforcement time (more probable responding) over some larger interval of time—in one case, by number of instances, and in the other, by duration of the instances. Now the rat has only to respond indifferently to variation in number and duration in order to make a neat, if small, contribution to parsimony; we are testing the matter now.

In progress for some time have been experiments in which equal total duration of reinforcement, produced by different combinations of rate and duration, are associated with the two bars in a two-bar choice situation. For example, associated with one bar are 30 4-sec. opportunities to drink water, and with the other bar, 60 2-sec. opportunities of the same kind. The predicted results are shown in Figure 3, right panel; the rate and duration scales on the abscissa have been pitted against each other in such a manner as to yield equal r x d products at all points; accordingly, responding is predicted to be equally divided between the two bars at all points. It seems little to ask, so little that after a year of technical difficulties our position on the matter has become: if the rat declines this invitation to parsimony, it is an ungrateful creature and not to be trusted further.

What relation, if any, can we now find between this proposed extension of the work on schedules and the other preference-measuring procedures that we have already considered? Since we have already indicated how it may be possible to change the rate measure, in which schedule problems are typically formulated, into a duration measure, the reader may wish to complete the parallel for himself. Perhaps, however, in order to assure that all parties complete the parallel in approximately the same way, it may be advisable to make our version explicit.

The transition from choice to the other procedures can be made via two further points. The first concerns the proportion of magazine time for which the birds actually eat in the Herrnstein, Reynolds, and Catania work. These durations have not been reported, but because of the parameters that have been used, it is reasonable to assume that the durations are essentially constant. That is, it is reasonable to assume that, first, the proportion of time the birds actually eat from one magazine presentation to the next is stable over the session, and second, this proportion is constant over the range of variables that have been tested. For example, these workers have not combined weak hunger with "long" magazine duration, which would be expected to lead to a within-session decrement (see Collier & Siskel, 1959; Collier, 1962), nor have they combined "short" magazine durations with "long" intermagazine intervals, which we have reason to suppose would substantially reduce the proportion of the possible magazine time that was utilized. In brief, though not commenting on the fact, these workers have restricted themselves to a narrow range of parameters—a range which makes the assumptions concerning constancy of the utilized proportion of magazine time quite reasonable. These expectations are supported to some extent by the report that the birds take all of the reinforcements that are offered by the schedules.

Now our concern with *actual* eating time, as opposed to the experimenter's parameters of rate and duration, which merely define a *possible* eating time, is to complete the transition from the variables in which the problem has been stated to the variable we consider to be critical (here no less than in the cases we have already examined). For this case, as for the others, we would make the same assumptions: (1) eating reinforces key pecking in the starved pigeon because eating is more probable than key pecking (this point is worth making because the tendency to speak of reinforcers as stimuli drawn from a special drawer marked "reinforcer" continues unabated), and (2) the relative reinforcement value of eating is equal to the relative total duration of eating.

That is, we expect possible reinforcement time to predict instrumental rate only when possible proves to be an unbiased estimate of actual. If, for example, the work on choice were extended to parameters beyond the narrow range used so far, we would *not* expect relative rate of responding to be a simple function of either relative rate or relative duration of reinforcement. Thus, in our present experiments, where the opportunity to drink water is used as the reinforcer, we do not expect 80 1-sec. opportunities to have the same effect as 20 4-sec. opportunities. Measures of drinking taken both within and outside the reinforcement situation show the proportion of time the rat drinks to be less with a 1-sec. magazine time than with a 4-sec. time. When actual magazine response time is *not* a fixed proportion of possible magazine time, we would predict the simple relations shown thus far to vanish. But we would expect these simple relations to be promptly restored, for all parameters, simply by plotting instrumental responding as a function of actual rather than possible magazine response time.

Turn now to the last point upon which completion of the

parallel depends. This concerns the manner in which the experimenter determines the proportion of time an organism spends responding to one of several alternatives. The reader may have observed that this proportion is determined more directly in the pigeon experiments than in the experiments considered earlier. In the former, the bird cannot eat more than, say, 20 per cent of the total eating time in association with one key for the simple reason that 20 per cent is all the experimenter provided on that side. In the experiments considered earlier, however, the animal could respond in all possible proportions to either alternative, for this was not limited by the experiment. It was not limited directly, at least, as in the pigeon experiments, but only indirectly by stimulus and/or deprivation factors. Although the animal was operated upon indirectly by being given particular stimuli to choose between, or being allowed to choose after varying deprivation periods, it could nonetheless divide its responding in all possible proportions rather than according to limits set by the experimenter.

In the one case, the experimenter bakes a pie, smaller than the bird can eat, and divides it making, say, 20 per cent available on one side. By making the pie smaller than the bird can eat (and serving it in small pieces at suitable intervals), he assures that the momentary probability of eating remains constant, and thus assures that the bird makes good on the 20:80 split. This represents a direct way of predetermining the distribution of the more probable response event, in this case eating, over the several alternatives. It may be seen to contrast with the relative indirection of giving the subject two pies, both larger than it could eat, and measuring the duration for which it eats one or the other.

Nevertheless, both the direct and indirect procedures affect the same variable, viz., the distribution of the more probable response events over the alternatives. Consequently, we are obliged to predict that their effects will be the same. That is, unless we introduce special assumptions, we are obliged to predict that whether the distribution is forced upon the animal by rate and/or duration parameters or generated by the animal's own dispositions, the effect upon instrumental responding will be the same. That is,

$$\frac{P(RA)}{P(RB)} = \frac{cFa}{cFb} = \frac{Ta}{Tb}, \quad \text{where} \quad \frac{Ta}{Tb} = \frac{\dfrac{ta}{ta + tb + k}}{\dfrac{tb}{ta + tb + k}}.$$

P(RA) is probability of A instrumental responses, c is a constant determined by magazine duration, F is frequency of magazine presentation, ta is duration of S's response to item a, and k is a constant equal to session time minus ta plus tb. An experimental example may be clarifying.

Picture a Skinner box temporarily bereft of levers but containing both a right and left magazine (or one magazine sometimes accompanied by a red light, other times by a green light). The two magazines are operated successively, each according to some predetermined schedule. The organism is hungry beyond the possibility of satiating on what the magazine opportunities provide. Measurements are made of the duration to which S responds to each of the magazine opportunities; the Skinner box regains its levers, and the subject is advanced to the second step of the experiment, where it is obliged to respond instrumentally for the same magazine opportunities it experienced without an instrumental requirement at step 1. For some parameters, Ta/Tb will simply equal Fa/Fb, the ratio of the reinforcement schedules, but whether or not this special condition obtains, we predict

$$\frac{P(RA)}{P(RB)} = Ta/Tb.$$

In a second experiment, the Skinner box, again bereft of levers, offers the subject a choice between any pair of stimuli to which the species responds, e.g., run and drink, manipulate and eat, eat a on one side and eat b on the other. Here, too, the duration for which S responds to the alternatives is measured, and the experiment is then concluded as before. Although Ta/Tb is now determined by subject disposition rather than by experimenter limit, we again predict $\dfrac{P\,(RA)}{P\,(RB)} = Ta/Tb.$[9]

It should not be thought that the two experiments differ importantly in that the stimuli are available discontinuously in one case and continuously in the other. This difference is trivial. The alternatives can be presented discontinuously no less in the one design than in the reinforcement-schedules case, though in the latter, discontinuous presentation is a necessity rather than an option. Custom presents stimuli continuously in the operant-level session. But stimuli need not be present throughout the session in order that their availability to the organism be noncontingent, i.e., independent of an instrumental requirement. The operant level for a discontinuously available stimulus can be used to predict the reinforcement value of the stimulus (relative to some other stimulus) no less well than can the operant level for the typical continuously present stimulus. Indeed, the former will afford a somewhat more accurate prediction than the latter. The very procedure of reinforcement imposes a discontinuity upon the availability of the contingent stimulus, a discontinuity which may affect the animal's probability of responding to the stimulus. The correction here is possibly small, a nicety at the present stage, though data can be shown in support of the possibility. Figure 4 shows amount drunk per session for three independent groups of thirsty rats that encountered a drinking tube which was (1) continuously available for 20 min., (2) in and out of the test cage alternately for 7 and 21 sec., respectively, and (3) in and out of the test cage alternately for 28 and 5 sec., respectively. The total period of availability (20 min.) was the same for all three groups; nonetheless, as Figure 4 shows, the groups drank different amounts (P < .01). Interestingly, discontinuous presentations were found that both increased and decreased total intake relative to that for the continuous stimulus.[10]

[9] This prediction obviously cannot require that responding be constant over the considered interval, but it can and does require that the decrements in responding to the alternatives offered occur at approximately comparable rates. Ways of coping with responses that decrement or habituate at different rates have been suggested in Premack (1961) and, more generally, in Hundt (1964).

[10] These data were collected by S. Manaster in 1961.

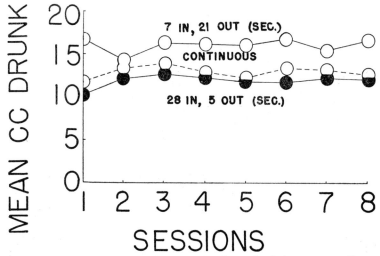

Fig. 4. Total amount drunk per session by each of three groups of rats that differed as to the manner in which the drinking tube was available to them, e.g., continuous *versus* discontinuous. See text for further explanation.

It is clear that the reinforcement schedule in the conventional problem will affect the distribution of the availability of the contingent stimulus. This effect will be direct in the interval schedule, more so than in the ratio schedule, though whether direct or not, all reinforcement schedules will have some effect upon how the availability of the contingent stimulus is distributed. What effect will the reinforcement schedule have upon the reinforcement value of the contingent stimulus? Perhaps no effect or perhaps a large one, in any case an amount that will depend, according to the present account, upon the degree to which the reinforcement schedule affects the animal's probability of responding to the stimulus. That is, if the schedule affects the animal's probability of responding to the stimulus (as in Figure 4), it will likewise affect the reinforcement value of the stimulus; otherwise it will have no effect. The time distribution of the stimulus thus joins other stimulus parameters, e.g., sucrose concentration, in being a parameter of reinforcement only insofar as the stimulus property is a parameter of

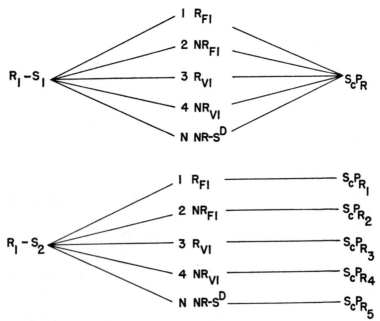

FIG. 5. Discriminative stimuli, S_1 (upper panel) and S_2 (lower panel), are associated with a common event, S_c, to which the species responds. The nature of the association varies, in one case affecting (lower panel) and in the other not affecting S's total duration of responding to S_c. The prediction is made that the acquired reinforcement value of S_2 will vary over conditions, while that of S_1 will be constant over conditions.

response probability. This point is brought out graphically in Figure 5.

The upper portion of Figure 5 shows a discriminative stimulus, S_1, to be associated with S_c, any event to which the species responds, e.g., mate, wheel, food, manipulandum. The nature of the subject's access to S_c varies markedly. In two cases, R_{FI} and R_{VI}, access to S_c depends upon instrumental responses that pay off according to fixed- and variable-interval schedules, respectively. In two other cases, NR_{FI} and NR_{VI}, S_c is independent of an instrumental requirement, being programmed, like the drinking tube in the experiment above, according to fixed or variable schedules. Finally, in NR-S^D a signal is added indicating the advent of S_c. The assumption depicted in the top half of Figure 5 is that none of these differences in manner of access yield differences in total duration of S's response to S_c; the bottom half of the figure depicts the opposite assumption. The prediction then made is that the reinforcement value of the discriminative stimulus will be constant over conditions in the first case, and variable in the second. Data bearing suggestively on this prediction have been reported (Catania, 1963a). In a choice situation, the rate at which pigeons pecked on key_A was shown to depend, not upon rate of responding to key_B, but solely upon rate of reinforcement received on key_B.

NEGATIVE REINFORCEMENT

Our basic measure for predicting positive reinforcement has been the duration for which a subject puts itself into a given state, relative to the duration for which it puts itself into some other state. It would seem reasonable to use the complement of this measure as a basis for predicting negative reinforcement, viz., duration for which a subject removes itself from a given state (into which the experimenter has forced it), relative to the duration for which it removes itself from some other state. Unfortunately, we have collected no relevant data, though a former student, A. G. Hundt, has formulated what would seem to be a basic question for this position. If the probability of S's remaining in one state is numerically equal to the probability of S's removing itself from another state, are the reinforcement values of the two responses equal? The present position requires an affirmative answer, and the question is now being tested with the use of food and electric shock, respectively.

Although, typically, negative reinforcement looks only at the offset of an event and positive reinforcement only at the onset, it should be observed that organisms both turn on and turn off virtually all stimuli to which they respond at all. Animals not only start eating but obviously also stop; as was clear in the ad lib case, eating is highly discontinuous, occurring in bursts and pauses. Although it apparently took intracranial self-stimulation (ICS) to call attention to the fact of on-off (Roberts, 1958;

Bower & Miller, 1958), it should now be evident that on-off is not a unique property of ICS, but rather is a general property of free responding. This leads to a further conclusion as regards the reinforcement possibilities for any stimulus to which the species responds; it should be possible to use the same stimulus both as a positive and as a negative reinforcer.

To demonstrate that the same event can be both positive and negative reinforcer, we require, first, an arrangement in which the onset of the event be more probable than the onset of some other event, and second, that the subsequent offset of the event be more probable than the onset of some other event. In the consummatory cases, this kind of arrangement could doubtless be made by the appropriate surgical preparation, for example, by tubing liquid directly into the animal. We have used instead a locomotor case, which retains the advantage of an intact animal. Two findings led to the arrangement: (1) for the rat, the opportunity to force itself to run is reinforcing, and (2) the rat is able to drink while running.

The rat is placed in a modified wheel containing a bar and a drinkometer (Hundt & Premack, 1963). The wheel is not free to move but is connected to a motor which the rat can turn on by pressing the bar. When the rat presses the bar, the motor is activated, the wheel rotates, and the rat is forced to run—has forced itself to run. It must continue running until it licks the drinkometer some predetermined number of times, which turns off the motor, stopping the wheel and allowing the rat to stop. The rat thus both forces itself to start and stop running by bar pressing and licking, respectively.

In one such experiment, an additional question was answered by using a fixed ratio of from 1 to 19 licks on the off response, viz., how does the "difficulty" of turning off a response affect the likelihood of its being turned on? Figure 6 shows the main results for a representative subject. Shown as a function of the fixed-ratio requirement on the off response are (1) frequency of the on response, (2) duration of the off response, and (3) duration of running. It may be seen that forced running increased bar pressing and that the frequency of the bar press (on response)

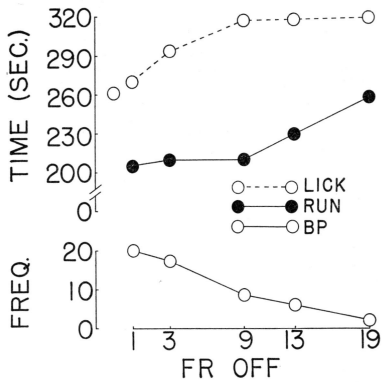

FIG. 6. Shown as a function of the number of licks required to turn off the wheel (FR OFF) are (1) average bar presses per session, (2) average duration of licking per session, and (3) average duration of running per session. The point to the left of the lick curve gives the base duration of licking (after Hundt & Premack, 1963).

was inversely proportional to the FR of the off response. The rat turned the wheel on only about twice per 20-min. session when 19 licks were required to turn it off, but turned it on upwards of 20 times per session when only one lick sufficed to turn it off. The average duration of licking and of running are both shown to increase over the FR variable, that of licking beyond the base duration (shown by the unconnected circle), so that we may conclude that the offset of running reinforced licking quite as the onset reinforced bar pressing. The total duration of running per session increased over the FR variable despite the fact that the number of times the rat turned the wheel on decreased over the same variable. The increase resulted from a marked increase in the average duration of the burst; though the rat started running less often, once started, it continued for notably longer—e.g., average burst duration for FR 19 was 140 sec., compared to 10 sec. for FR 1. This did not result from the rat's trying to stop but being unable to do so because of the large lick requirement: the *first* lick did not occur for about 134 sec. after the animal started running in the FR 19 case, as compared to about 10 sec. for the FR 1 case.

These results indicate how a generalization that was stated originally for positive reinforcement may now be broadened to include negative reinforcement as well. Originally, the generalization read: for any pair of responses, the more probable one will reinforce the less probable one. But this fails to distinguish between the onset and offset of an event. The generalization should now read: if the onset or offset of one response is more probable than the onset or offset of another, the former will reinforce the latter—positively if the superiority is for "on" probability and negatively if for the "off" probability.

ACQUISITION

So far we have looked only at asymptotic responding, giving no attention to the manner in which reinforcement is acquired. Tolman[11] once remarked of the Skinner box that its data were of relatively little interest to him in that the learning that takes place there is over after the first or second bar press. The rest, he suggested, is performance and thus of less than vital interest to him. This may be seen as a comment on the efficiency of the apparatus. On the other hand, Tolman's comment may be viewed as a perceptive complaint—as noting that the steps taken to make the organism susceptible to reinforcement, to prep it, as it were, are buried in the artistry of the laboratory; these steps need instead to be made an explicit part of theory.

Consider that we have two events, one of them incontro-

[11] Personal communication, 1960.

vertibly reinforcing (H) and the other incontrovertibly reinforcible (L). What is the minimal relation that can obtain between H and L that will produce reinforcement? How slightly can they contact each another and the contact still be effective? This is the question we want to examine now, as opposed to the matter of what are reinforcing and reinforcible events. We have already urged that the latter consists of any two responses that differ sufficiently in their probabilities of occurrence. Let us suspend debate on that topic in order to ask: What is the weakest relation that more and less probable responses can have that will eventuate in reinforcement?

We all know one sure-fire procedure for producing reinforcement: the contingency, the "if L, then H" operation which is used to produce virtually all reinforcement. But is the contingency a minimal or even a weak operation? Does it provide only temporal contiguity between H and L—the incontrovertibly reinforcing and reinforcible events—and nothing else?

Consider an ordered set of operations, all of which may conceivably produce reinforcement. The weakest will be pure temporal contiguity between L and H, while the strongest we need consider here will be the contingency. There are more than a few ways to produce temporal contiguity between L and H, and these vary in strength according to the number and perhaps kind of additional conditions they superimpose upon temporal contiguity. Pure temporal contiguity, we will show in a moment, is rare or unknown.

In order to locate the weakest possible effective operation, we will start with the strongest operation in the set—which will give us the assurance that reinforcement is possible with the materials in question—and progressively denude the strongest operation of its surplus conditions until a point is reached where reinforcement is no longer produced. This point may be on either side of temporal contiguity.

What are the major surplus conditions of the contingency? Embodied in the contingency are at least three first-order conditions over and above simple temporal contiguity, not to mention some second-order conditions that are less evident though possibly important. Consider the first-order properties more or less in the order of their visibility. *First*, the heart of a contingency, which is a response requirement: the reinforcing event can occur only if L occurs first; this is a special constraint, for if a contingency did not obtain, the animal might enter H from any of a number of antecedents. But a typical contingency prescribes that H can be reached only through a preselected L. *Second*, the distribution of the organism's responding to H is circumscribed. The animal has a characteristic way of responding to H, both in terms of burst durations and intervals between bursts, but a contingency limits both maximum burst duration and minimum interburst interval; it sets these limits dramatically when the schedule is intermittent, though even to some extent when the schedule is continuous. That is, by its very nature a contingency involves intruding an experimenter-selected event, L, between the organism's successive responses to H, thereby disturbing to one degree or another the organism's response distribution on H. *Third*, a typical contingency leads to a reduction in the total amount or duration of responding to H, relative to what would occur were H free. The amount of food the animal eats, for example, in a typical contingency is substantially less than the amount it would eat were food freely available for a period of time equal to that of the contingency session. This reduction is not a necessary consequence of a contingency; as we shall see, a contingency can be arranged that leads to no such reduction, but historically the reduction appears to be an invariant concomitant of the contingency procedure, and thus it remains to be seen whether the reduction plays a role in reinforcement. To be sure, any of the constraints described above may be as inconsequential as they appear to be accidental; the mere fact that we find them in the test tube does not prove that they are active ingredients; they may be inert accompaniments and temporal contiguity the only active factor.

The three above are simply the most visible surplus conditions of the contingency; we may mention at least one of the less evident possibilities. The response requirement, which allows H to be reached only through L, may be conducive to "errors" or nonreinforcement, and these may be potentiating. That is, if L is not high in the animal's hierarchy, other responses may precede L and of course fail. These failures may call attention to the effectiveness of L. Speaking loosely, except as I have first failed on x, y, and z, I may not recognize the effectiveness of L when at last H is obtained through L. However unlikely a noncognition theorist may consider such a mechanism, it should at least be recognized that its occurrence is more or less built into the contingency procedure.

This characterization of the contingency is intended to establish what is already suspected, viz., that the contingency is not a simple procedure, certainly not one whose effectiveness permits citing temporal contiguity as a sufficient condition. We know that the contingency works, but, in view of all that it contains, we hardly know why. We need to begin peeling off the surplus conditions.

A procedure which is weaker than the contingency and which is said to demonstrate that temporal contiguity is sufficient, is Skinner's (1948) noncontingency or superstition case. This procedure differs from a contingency principally in that it drops the response requirement. As you will likely recall, grain was available to pigeons in Skinner's classical demonstration according to a temporal schedule that was independent of the bird's responding. Since this procedure does not prescribe the path through which H is reached, the animal could enter H by any of a number of antecedents, different from bird to bird. Skinner reported pigeons to be reinforced by this procedure, to increase in the frequency of turning about or pecking the ceiling—any of a number of idiosyncratic responses which, though not required, occurred prior to H. Skinner concluded that temporal contiguity is a sufficient condition for reinforcement.

But we may note that although Skinner's procedure is weaker than the contingency, it is not yet a pure case of temporal contiguity. On the contrary, it retains from the surplus conditions of the contingency both a circumscription on the distribution of responding to H and a reduction in the total amount of responding to H. That is, the grain was not free but was available to the birds according to some program, and the amount they ate was almost certainly markedly less than they would have eaten in an equal period of time had grain been freely available.

Can temporal contiguity be achieved without either a response requirement or any restriction on H? The free pairing of stimuli to which the subject has different probabilities of responding would appear to be one way. For example, suppose a rat is given unrestricted access to both an activity wheel and a source of water. Previous tests have established that with suitable water deprivation, the total duration for which the rat drinks when only water is available is greater than the total duration for which it runs when only the wheel is available. Accordingly, in this case, drinking will instance H, running will instance L.

Now when the rat is given both the tube and wheel at the same time, it will occasionally run and then drink—in the case of some of our rats, repeating this run-drink sequence perhaps 20 or more times in a 15-min. session. There will thus occur a temporal contiguity between incontrovertibly reinforcible and reinforcing events. That is, if, with identical parameters, drinking were made *contingent* upon running, running would increase without question. The temporal contiguity that interests us now, however, is one that occurs without the encumbrances of the contingency. If there is no response requirement, no circumscription upon the distribution of H responding, and no reduction in the amount of H responding, is temporal contiguity between H and L still a sufficient condition?

All the evidence we now have on this question is negative. Pure temporal contiguity has never proved to be a sufficient condition. By now a fair number of rats, upwards of 40, have been placed in a wheel containing a drinkometer and their running and drinking recorded on Esterline Angus tape. Despite the relatively large number of times these records show an instance of drink to follow (within 2 sec. or less) an instance of run, there are no cases in which the amount of running has increased over the base amount—the amount run when only the wheel is available; in fact, the rat typically runs more *before* the tube is inserted. Table 2 affords some idea of the number of times the

TABLE 2
NUMBER OF NONCONTINGENT RUN-DRINK CONTIGUITIES/15 MIN.

Subject				
1.	25		7.	19
2.	24		8.	17
3.	22		9.	13
4.	11		10.	23
5.	13		11.	21
6.	8		12.	23

would-be effective temporal contiguities occur in this situation. This number of contiguities in a contingency situation would be more than sufficient to produce an increase in the frequency of running. Further, the number shown is an average per session, and many sessions are run before a negative outcome is accepted.

It might be considered that when the rat can both drink and run and drinking is more probable, running fails to increase simply because drink suppresses run. That is, although run is reinforced by drink, the increased disposition to run is not manifested because of response competition. This would make more sense if the total duration of run plus drink approximated total session time, which it does not; even so, since a direct test can be made so simply, the point is worth considering. The possible suppressive effect of drinking can be removed altogether simply by removing the tube. When this is done, the animal being placed in the wheel with the drinkometer removed, the amount it runs is not different from the base amount. Thus, no increase in running is seen either during a potential learning situation or subsequently during a potential extinction situation.

Thus far we have described three temporal contiguity–producing operations, ranging from the strong contingency to the weak pairing of two stimuli (wheel and tube); intermediate is Skinner's superstition paradigm, which appears to differ from the contingency only in dropping the response requirement. Since the latter produces reinforcement and the free-pairing procedure does not, this leaves in doubt the effect of the other two principal encumbrances of the contingency—circumscription of the H distribution and reduction of H total. Both are retained in the superstition paradigm, which is effective, and both are dropped in the free-pairing design, which is not effective. Accordingly, at least one and perhaps both of these conditions are necessary, i.e., must accompany temporal contiguity in order for reinforcement to occur.

One way to proceed now is to attempt to pervert the purpose of the contingency. Normally, a contingency is used to produce reinforcement, but is it possible to establish a contingency relation and yet not produce reinforcement? The instructive consequence of attempting to divert the contingency from its usual end is that it leads to the abandonment of one of the normal surplus conditions of the contingency—specifically, the reduction in H. Although a circumscription on the distribution of H is all but inevitable, a result of the instrumental requirement, contingencies can be formed that do *not* reduce the animal's normal amount of responding to H. Indeed, the characteristic reduction in H is a coincidental by-product of another accidental feature of the standard contingency. The typical instrumental response, e.g., bar press, has a low operant level, and when access to H is made contingent upon such an instrumental event, a reduction in H, particularly when the contingency is first instated, is nearly inevitable. For example, when the rat can obtain a pellet only following a bar press, the low operant level of the bar press will almost certainly reduce the number of pellets the rat eats in the beginning (whether the reduction obtains after bar pressing has increased in frequency is immaterial; at that point reinforcement has taken place, and we are concerned with whether the initial decrement in H played any role in the ultimate increment in L).

The reduction in H can be avoided from the outset, however, by using an atypical instrumental response, one that has a substantial operant level. For example, consider drinking to be made contingent upon running at a time when running has a high pre-reinforcement level, a thing which is easily established in the rat. By requiring only a "little" run for each relatively "large" drink, the arrangement can be made whereby the rat can provide itself the opportunity to drink the normal amount by running no more than the normal (base) amount. Now the striking thing about this kind of contingency is that it produces no reinforcement, no increase in the frequency of running. But, indeed, why should it? Without running more than it would otherwise, the animal can (and does) drink essentially the normal amount. We are thus led to see that a contingency per se is not a sufficient condition for reinforcement. Moreover, this completes the devaluation of the response requirement: Skinner's superstition paradigm showed that it is not a necessary condition for reinforcement, and the present design shows that it is not a sufficient condition.

More instructive is the suggestion that, specifically, a reduction in H is needed in addition to temporal contiguity if reinforcement is to occur. Circumscribing the distribution of H is clearly not a sufficient condition (though it may be necessary), for the contingency will have this effect; yet if, despite the partitioning of H, H occurs in normal amount, there is no increase in instrumental responding.

But a main point may be considered to remain: if the rat drinks its normal amount, there is no reason for it to run more than its normal amount, but what if the tube is removed? Here, too, there is no increase. After numerous sessions in which instances of run led repeatedly to instances of drink, but with no decrease in drink and no increase in run, the drinkometer was removed, as in extinction, and the animal given only the opportunity to run. No increase in running was observed in three such studies involving 19 rats.

The failure of this kind of contingency to increase instrumental responding, during either a potential learning situation or, more strikingly, a would-be extinction situation, is illuminating on still another score. Data from these contingencies can be shown essentially to rule out the possibility that, during the contingency, runs occur which do not lead to drink and thus are extinguished. We have not mentioned this point earlier, having waited for the present case, where an especially strong test of the point is to be found. In the present data, run is followed (within 2 sec. or less) by drink an average of about 50 times per session. Run is not followed by drink—being followed either by another burst of run or by neither run nor drink for a period greater than 8 sec.—only about 6 times per 15-min. session. Moreover, 6 times per 15-min. session is about the same frequency with which this kind of event, an "unprotected" run in Guthrie's sense, occurs in contingencies that are effective, that do reduce drink and do produce an increase in run. It is therefore difficult to argue that the effectiveness of the temporal contiguities between run and drink is dispelled in the present case by extinction from runs that are unaccompanied by drinks. On the contrary, run is followed repeatedly by drink—it is rarely followed by any other event—nevertheless, when drink is not reduced, run is not increased, and run shows no increment in subsequent would-be extinction sessions.

In summary, a set of operations were shown that lead to temporal contiguity between events that are incontrovertibly reinforcing and reinforcible. If all such operations produced reinforcement, temporal contiguity could be accepted as a sufficient condition. As it turns out, however, only some of the operations produce reinforcement; we are thus led to search among the operations to discern the further conditions they embody. The present search indicates that a reduction in the total amount of H is a necessary condition. A response requirement, which is an essential part of the contingency, proved to be neither a necessary nor a sufficient condition. For example, if H is reduced, reinforcement can be produced without a response requirement, as in Skinner's superstition paradigm. Conversely, if H is not reduced, then, despite the presence of both a response requirement and a circumscription on the distribution of H, reinforcement apparently cannot be produced, as shown by the special run-drink contingency where drink occurred in normal amount. Without doubt the contingency is the most widely used means of producing reinforcement. Apparently, an invariant though unrecognized component of the contingency is a decrement in the amount of responding that occurs to the contingent stimulus, relative to what would occur were the stimulus free. Our results suggest that this reduction is vital, that reinforcement cannot be initiated without it. We are thus led to suppose that although the reduction is not, like the response requirement, a necessary feature of the contingency, it nonetheless occurs as a routine part of the reinforcement procedure. It would be preferable to elevate this factor from its obscure status as a hidden concomitant to that of a public operation where its consequences for theory can be examined.[12]

SUMMARY: COUNTEREXAMPLES

The argument has been too long to recapitulate easily, so let us summarize instead by briefly considering outstanding counterexamples.

Classical Conditioning

That the reinforcement value of a chain of operant behavior (or of the initiating discriminative stimulus) is proportional to the strength of the terminal respondent is a view that claims surprisingly many adherents, surprising given the slight evidence the view so far commands (for adherents, see Spence, 1956; Mowrer, 1960). Is this model compatible with the present one? Let us suspend that question to look first at the basic assumption of the model. Do operant chains terminate in reflexes? It is not necessary that all operant chains terminate in reflexes, but the view does require that those chains which participate in reinforcement do so terminate. In other words, the adequacy of the view requires that its domain be at least as broad as that of reinforcement. We can comment on that adequacy by looking at several of the operant chains which were shown here to participate in reinforcement.

Thus, we may ask what is the terminal respondent in manipulation of monkeys. Is it possible, in the case of the lever-pressing

---

[12] A sequel has shown that although such "weak" operations as pairing stimuli that control responses of different probabilities do not produce changes in frequency, they may nonetheless affect distributional properties; e.g., they may produce a quasi-permanent change in average duration of the burst. However, we have considered it to be less confusing to restrict the meaning of "reinforcement" here to the traditional frequency change. Elsewhere we shall deal with reinforcement under various relaxations of the standard definition.

or plunger operation of the present monkey experiment, to delineate the reflexes in which these undeniably operant chains terminated? What is the terminal respondent in wheel turning in rats? The impression grows that these questions, and more like them, may not be easily answered, especially when it is observed that a proper answer will require a description of the unconditioned stimulus, the location on the animal's body where it is to be applied, and the form of the response that is to result. Once reinforcement is loosened from eating and drinking—a loosening unlikely in those cases where the tie is essentially umbilical—we encounter cases where there is no visible respondent, no unconditioned stimulus to apply, no unconditioned response to measure. The adequacy of the view would thus seem to be confined mainly to the ingestive cases that spawned the view. But a theory of ingestion cannot be equated with a general model of reinforcement.

There is a more important point. The facts of classical conditioning are themselves in need of explanation. Rather than attempting to explain operant reinforcement with classical conditioning, we might instead look to the possibility of accounting for classical conditioning. It is at this point that an interesting possibility arises, viz., accounting for both classical conditioning and operant reinforcement by the same principle.

Standard treatments of operant reinforcement fail to make contact with the strong question "Why does (say) food reinforce the bar press?" being sidetracked instead by the weak question "Why is a large piece of food more effective than a small one?" But if one can answer the question of why X will reinforce Y, it should not be too difficult to explain why a large X may be more effective than a small one. An answer to the strong question is far more likely to include an answer to the weak question than vice versa.

Likewise, in classical conditioning the strong question tends to be overlooked in favor of the parameters of conditioning. Why are the responses elicited by some stimuli conditionable to other stimuli and not vice versa? That is, what makes some stimuli (utilizable as) unconditioned stimuli and others (utilizable as) conditioned stimuli? The latter has been rather neglected, though Pavlov (1927) would appear to have regarded the question as basic and, along with Sherrington (1906), attempted to answer it. In fact, these men gave similar answers, both stressing the dominance of one stimulation relative to that of the other. More recent versions of dominance theory have been provided by Razran (1957) and Grings (1960).

We may now discern an evident similarity between the Pavlovian account of classical conditioning and the present one of operant reinforcement. A process is considered to depend upon a relationship between two events—US and CS in one case, base and contingent response in the other—and to require that one event be dominant relative to the other. It will be observed, however, that in order to complete the formal parallel, we must specify the dimension on which dominance is to be measured in the classical case. Pavlov does not appear to have made any operational provisions, having considered dominance mainly in neurological terms. There are only two operational alternatives: stimulus or response properties. If stimulus properties are used, dominance will be restricted to a few (though possibly paradigmatic) cases where US and CS can be located on the same scale. This is a restriction we specifically sought to overcome in the operant case by the use of response probability. But can the classical case be formulated in other than stimulus terms?

If analogues of the two responses in the operant case can be found in the classical one, the classical case too could be stated in response terms. There is no problem with the UR, for it is quite explicit and in fact sometimes measured; rather, the problem is with the response to the CS—not the CR, but the unconditional response to the CS. Is there such a response? Typical CSs such as lights and buzzers elicit reactions, of a lesser magnitude than those elicited by the typical US, which characteristically are ignored but which might instead be measured. The appropriate scale for their measurement has already been established, should measurement prove worthwhile, for the response rationale worked out for the operant case can be applied here without revision. That is, in the classical case, too, one will encounter a set of physically different movements, all of which, however, will have duration or temporal extent in common. Thus, in principle at least, the decision as to dominance can be made on an equivalent basis in both cases.[13]

"Yes" as a Reinforcer

A case which questions the exhaustiveness more than the validity of the present account arises from a category of stimuli that are effective through another agent applying them to the subject rather than through the usual self-application. A simple example is the experimenter saying "yes" (or, for that matter, "wrong"; Buchwald, 1959) to a human subject. "Yes" does not appear to give rise to any determinate response on the part of the subject, and moreover it is not clear how to estimate the probability of S's responding to E's "yes." If we were to provide the subject with a "yes" machine—a box emitting "yes" whenever touched—S would seem unlikely to make extensive use of it, in particular, a use proportional to the reinforcement value of "yes" as applied by the experimenter. But if so, this would appear to refute the present account, not merely question its exhaustiveness. On the other hand, all that may be at stake here is a secondary reinforcer whose effectiveness depends upon a context more complex than that found in the usual animal example. A light made effective by association with a food pellet should display its effectiveness in any situation which sufficiently approximates the training one. Similarly, "yes," having acquired its potency in a distinctive linguistic relation, could be expected to reveal its effectiveness only in contexts that approximate the original linguistic relation. A "yes" box would not sufficiently approximate that relation. Furthermore, we would trace the

[13] One immediate prediction which follows from thus equating the classical and operant cases is that the US and CS will no longer be seen as categories with fixed membership; on the contrary, if appropriate parameters can be found, it should be possible to reverse the classical conditioning relation in a manner comparable to the reversal of the reinforcement relation shown earlier in the operant case.

original effectiveness of "yes" to association with high-probability events.[14]

Nonresponse Reinforcement

A more blunt objection is found in data showing that, for example, fistula feeding is reinforcing (e.g., Miller & Kessen, 1952). Here the R-R paradigm is visibly no longer applicable: reinforcement occurs without a response. Such cases cannot be gainsaid, and we must instead take into account their one irrefutable implication. Organisms are of such a design that their responses can be circumvented. Indeed, the circumvention of all responses would seem only to await sufficient knowledge. In due time, the effects of, say, running will doubtless be duplicable without running, by neurological intervention, and these effects no less than those of eating or of any other behavior. To a nonspecialist such as myself, the wholesale extent to which this intervention may be possible was nowhere better suggested than on a Sunday television program that showed a robot learn a maze. Having first struck nearly every blind, but finally learning to sail down smoothly, the little device was picked up and its head promptly opened. There were the dread insides—though in this case the black box *was* nearly empty—perfectly open to direct intervention. Never was it more clear that behavior is expendable. Although behavior is the locus of morality (that without which Conrad would have had no subject matter), it is nonetheless susceptible of total circumvention, contingent only upon sufficient knowledge. Strictly speaking, therefore, one cannot say, as we have, that a response is a necessary condition for

---

[14] L. Homme (personal communication, 1965) has described an ingenious set of studies (using both normal children and mental defectives) in which speech was reinforced, not with the standard approval or attention, e.g., "yes," "umhum," but by making the opportunity to talk about a topic for which the probability of speech was high contingent upon talking about another topic for which the probability of speech was relatively low. For example, the opportunity to talk about baseball was made contingent upon the solution of arithmetic problems.

anything; in principle, one can always reach inside and pull a string.

Still one can ask whether it is possible to predict under what circumstance fistula feeding will be reinforcing. The present assumptions may regain their relevance at this point, for, although responses can indeed be circumvented, when they are not, measurements which they permit may yield generalizations that hold about as well for the surgical puppet as for the intact organism. Fistula feeding may prove to reinforce, say, bar pressing only if the probability of normal eating is greater than that of bar pressing. Alternatively, an organism that is less apt to eat than, say, scrutinize the passage of pinballs may be increased in the frequency with which it feeds itself through a fistula if the pinball opportunity is contingent upon self–fistula feeding. The response is not a necessary condition so much as an opportunity for measurement, one that would be regrettable to neglect for the information it may provide and the theory to which it may lead.

REFERENCES

Bower, G. H., & Miller, N. E. Rewarding and punishing effects from stimulating the same place in a rat's brain. *J. comp. physiol. Psychol.*, 1958, **51**, 669–674.

Buchwald, A. M. Experimental alternations in the effectiveness of reinforcement combinations. *J. exp. Psychol.*, 1959, **57**, 351–361.

Catania, A. C. Concurrent performances: reinforcement interaction and response independence. *J. exp. Anal. Behav.*, 1963, **6**, 253–264. (a)

Catania, A. C. Concurrent performances: a baseline for the study of reinforcement magnitude. *J. exp. Anal. Behav.*, 1963, **6**, 299–301. (b)

Collier, G. Consummatory and instrumental responding as a function of deprivation. *J. exp. Psychol.*, 1962, **64**, 410–414.

Collier, G., & Siskel, M., Jr. Performance as a joint function of amount of reinforcement and inter-reinforcement interval. *J. exp. Psychol.*, 1959, **57**, 115–120.

Dethier, V. G. Microscopic brains. *Science*, 1964, **143**, 1138–1145.

Grings, W. W. Preparatory set variables in the classical conditioning of autonomic variables. *Psychol. Rev.*, 1960, **67**, 243–252.

Herrnstein, R. J. Relative and absolute strength of response as a function of frequency of reinforcement. *J. exp. Anal. Behav.*, 1961, **4**, 267–273.

Hodos, W., & Valenstein, E. S. An evaluation of response rate as a measure of rewarding intracranial stimulation. *J. comp. physiol. Psychol.*, 1962, **55**, 80–84.

Holstein, S., & Hundt, A. G. Reinforcement of intracranial self-stimulation by licking. *Psychonomic Sc.*, in press.

Hundt, A. G. Instrumental response rate and reinforcement density. Unpublished doctoral dissertation, Univ. of Missouri, 1964.

Hundt, A. G., & Premack, D. Running as both a positive and negative reinforcer. *Science*, 1963, 142, 1087–1088.

Kintsch, W., & Premack, D. Stochastic analysis of free responding. Paper read at Psychometric Society, Niagara Falls, 1965.

Meehl, P. E. On the circularity of the law of effect. *Psychol. Bull.*, 1950, 47, 52–75.

Meehl, P. E. Schizotaxia, Schizotypy, Schizophrenia. *Amer. J. Psychol.*, 1962, 17, 827–838.

Miller, N., & Kessen, M. L. Reward effects of food via stomach fistula compared with those of food via mouth. *J. comp. physiol. Psychol.*, 1952, 45, 555–564.

Mowrer, O. H. *Learning theory and behavior.* New York: Wiley, 1960.

Parzen, E. *Modern probability theory and its applications.* New York: Wiley, 1960.

Pavlov, I. P. *Conditioned reflexes.* (Trans. by G. V. Anrep) London: Oxford Univ. Press, 1927.

Premack, D. Toward empirical behavioral laws: I. Positive reinforcement. *Psychol. Rev.*, 1959, 66, 219–233.

Premack, D. Predicting instrumental performance from the independent rate of the contingent response. *J. exp. Psychol.*, 1961, 61, 163–171.

Premack, D. Reversibility of the reinforcement relation. *Science*, 1962, 136, 255–257.

Premack, D. Rate differential reinforcement in monkey manipulation. *J. exp. Anal. Behav.*, 1963, 6, 81–89. (a)

Premack, D. Prediction of the comparative reinforcement values of running and drinking. *Science*, 1963, 139, 1062–1063. (b)

Premack, D., & Bahwell, R. Operant-level lever pressing by a monkey as a function of interest interval. *J. exp. Anal. Behav.*, 1959, 2, 127–131.

Premack, D., & Schaeffer, R. W. Distributional properties of operant-level locomotion in the rat. *J. exp. Anal. Behav.*, 1962, 5, 89–95.

Premack, D., & Schaeffer, R. W. Some parameters affecting the distributional properties of operant-level running in rats. *J. exp. Anal. Behav.*, 1963, 6, 473–475.

Pribram, K. H. Reinforcement revisited: a structural view. In M. R. Jones (Ed.), *Nebraska symposium on motivation: 1963.* Lincoln: Univ. of Nebraska Press, 1963. Pp. 113–150.

Razran, G. The dominance-contiguity theory of the acquisition of classical conditioning. *Psychol. Bull.*, 1957, 54, 1–46.

Reynolds, G. S. On some determinants of choice in pigeons. *J. exp. Anal. Behav.*, 1963, 6, 53–62.

Roberts, W. W. Rapid escape learning without avoidance learning motivated by hypothalamic stimulation in cats. *J. comp. physiol. Psychol.*, 1958, **51**, 391–399.

Schaeffer, R. W. The reinforcement relation as a function of the instrumental response base rate. *J. exp. Psychol.*, in press.

Schaeffer, R. W., & Premack, D. Licking rates in infant albino rats. *Science*, 1961, **134**, 1980–1981.

Sherrington, C. S. *The integrative action of the nervous system.* New Haven: Yale Univ. Press, 1906.

Skinner, B. F. The measurement of spontaneous activity. *J. gen. Psychol.*, 1933, **9**, 3–24.

Skinner, B. F. *The behavior of organisms.* New York: Appleton-Century-Crofts, 1938.

Skinner, B. F. "Superstition" in the pigeon. *J. exp. Psychol.*, 1948, **38**, 168–172.

Spence, K. W. *Behavior theory and conditioning.* New Haven: Yale Univ. Press, 1956.

Stellar, E., & Hill, J. H. The rat's rate of drinking as a function of water deprivation. *J. comp. physiol. Psychol.*, 1952, **45**, 96–102.

Comments on Dr. Premack's Paper

Robert Ward Leeper

There are a few questions I want to raise about Dr. Premack's paper, but let me say, first, that I regard this as an unusually keen and interesting paper—one that makes some enduring contributions to the psychology of motivation. Let me speak first about the features that prompt this remark.

First of all, I must confess that I am highly sympathetic with certain temperamental characteristics that run through Premack's paper. I like his readiness—his eagerness, even—to challenge traditional conceptions in psychology and to seek better alternatives. I admire his predeliction for casting his hypotheses in very broad, abstract terms rather than timidly confining his statements to the particular conditions of his particular experiments. I would have preferred for him to state these abstract propositions in simpler, plainer terms, and without the shifting meanings he gives to "reinforcement" and to his "H" and "L." But these matters are relatively incidental. The two positive features of his approach that I have mentioned are ingredients, it seems to me, that are much needed in any scientific field.

Second, in the experimentation which Premack reports, and in his generalizations from his data, there are some strikingly interesting products. Thus, he has made a simple and yet remarkably important suggestion in his proposition that, under at least many conditions, the relative strength of the motives lying back of different activities may be measured in terms of the relative amount of time that the organism would spend in engaging in these activities. (On this point, as in the others that follow, I am rephrasing Premack's propositions in somewhat different terms than he would use, partly to simplify my discussion and partly to show the relationships of his ideas to more traditional interpretations; I may also be stating some of them a bit more cautiously than he does.) As Premack points out, we have needed a means of making comparisons between different activities that, in many cases, are drastically different qualitatively from one another. I can envisage possible uses of his concept in much more complex matters than he has explored (e.g., when we try to help persons to reach decisions about vocations or try to decide whether they are sufficiently motivated to attempt college work). Much of laboratory research can be facilitated by this methodological tool which he has explored to some extent.

It is highly worthwhile, furthermore, to have his conceptual and empirical clarifications of the point that activities of the organism cannot be divided into fixed categories of rewarding activities and possible instrumental activities, but that the properties of any activity, in this connection, depend on the larger context.

Naturally I appreciate, as well, the evidence he provides that (as I would phrase it) activities which rest on emotional factors (like interest in playing a pinball machine) serve as motivational factors in just as natural and true a sense as interest in eating chocolate drops, or that the rat's activity of running can be just as truly rewarding as the activity of drinking or eating. His demonstration is interesting, furthermore, that rats could learn, as instrumental responses to make a water tube available, bar-pressing responses that produced intracranial stimulation which, in itself, seemed to have reinforcing properties (although, from the description Premack gives here, I am not sure that the rats were learning anything except bar pressing and would have learned this regardless of whether intracranial stimulation was involved).

So, on these various scores, as well as on his proposals of the three abstract concepts of relativity of reinforcement relation-ships, reversibility of reinforcement relationships, and the "in-difference principle," the paper seems to me to be a notable con-tribution to motivational psychology.

On the side of skeptical comments, the main points I would make would be the following: In his general approach, Premack has used what may be called a miniature-area approach, rather than a broad-area approach. He indicates at some points that since he is stating his hypotheses in sweeping terms, they will need some far-ranging corroborations before they can be taken with confidence. But he has not been much inclined, himself, to check his generalizations against some broader reaches of material. As a consequence, it seems to me, he is using his time to propose generalizations which, in some cases, he ought already to be able to qualify or discard. In some other matters, he fails to consider some further factors and relationships that might be important additions to the variables he has recognized.

Let me illustrate. If I understand him correctly, Premack is suggesting that the minimal conditions for learning are these: (1) There must be two activities that have different probabilities of occurrence (as measure by total time in which each would be engaged under conditions such as are being used in the experiment). (2) The less probable activity is made closely ante-cedent to the other by some circumstances or other. (3) There are restrictions of external sorts introduced which keep the second (what we might call the "rewarding") activity from being engaged in as fully as it would be at that time were it not for external interferences. Thus, he said, he could teach rats to run more extensively to get water if he put some restrictions on how adequately the rats could satisfy their thirst within each given training period, but got no such learning when comparable running activity frequently was antecedent to drinking but when the total amount of drinking was unrestricted. From his informal comments at Lincoln, I understand also that this latter effect occurred even when each individual burst of drinking activity was restricted externally, but the possible total number of bursts of drinking within each training period left the rat finally satiated. As Premack states it: "The present research indicates that a reduction in the total amount of H [e.g., of drinking by a thirsty rat] is a necessary condition [for reinforcement or learning]."

This whole interpretation seems equivalent to the proposition that rewards are essential for learning but that the rewards must be restricted (or, as we might say, "stingy") rewards. Both phases of this interpretation seem counter to findings of other experiments. Particularly does this seem the case since Premack intends this interpretation to apply generally. For example, during the symposium, I asked whether he meant that rats should fail to learn a maze if, at the conclusion of each run, they were allowed to eat or drink until they were satiated. He accepted this implication, but said that, to the best of his knowledge, all maze experiments and other learning experiments had used restricted rewards.

Now, unquestionably, most experimenters, to economize their time, have given only limited rewards in the experimental apparatus, regardless of whether this is a maze, a Skinner box, a conditioned-salivary situation, or whatnot. But many situations in natural life afford unlimited reward materials. For example, when an animal finds a stream or pond from which to drink, normally there are no restrictions on its consummatory activity. It seems extremely doubtful that no learning of "routes to water holes, streams, or the like" would occur under such frequently recurring natural conditions and that the animals would learn the routes only in case some interference occurred to prevent the animal's drinking its fill. Such appeal to natural circumstances of course does not conclusively disprove Premack's proposition. But when one checks back over various experimental studies, there do seem to be cases where learning occurred despite the lack of such restrictions. For example, going back to R. C. Tryon's experiments (as reported in *J. Comp. Psychol.*, 1930, 11, 145–170), I find the following: on one of his 20-unit mazes, with one trial a day, "animals were permitted to eat at a filled food pan in their end chamber until they definitely turned away from their food pan." Yet this was an efficient training situation.[1] Furthermore, spurred by Premack's comments, I've gone back and read (for the first time) the account of the pioneer maze experiment by Willard Small (*Amer. J. Psychol.*, 1901, 12, 206–239). The rats were apparently allowed more than sufficient stores of milk and bread in the end-box, and could wander in and out of the end-box and consume as much as they wanted, and on their own schedule. Yet, with the Hampton Court design he used, Small found that they developed high proficiency at running the maze.

Those psychologists who are more thoroughly familiar with operant conditioning work than I am might be able to cite experiments with lever-pulling apparatus where rats were allowed to keep working and eating until they were thoroughly satiated. I would presume that rats would learn under this arrangement. In fact, it would seem hard to believe that this would not be the case, because Skinner found such considerable resistance to extinction in many rats after merely a single rewarded lever pull that

[1] From a personal discussion with Dr. Tryon when the galley proofs of this commentary arrived, I learned that he has some notable further data which he has never published. In 1940, with his twenty-second generation of rats, he trained 41 maze-bright rats as follows. After each daily run, each rat was left in its goal-box for some hours with more than seven times the amount of wet mash given under the standard training conditions. This was much more than any rat could consume, and surely permitted unlimited consummatory activity. Nevertheless, these rats not only learned to run the 17-unit maze, but performed almost as efficiently as other maze-bright rats under the standard restricted reward, and performed dramatically better than the maze-dull rats under either the normal deprivation schedule or under a schedule where they received only about half the standard food reward.

he drew this conclusion: "I think it may be concluded from the high frequency of occurrence of the instantaneous change that a single reinforcement is capable of raising the strength of the operant to essentially a maximum value" (*The Behavior of Organisms*, p. 69). If the rats would show no enduring habit-formation after having been allowed to continue bar pressing and eating until they were thoroughly satisfied, this would then mean that the rats would have learned if they had been interrupted after their early trials, but somehow would have unlearned all this if they had been allowed to continue till they desisted of their own accord. This hardly sounds possible.

Another angle of attack on the question of the minimal conditions for learning might have been used by Premack. There are various experiments in which no recognizable rewards occurred and yet where learning occurred anyway. Thus, in long-continued testing for perceptual thresholds, it is a commonplace finding that the subjects get better and better in the early part of their work even though they never receive any feedback as to whether their judgments are correct or wrong. In his work on the two-point tactual threshold in 1868, Volkmann had laboratory evidence of this point almost two decades before the monograph by Ebbinghaus which we usually cite as the pioneer experimental study of learning. Similarly, it seems that learning occurs in the figural-aftereffect experiments, even though the conditions suggested by Premack as minimal do not occur.

As I have suggested in discussing this same basic question in Volume 5 of S. Koch's *Psychology: A Study of a Science*, it can be granted that rewards are indispensable for the establishment of reward-expectation habits and punishments are normally essential for the establishment of punishment-expectation habits. But other habits can be learned that require neither rewards nor punishments, and all that seems essential for learning is that (1) some new perceptual organization must be brought into existence, and (2) some conditions of vividness, frequency of repetition, or duration must be provided which will give sufficient neural perseveration so that habit-consolidation can occur. Furthermore, it seems that the influences of rewards and punishments on learning come through properties that are shared with some situations that lack both of these, rather than from any basic properties peculiar to rewards or punishments.

Speaking more broadly, it seems to me that Premack's reflections on his running-and-unrestricted-drinking experiment illustrate some limitations that tend to plague the S-R approaches to motivation and learning that Dr. Kendler also is partial to. The S-R modes of thought tend to assume that the sufficient conditions for learning are provided when stimulus, response, and reward come in close temporal succession, regardless of other considerations. From the standpoint of a cognitive or perceptual theory of learning, on the other hand, it is assumed that the specification of conditions must be much more specific. It is assumed that what is learned depends on the perceptual organization in the situation and that rather minor-looking factors might make major changes in the organism's perception of the situation. Thus, in Premack's situation, a perceptual theory would not assume that the rat would develop a perception of a means-end relationship between running and drinking merely because the rat had had a separate perception of the wheel as something in which it might run and another separate perception of the water tube as something from which it might drink. There would have to be some special factors which would produce a more complex perceptual organization which the rat, if it could verbalize, might express by saying, "Running in that wheel seems to be the necessary condition for making the water available." The crucial question really is: "What conditions would help to develop—or, contrariwise, tend to preclude—the development of such a means-end perception?"

It is easy to arrange conditions to obstruct the development of means-ends or sign-significate perceptions. To illustrate this point, one of the simplest and surest situations that I know of is the following: With a large group of students, you tell them their task will be to learn to predict whether you will say "this is an A" or "this is a B" when you point to different objects in the room. Then, using an exaggeratedly visible pointer, you point to a long succession of objects about the room, at various heights, but always holding the pointer inclined upward when pointing to As and sloping downward when pointing to Bs. All sorts of hypotheses get formulated, tested, and discarded by members of the group; but the one invariable stimulation property that precedes the pronouncements that "this is an A" or "this is a B" proves very difficult for any of such subjects to learn to use, even though there is the sequence of "discriminable stimulation, then response, and then restricted reward" which Premack is assuming is the minimal condition for learning.

In the experimental situation which Premack used, it may be hard to say what factor prevented the rats from developing a means-end habit. But the point would be that a cognitive theory would say that the variables involved in such a situation are apt to be much more diverse than those recognized by S-R theorists *to date*, and, among such diverse factors, there are many that tend to obstruct perceptual reorganizations rather than facilitate them. It is much easier, as physiological psychologists recognize, to destroy than to create, to hamper than to facilitate. If I might hazard a guess, I would say that the rats were failing to develop a perception of "running as a means to drinking" because of the fact that they were allowed to drink occasionally at various sizable delays after running. The rats therefore had the conditions for perceiving the water tube as something unrelated to the running activity. Or, to phrase the matter in probably better terms, using some of the mode of thought which I described in my paper as increasingly characteristic of perceptual theorizing: the rats had nothing to force them into developing the rather more complex perceptual hypothesis that the running and drinking had anything to do with each other. Instead, the hypothesis they would tend to develop would be one which, if it could be verbalized, would state that "whenever you want to use the drinking tube, it is available, even though—sad is the lot of a rat—the damn thing usually runs dry each time before you get satisfied and you have to keep coming back over and over again." And, as in other matters, as I was saying near the end of my own paper, whatever perceptual organization gets developed first will tend to obstruct the development of any other organization, even though the latter might otherwise have been easily achieved.

There are some other points that I might make, too, but they are relatively minor. The above may well illustrate the main idea I would like to suggest—to wit, there are some very considerable values in what Premack has done, both experimentally and theoretically, but there are some additional values that I believe would have come through using a broad-area type of approach that would try to utilize many different sorts of examples in trying to deal with theoretical questions. Some of such knowledge, at that, needs to come from outside experimental laboratories. Thus, Premack has spoken as though it is somewhat new knowledge that we cannot divide activities into two categories—those that are merely reinforcing and others that are merely reinforcible or that might be learned as instrumental responses. However, he might well have considered that the Second Oldest Profession has given abundant proof, from time immemorial, that what are normally consummatory activities can be used as instrumental means to other goals.

Intrinsic Motivation and Its Role in Psychological Development[1]

J. McV. HUNT

University of Illinois

In the history of thought, the nature of human nature has been characterized largely on the basis of the answers assumed to the motivational questions. Human nature has been conceived as fixed or free, bad or good, irrational or rational, selfish or altruistic, pugnacious or peaceful, according to the assumptions made about the springs of human conduct and thought. In turn, these assumptions about man's nature have figured in the structure of political and economic institutions, and these same assumptions have helped to shape ends and means of education. On the side of political structure, for instance, Machiavelli justified the need for a powerful autocracy by his assumption of the irrational, selfish, and pugnacious nature of man, who could be socialized into proper conduct only by trickery and coercion. Contrariwise, the founding fathers of these United States based their innovations of governmental structure on the assumption that man is free to make rational choices. They feared most a tyrannical coercion from either leaders or majorities. The result is our system of checks and balances. On the side of education, Calvin's assumption of an "evil" human nature, implicit in the doctrine of original sin, gave conceptual justification for stern discipline and strong punishment in child rearing and education.

[1] This paper has been prepared with the support of a grant from the Carnegie Corporation of New York and of USPHS Career Award MH K6-18,567.

189

Contrariwise, Rousseau assumed that man is by nature "good," and he employed this assumption to justify a nurturant approach to child rearing and education.

These assumptions about human nature may well derive from general attitudes toward life and existence, as Tomkins' (1964) "psychology of knowledge" would indicate. Even so, there is a peculiar contemporary conflict. The conceptual synthesis dominant in psychological science over much of the past century has answered the motivation questions in ways that lend support to the pessimistic view of human nature. It is ironic, then, a special case of C. P. Snow's "two cultures," that democratic political institutions have continued to function reasonably well in a number of Western countries. (Indeed, the word *democracy* has such status over the world that even the modern guises of tyranny must be cloaked in its terms.)

As another special case of the "two cultures," a *laissez faire* approach to child rearing has grown in prominence during this same period. Its growth appears to have derived from the confluence of four streams of thought and social movement. One begins from Rousseau and has come down to us through the work of Pestalozzi and Froebel in the kindergarten movement. Another traces from the recapitulation assumption in the thought of G. Stanley Hall and comes via the child-study movement, which merged in many places with the Froebel Societies just before the turn of the century. A third stream derives from John Dewey and the reform-Darwinism of Lester F. Ward and Albion Small (see Cremin, 1962) and has come down through the progressive-education movement. A fourth moves from Freud and comes to us through the application to kindergarten and primary education of the principle that a strong superego is bad for mental health. Again, it is ironic that these streams of influence converged, in America, just before and after World War I, when the pessimism of *unconscious motives* and drive-reduction theory came to dominate both psychological and psychoanalytical theorizing.

The result is a kind of cultural schizophrenia. The assumptions underlying our legal, political, and economic institutions and our educational practice have lacked congruence with the theory of motivation from behavioral science. Since the concern of behavioral science is with "what is what" about motivation, and about human nature in general, this lack of congruence neither impugns nor supports what has become the dominant scientific view of motivation. On the other hand, this dissonance between social practice and the scientific view should not endure. Either legal, political, and economic policies and educational practice should be changed to fit the real nature of human nature or behavioral science's empirical observations should be correcting the dominant scientific conception of that nature. Moreover, this cultural schizophrenia lends extrascientific import to the evidence which has been accumulating, especially since World War II, to indicate that the dominant scientific conception of human nature is far from established and to suggest that the theoretical underpinning for democracy and education, while inadequately formulated for our day, may be closer to a valid conception of human nature.

What I wish to do here comes under four headings. First, I wish to synopsize the traditionally dominant answers to the chief motivation questions. Second, I wish to synopsize the conceptual and empirical basis for intrinsic motivation, *i.e.*, motivation inherent in the organism's informational interaction with the environment, especially through the eyes and the ears. Third, I wish to present a hypothetical view of the role of this intrinsic motivation, so defined, in psychological development. Finally, fourth, I want to present some issues, some methodological suggestions, and some evidence generated by this hypothetical view.

The Dominant Answers to the Motivation Questions

The first motivation question, as I have them ordered, asks what instigates the activities of organisms and what stops them. According to the traditionally dominant conceptual scheme, the instigators of action are of three kinds: (1) strong and painful external stimuli, (2) such homeostatic needs as hunger and thirst, and (3) sex. In addition, there are those acquired drives based upon experiences in which originally innocuous stimuli have been associated with, and have become conditional stimuli for, those emotional responses evoked by the various primary drive-stimuli. These various instigators have been presumed to produce a generalized inner state of arousal or excitement, which has been called *drive* ever since Woodworth first introduced the term in America. Drive impels action. When such primary or acquired drive-stimuli cease to impinge on an organism, the behavior is presumed to stop.[2]

The second motivation question asks what energizes activity and controls its vigor. An answer has been found in the intensity of the painful stimuli, in the degree of homeostatic need, and/or in the intensity of those emotional responses which were originally part of the total reaction to the primary drive-stimuli.

The third motivation question concerns the direction-hedonic issue. Its answer has come in terms of drive-reduction. Organisms withdraw from and avoid situations which will increase the level of drive. Conversely, they approach and seek situations which will reduce the level of drive. In animals without speech, withdrawal from and avoidance of a situation has been presumed to indicate a negative, distressing hedonic value. Conversely, approach to the source of stimulation and the seeking of certain situations is presumed to be associated with positive, pleasant hedonic value. It is perhaps impossible to separate the directional from the hedonic in animals without speech, so I have combined the issues. On the other hand, in human beings with speech, the equivalence of direction to hedonic value becomes an issue for investigation.

The fourth motivation question asks what accounts for cathexis, emotional attachment, or love. It too has been answered in terms of drive-reduction. An organism is presumed to develop emotional attachments for those objects, persons, and places that are associated with drive-reduction or that have led to drive-reduction. It is thus that the human infant is presumed to become attached to the mother, who reduces his hunger, his various discomforts, and his anxieties based on past experience with them

---

[2] Since I have documented these statements extensively elsewhere, I refer the reader to that paper (Hunt, 1963b).

(Freud, 1926). Similarly, the "secondary reinforcements" of behavior theory are innocuous stimuli which, having been associated with drive-reduction, are presumed to signal relief from either primary drive or anxiety (see Mowrer, 1960).

The fifth question concerns choice of response. It has been answered in terms of the kind of drive-stimulus operative and the organism's past experience with it. For each drive-stimulus, there is presumed to be a hierarchy of responses innately associated with it, and the response chosen is the one that has served effectively to reduce the drive in past encounters with the situation (see Hull, 1943).

The sixth question asks what controls choice of goals. In the short run, this question is the same as the instigation question already answered. In the long run, however, it concerns those relatively distant objectives characteristic of human conduct. From the generic standpoint, this question too has also been answered in terms of drive-reduction, for this is what Freud (1905, 1915) considered to be the "aim" of all behavior and thought. Inasmuch as a major share of the evidence on this long-run goal-choice question has come either from observations of distressed people in psychotherapy or from experiments with such laboratory animals as rats, the attempted answers at best have been extrapolative. These extrapolated answers, stated largely in terms of the notion of acquired drive (see, *e.g.*, Dollard & Miller, 1950; Mowrer, 1960), however, have posed puzzling quandaries, as Brown (1953) pointed out in the first of these Nebraska Symposia on Motivation.

The seventh question concerns the basis for behavioral change or learning. Frustration has been the answer given in the dominant conceptual scheme. When the conditions are so changed that any given mode of response ceases to reduce drive, the result is frustration. That mode of response is presumed to be weakened relative to the other responses in the ready-made hierarchy. These are tried out in turn until one serves to reduce the drive (Hull, 1943; Melton, 1941; Miller & Dollard, 1941) or the emotional distress based originally on the drive (Mowrer, 1960, pp. 307 ff.).

The eighth question asks why organisms persist in utilizing a given response or in seeking a given goal when conditions have changed. The answer has been given in terms of the number of times that the action has met with success in reducing the drive (Hull, 1943, pp. 102, 112) or in terms of what Mowrer (1960) has called *counterconditioning*. In the case of counterconditioning, frustrations which have been followed by relief are reduced in their inhibitive power by virtue of their tendency to signal relief or, as Mowrer terms it, hope.

The Basis for Intrinsic Motivation

The simplicity of the answers which this traditionally dominant theory has given to most of these motivation questions has lent the theory considerable elegance. Moreover, the evidence from a substantial body of experimental investigation has lent these answers a bulwark of empirical support. They are true—within limits.

On the other hand, the theory is inadequate. It has commonly been asserted that all behavior is motivated. Implicit in this statement is the notion that all behavior is motivated by the extrinsic forces of painful stimulation, homeostatic need, and sex or the acquired drives based upon them. Without the action of such extrinsic drive-stimuli, organisms presumably become quiescent (Freud, 1915; Hull, 1943). Such is clearly not the case. Various studies, done largely since World War II, have described animals playing, manipulating things, exploring new regions of space, and seeking new sources of perceptual input in the absence of these primary drives and of the acquired drives based upon them (for documentation, see Hunt, 1963b). In fact, it is precisely when painful stimulation, homeostatic needs, and sex are absent and when any acquired drives based upon them are minimized that play, exploration, manipulation, and curiosity behaviors are most likely to occur. This, coupled with the facts that animals will not eat when in pain or indulge in sex when hungry, lends credence to Maslow's (1954) hypothesis of a hierarchy of motivational sources. In spite of the evidence illustrating the traditional answers to the various motivational questions, this dominant theory does not account for all behavior.

Moreover, the existence of a system of motivation inherent in the functioning of the distance receptors, the eyes and the ears, has long existed without proper theoretical notice. Such a system was implied in the investigations of the "orienting reflex" begun by Pavlov very shortly after he began his famous work on salivary conditioning (see Berlyne, 1960; Razran, 1961). Also unheeded were such objections to traditional drive theory as Nissen's (1930), which was based on his finding that rats would leave their familiar nests and cross an electrified grid to get to a Dashiell maze filled with objects fresh and novel to them. The neglect of such early evidence was itself probably intrinsically motivated by what Festinger (1957) has termed "cognitive dissonance." The various bits of evidence were simply too dissonant with the dominant conceptual beliefs of drive theory to be credible.

In the period following World War II, it was Harlow (1950) who first gave vigorous emphasis to the dissonant evidence, and particularly to that from his own laboratory. He made his strongest and most generalized presentation from this platform in the first of the Nebraska Symposia on Motivation (Harlow, 1953). Since then a heavy bulwark of evidence has derived from the work of Berlyne (1960) on curiosity, the investigations by Montgomery (1952, 1953a, 1953b, 1954) on spontaneous alternation and exploratory behavior in the rat, the work of Butler (1953, 1954, 1958) on the incentive value of visual exploration in monkeys, and the McGill finding that human beings can hardly tolerate homogeneity of input for more than three or four days (see Bexton, Heron, & Scott, 1954; Heron, Doane, & Scott, 1956). In sum, this evidence makes untenable the contention that all behavior is motivated by forces extrinsic to information processing.

Nevertheless, several modes of theoretical recognition for behavior in the absence of pain, homeostatic need, and sex and of acquired drives based on these seem to me to be unfortunate. The first consists in the naming of drives to account for each of such various activities as play, exploration, manipulation, and curiosity; in the naming of such needs as those for stimulation and variation; and in the naming of such urges as those for contact and locomotion. Such naming of drives, needs, and urges seems to revisit the instinct-naming of McDougall (1908). After our soul-searching professional excursion into theoretical methodology in the thirties and forties, we should know better. Insofar as the drives, needs, and urges named are accepted as explanations of the activities, they are theoretically unfortunate. Even though they are mere logical shuttles, they may delay the thought and investigation required for genuine understanding.

A second mode of theoretical recognition of behavior in the absence of extrinsic forces consists in naming the telic significance of activities. Thus, we have an "urge to mastery" (Hendrick, 1943) and, more recently, the "competence motivation" proposed in his splendid reviews of the evidence by White (1959, 1960), the latter from this platform. Such terms of telic significance may be helpful as classifying and mnemonic devices, but they too may be unfortunate in the sense that they suggest no hypotheses about antecedent-consequent relations, and, when accepted, they too may delay fruitful thought and investigation.

A third mode of unfortunate theoretical acknowledgement consists in the postulation of spontaneous activity. For several years, it has become almost fashionable to say that "to be alive is to be active," and formulations by Cofer and Appley (1964), Hebb (1949), J. McV. Hunt (1960), Miller, Galanter, and Pribram (1960), and Taylor (1960) have recently entertained the assumption that the instigation question needs no answer because some activity is spontaneous. It was my colleague, L. I. O'Kelly, who convinced me that such an assumption may be just as malevolent for theoretical purposes as naming drives, needs, and urges, and for precisely the same reason. Reviewing the various lines of evidence for behavior in the absence of either primary or acquired drives, I believe I have found at least the outlines of a mechanism of motivation inherent in information processing and action—that which I like to call "intrinsic motivation" (Hunt, 1963b).[3]

Two years ago, in the Nebraska Symposium on Motivation, Neal Miller (1963), whose heroic defense of the drive-reduction theory on admirable heuristic grounds has been its main support for nearly a decade, offered reflections leading to an alternative conception of motivation. As another long-time believer in drive-reduction, my own conversion began somewhat earlier and has been somewhat more thoroughgoing. While I continue to consider that drive-reduction theory contains some truth, and is particularly true for situations giving rise to painful inputs, the main burden of my alternative formulation, suggested in part by the evidence referred to, is one acknowledging an intrinsic motivation or a motivation inherent in the organism's informational interaction with circumstances through the distance receptors and in its intentional, goal-anticipating actions (see Hunt, 1963b). Insofar as freedom and rationality mean actions and choices based on the organism's informational interaction with the environment, the newer evidence lends support to the claim that man is at least partly free to make decisions that are rational in the sense that they are based on the information available to him and on his ability to process it.

Intrinsic Motivation and the Instigation Question

One of the stumbling blocks for cognitive theories of motivation has been their inability to answer the instigation question. This is evident in the cognitive theory of Tolman (1938, 1945). The question was an easy one for drive theory. The instigator for a given pattern of activity was the onset of a drive stimulus. With the cessation of this stimulus, the activity stopped.

Drive theory accepted the notion of the reflex as the functional unit of the nervous system. Historically, this notion has

---

[3] I claim no originality for these terms. Harlow (1950) used the term "intrinsic motivation" for that in the puzzle manipulation of his monkeys. Taylor (1960) came very close to "motivation inherent in information processing and action" with his "information processing theory of motivation" presented at one of the Nebraska Symposia.

conceptual roots in Descartes' conception that the bodies of animals (men were presumed to have souls) are machines activated and energized by external forces. Anatomical foundations for the reflex arc came with Bell's discovery, in 1811, of separate ventral and dorsal roots of spinal nerves, combined with Magendie's discovery, about a decade later, that dorsal roots have sensory functions while ventral roots have motor functions. The concept of the reflex was explicitly formulated and identified with the anatomical conception of the reflex arc by Marshall Hall (1843). It was then extrapolated to brain function by the Russian, Sechenov (1863), whence was laid the conceptual foundation for the transcortical, reflex-analogous associations that Pavlov (1927) thought were the bases for conditioned reflexes. This extrapolation to brain function received empirical support in 1870 when Fritsch and Hitzig found that movements on one side of the body could be elicited by applying a galvanic current to the cortex of the gyrus anterior to the central sulcus on the opposite side. When, in 1875, Caton and, later, in 1890, Beck discovered electrical potentials in the primary sensory areas of the cerebral cortex associated with receptor stimulation, at least suggestive empirical foundations were established for a conception of transcortical, reflex-analogous connections between sensory input and motor output. It was largely the work of Sherrington, beginning in 1893 and culminating in 1906 with his *Integrative Action of the Nervous System*, that established the concept of the reflex, however. This is ironic because Sherrington worked only with spinal preparations and clearly recognized the reflex as an abstraction. Nevertheless, he established it so well that Dewey's (1896) trenchant criticism of the concept went unheeded.[4]

The major defect of transcortical, reflex-analogous associations of receptor input with motor output has been its vagueness on the matter of set and attention (see Hebb, 1949). In his famous textbook, William James (1890) noted that the relatively loud ticking of the clock might evoke neither response nor awareness until it stopped. Conversely, a faint sound of a child's distant

---

[4] Again I refer the reader to my earlier paper (Hunt, 1963b) for detailed documentation of these statements.

cry can bring a mother up quickly in the face of louder noises so long as they do not completely mask the cry. Such observations imply that the instigation of activity can hardly be completely a matter of the onset of drives or acquired drives.

Recently, moreover, neurophysiologists have demonstrated that the Bell-Magendie Law is overgeneralized, that efferent impulses from the brain feed back through nerve tracks previously thought to be completely sensory in function and serve to regulate the level of discharge in these sensory nerves at a point close to the peripheral receptors. For instance, Hernandez-Péon, Scherrer, and Jouven (1956) have found that the neural activity of the cochlea, recorded through electrodes imbedded in the cochlear nuclei of unanesthetized cats and evoked by exposure to tones of substantial intensity, can be markedly reduced by exposing the cats to the sight of mice in a bell jar or to the odor of fish. Such evidence of inhibition by visual or olfactory inputs clearly implies that there must be a direct feedback-loop through which central processes can regulate receptor inputs. Bruner (1957) has made use of such central control of receptor inputs to account for perceptual organization, and it is equally useful in answering the instigation question in motivation. Neurophysiologists have also found evidence of sensory fibers in various motor nerves, and it is thus that stretch-receptors in the muscles have a direct connection with which to influence the firing from the motor areas of the brain over the pyramidal tract. With evidence from both neurophysiology and neuroanatomy of direct feedback control of both receptor input to the brain and motor output from the brain, it is no longer necessary to try to stretch the transcortical, reflex-analogous notion of connection between sensory input and motor output in order to account for instigation when it will not handle the facts of set and attention (see Pribram, 1960; also Desmedt, 1962; Fex, 1962; Galambos, 1956; and Wiederhold, 1963).

Miller, Galanter, and Pribram (1960) have conceptualized the feedback-loop in the terms of their Test-Operate-Test-Exit (TOTE) unit to serve as a successor to the concept of the reflex arc (see Figure 1). Perhaps the most familiar prototype is the

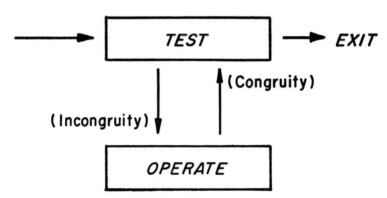

FIG. 1. Representation of the TOTE unit, a successor to the concept of the reflex (after Miller, Galanter, and Pribram, 1960, p. 26).

room thermostat. In this device, the *test*, or sensing mechanism, is a thermometer. Its setting constitutes a *standard*. When the *input*—here the temperature of the room—falls below the *standard*, the incongruity sensed by the device closes an electrical circuit that *operates* the furnace. Here it is an *incongruity* between the *input* and the *standard* of the *test* which instigates the operation. The furnace continues to operate until the temperature rises to the level of the thermostat setting which provides the *standard*; then the resulting *congruity* prompts the mechanism to break the circuit, and this operation of heating activity makes its *exit* from the scene of action. Establishing *congruity* between the *input* conditions and the *standard* stops the operation. It frees the organism for other activities.

Elaboration of TOTE unit with kinds of standards.—This motivational principle of the TOTE unit can be broadly generalized. So generalized, incongruity becomes a kind of generic instigator. Miller, Galanter, and Pribram (1960) have used the arrows in their TOTE-unit diagram to represent three levels of abstraction, namely, energy, information, and control. At the level of energy, the arrows represent nervous impulses, and the standards are thresholds. At the level of information, the arrows represent information flowing from one place to another, and the test is based on some informational standard. At the level of control, the arrows represent such a list of instructions as might comprise the program for an electronic computer, and the standard may become even a plan or an ideal.

One can readily conceive of a variety of standards. Various kinds exist within organisms at various phylogenetic levels or within human beings at various stages of development. One class of incongruities is based upon what one may call the "comfort" standard based on a threshold for pain. While no one need invent the TOTE unit to account for pain avoidance, the conception of a "comfort" standard will bring the facts of pain avoidance into a consonant relationship with the notion of the TOTE unit.

A second class of incongruities may be conceived to be based upon those innate standards which Pribram (1960) has termed the "biased homeostats of the hypothalamus." When, for instance, the concentration of blood sugar falls below a certain level, the on-receptors along the third ventricle are activated. At one level of incongruity, they serve to release glycogen from the liver; perhaps at a higher level, they prime the distance receptors to attend to the signs of food, which the organism follows with avid excitement. The organism is then said to be hungry, and he is avidly excited by his perception of things leading to food and eating. Again, for instance, when the concentration of sodium ions in the blood stream and spinal fluid rises above a certain level, the processes involved in the regulation of water balance are called into operation and the organism is primed to note the signs of water, which it also follows avidly. We say then that the organism is thirsty.

Although humoral factors figure also in sex motivation, I find it difficult to make the facts of sex nicely consonant with such a conceptual scheme. They appear to me to fit better the ethological notion of instinct as the *Erbkoordination* of Lorenz (1937) or the "specific-action-potential" of Thorpe (1951). It is in the case of sex that one most readily observes a build-up of a specific kind of tension, with a consequent lowering of the threshold for the stimuli effective in releasing the action pattern, and even the *Leerlaufreaktion*, or overflow activity, to be found in sexual dreams with or without orgasm. The orgasm does at least temporarily stop the action. Incidentally, this is a picture of sex function not very different from that presented by Freud (1905), wherein sexual excitement was seen as a source of pleasure. It is interesting that Freud seems not to have noted or remarked upon the discrepancy of this picture of the sexual instinct (Brill's unfortunate translation of *Trieb*) or of the libido, presented in the "Three Contributions" (Freud, 1905), with his picture of *Trieb* or primary function as something to escape from, presented in the last chapter of *The Interpretation of Dreams* (Freud, 1900) and in his paper on "Instincts and Their Vicissitudes" (Freud, 1915). In these latter formulations of *Trieb*, Freud was strictly an advocate of drive-reduction theory.

Coming to the organism's informational interaction with its circumstances, perhaps the most primitive of standards consists in the ongoing input of the moment. Whenever there is a change from this standard, the organism exhibits what the Russians have termed the "orienting reflex," consisting of attention to the changed input and arousal (see Berlyne, 1960; Razran, 1961). With repeated encounters with the patterns of change in input associated with specific objects, persons, and places comes the establishment of central processes that serve to represent them and to supply standards permitting recognition of them.

Within the domain of action, the basic standards are either the innately outlined standards of comfort and homeostatic need or those developing out of informational interaction. The latter are intentions and plans.

One important aspect of psychological development consists in the epigenesis of standards within the infant's informational interaction with circumstances. Although this is the topic of the third section of this paper, it should be said here that on the side of information processing, the standards may take the form of adaptation levels (Helson, 1964), of expectations, of conceptions, and of theories. On the side of intentional action, the goal-standards may take the form of task habits like "things should be recognizable" or "things have names," of intentions that anticipate the goals of action, of plans, and of ideals.

Separation of information processing from action.—The separation of information processing from action implied in the foregoing taxonomy of standards gets some support from recent neurophysiological work on brain function. When the transcortical, reflex-analogous view of brain function held sway, the telephone switchboard provided a mechanical model for the connections between stimulus and response. This telephone-switchboard model, which replaced the notion of the "neural groove," provided not only a conception of how various stimulus inputs could be connected with various responses but also a conception of how chaining one reflex to the next might account for complex activity. The model was so highly teachable that it persisted in spite of the fact that the neuroanatomical work of Cajal and the neurophysiologizing of Hughlings Jackson at the turn of the century made it already untenable when it was adopted. It persisted in spite of the fact that Lashley (1917) early pointed out that, given the speed of the nervous impulse, it would be impossible for the movement of a pianist's finger to be the stimulus for the motion of the next finger in the execution of a rapid cadenza. Nevertheless, even in 1943, Hull considered it self-evident that the brain "acts as a kind of automatic switchboard" (pp. 18, 384). In view of the professed objectivity and rigor of behavior theorists, it is ironic that in a logical sense this automatic switchboard had essentially the same properties as the mental faculties which Romanes (1883) had used to explain the problem-solving of intelligence in animals when C. Lloyd Morgan (1894) noted their logical circularity and when he and Thorndike (1898) attempted to explain problem-solving without recourse to such mental constructs as trial-and-error activity. The fact that it is only with the advent of the electronic computer, that dramatic mechanical model of the mid–twentieth century, that the notion of the switchboard has been displaced by the notion of active information processes nicely illustrates Conant's (1951) principle that "a theory is only overthrown by a better theory, never merely by contradictory facts" (p. 48).

No sooner had electronic computers been developed than Wiener (1948) and others were struck by the analogy between computer processes and human thought. Moreover, the programing of electronic computers to solve logical problems has led to a generalized consideration of what kinds of processes must go on within a brain to permit animals and human beings to do what they are observed to do. Computers solve a wide variety of problems. When they solve problems, they are said to process information. It was this fact that suggested to me the too-long and uneuphonious term "motivation inherent in information processing." The kinds of processes that must be involved have been seen by Newell, Shaw, and Simon (1958) to have the following components: (1) a control system consisting of a number of memories which contain symbolized information and which are interconnected by various ordering relationships; (2) a number of primitive information processes which operate on the information in the memory and each of which is a perfectly definite operation for which no special physical mechanisms exist; and (3) a perfectly definite set of these processes organized into whole programs of processes for each of which it is possible to deduce unequivocally what externally observed behaviors will be generated.

The suggestion that such components are required for solving logical problems has prompted certain neuropsychologists to look for their counter parts within mammalian brains. Pribram (1958, 1960), for instance, has suggested that analogues of these computer, control-system components may reside within what Rose and Woolsey (1949) have termed the intrinsic portions of the cerebrum. Rose and Woolsey have divided the cerebrum into an extrinsic portion and intrinsic portions (see Figure 2). The extrinsic portion is directly connected to receptors and to effectors. It consists of the ventral and geniculate nuclei of the thalamus, and of the sensory regions of the cortex receiving the thalamus relays from the eyes, the ears, the various receptors in the skin, etc. It consists also of those portions of the cerebral cortex giving rise chiefly to the motor tracts to the muscles and glands.

The intrinsic portions are two, and the division is based on both anatomical and functional grounds. One is the frontal intrinsic sector, consisting of the dorso-medial nucleus of the

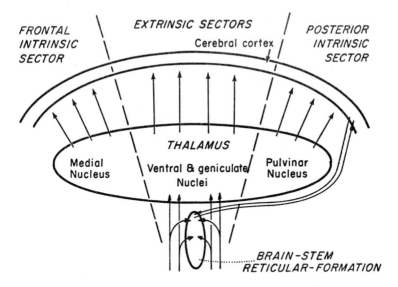

FRONTAL INTRINSIC SECTOR

EXTRINSIC SECTORS
Cerebral cortex

POSTERIOR INTRINSIC SECTOR

THALAMUS

Medial Nucleus

Ventral & geniculate Nuclei

Pulvinar Nucleus

BRAIN-STEM RETICULAR-FORMATION

INPUTS FROM RECEPTORS

FIG. 2. Diagrammatic representation of the division of the cerebrum into an extrinsic sector and two intrinsic sectors based on the absence or presence, respectively, of peripheral connections. The extrinsic sector consists of the geniculate and ventral nuclei of the thalamus. These receive direct afferents from peripheral receptor systems, and of the various sensory regions of the cortex (auditory, somesthetic, visual, etc.), to which they send inputs, and also of such motor centers of the cortex as the precentral gyrus, from which the pyramidal tracts originate and descend to the cells in the ventral gray portions of the spinal cord. The frontal intrinsic sector consists of those portions of the frontal lobes that do not give rise to direct motor fibers, the dorso-medial nucleus of the thalamus, and the hypothalamus. The posterior intrinsic sector includes those portions of the parietal and temporal lobes receiving no direct receptor inputs and their connections with the brain-stem reticular-formation (after Pribram, 1958, with modifications).

thalamus, the frontal association areas of the cerebral cortex, and the limbic system, with its various connections to the centers of homeostatic need around the internal core of the brain and in the hypothalamus. These centers Pribram has termed the "biased homeostats of the brain-stem core." The other is the posterior intrinsic sector, composed of the pulvinar nucleus of the thalamus, those portions of the parietal and temporal lobes that receive no sensory-input fibers from the ventral and geniculate nuclei of the thalamus, and tracts to and from the brain-stem reticular-formation (see Figure 2).

These two intrinsic portions of the brain may be seen to have the same general functional significance as traditionally attributed to the association areas. One might well translate Hebb's (1949) conception of the A/S (association *versus* sensory motor portions) ratio into a corresponding ratio between the intrinsic portion of the brains of various species to the extrinsic portion, *i.e.*, an I/E ratio. This ratio is low in such vertebrates as reptiles and amphibia, where the anatomical provision for semi-autonomous central processes intervening between receptor inputs and motor outputs is highly limited. It increases up through the orders of mammals, reaching its maximum in man.

The differing functional significance of these two intrinsic sectors may be shown by interrupting the tracts leading from the cortex to the structures nearer the core of the brain. Interrupting the tracts under the frontal lobes of the cortex produces confusions of executive function: such lesions have been found to disorganize delayed reaction and double alternation in primates (Jacobsen, Wolfe, & Jackson, 1935) and in a human patient (Nichols & Hunt, 1940). Human patients can have normal memory for events prior to surgery and they can readily recall a series of digits or of instructions immediately after they are given, but they cannot carry out a sequence of actions or develop plans. From such evidence, Pribram (1960, pp. 12, 22) has tended to localize here the hierarchical arrangements of TOTE units mediating intentions and plans, especially those based on the interconnections among the biased homeostats of the brain-stem core. From such considerations, one can associate action especially with the frontal intrinsic portion.

Interrupting tracts under the posterior intrinsic sector interferes especially with the recognitive intelligibility of receptor inputs. While injury to regions very close to receptive centers results in behavioral effects closely related to the specific receptor modality concerned (Pribram, 1958), these effects differ from those deriving from injury to the receptive centers themselves. Lesions in the visual projection system, for instance, result in damage to discriminations based on contour and brightness. Monkeys with such lesions can discriminate only total light intensity (Klüver, 1941). Monkeys with lesions in the posterior intrinsic sector can readily make such discriminations, but they cannot identify objects or make alternative responses to differing patterns or contours (Chow, 1952; Mishkin, 1954). Monkeys with lesions in the posterior intrinsic sector can readily catch gnats in mid-air, evidence of capacity to discriminate contours and brightness, but they lose habits based on the identification of objects. From such evidence, one gleans that this posterior system may well contain hierarchically arranged stores of coded representations of the various invariant properties of receptor input from objects, persons, and places viewed from various angles. Such stores correspond functionally to Hebb's (1949) notion of the cell assemblies that derive from "primary learning." I shall refer to them as *the storage,* and consider them a repository especially for past inputs from the eyes and ears. This posterior intrinsic sector appears to be especially important for recognitive and intelligibility functions.

Intrinsic Motivation and the Energization Question

In the case of action, the standard which provides the basis for the test of incongruity or congruity is the plan, generically considered. At the lowest level, plans may derive from the incongruity between conditions of the internal environment and the biases of the "homeostats of the brain-stem core." On another level, plans may derive from such a "learning set" as "things should be perceptually recognizable." Such a "learning set" may well be the basis for that clarity of recognitive perception which Woodworth (1947) has pointed out as the goal of perceptual search. At still another level, plans may have their bases in intentions whose complexity and temporal characteristics depend upon the cognitive organization which the organism or person has developed.

Cognitive theories of behavioral control have been notoriously "cold," but it is more than a verbalism to note that in the terms of such a conception of action as that outlined, an incongruity between circumstances and plans constitutes either an unfinished task or a frustration. Both unfinished tasks, or unfulfilled intentions, and frustrations have long been recognized to be sources of both motivation and emotional arousal.

As long ago as 1675, Spinoza's *Ethics* spelled out with remarkable clarity the relation of certain emotions to desire; and Spinoza's desires had the character of plans and intentions. In a sense, he anticipated Festinger's (1957) concept of cognitive dissonance, moreover, in pointing out that "in no case do we strive for, wish for, long for, or desire anything because we deem it to be good, but on the other hand we deem a thing to be good, because we strive for it, wish for it, long for it, or desire it." Also, the tendencies to resume uncompleted tasks (Zeigarnik, 1927) and to recall uncompleted tasks (Rickers-Ovsiankina, 1928) more commonly than completed tasks attest the motivational power of the incongruity involved in an unfinished plan.[5]

Frustration is commonly recognized as a basis of distress. Although Dewey (1894) formulated a frustrative theory of emotional distress and although Freud's (1917, p. 335) early theory of anxiety as a "souring" of unsatisfied libido is a frustrative conception of such distress, such formulations have only recently been tested. On the behavioral side is a series of studies by Amsel (1958) and his collaborators. In the first experiment in this series, Amsel and Roussel (1952) arranged two mazes in tandem. Hungry rats were trained to run down a straight alley-maze into a goalbox for food and then to leave this goal-box and run down another alley into a second goal-box, which differed from the first. The dependent variable was the time required to run from Goal-Box 1 to Goal-Box 2. When this time had achieved an

[5] Since writing this, I have come upon George Mandler's (1964) interesting paper of last year's Nebraska Symposium on Motivation. There is much that is congruent between our formulations, even though the centers of concern differ. We agree on the unitary, Gestalt-like character of "an integrated or organized response sequence," even though he is unconcerned either with the various categories of motive systems or with a distinction between action and information processing. We also agree that interruption of such a response can be emotionally arousing. We cite some of the same studies from the past, but his data go well beyond those brought in here.

asymptotic stable minimum, the rat-subjects were frustrated by omission of food in the first goal-box on intermittent trials. Thus frustrated, the rats ran faster through Maze 2 on those trials when food was omitted from Goal-Box 1 than they did on trials when food was present there. They also ran faster on the average than did unfrustrated controls on the same-numbered trials.

Investigations utilizing physiological indicators of emotional arousal in subjects submitted to frustration are relatively scarce, but two Japanese investigators (Yoshii & Tsukiyama, 1952) have reported an increase in frequency and a decrease in amplitude of EEG waves in rats when food is unexpectedly—on the basis of the rats' previous encounters—omitted. Unfortunately, it is not certain that such emotional arousal comes, as claimed by Miller, Galanter, and Pribram (1960), merely from interference with a plan. From the standpoint of drive-reduction theory, the activity being interfered with is presumably reducing some primary or acquired drive. Thus, interfering with the progress of an instrumental activity may be interpreted merely to reinstate the original drive. Such an interpretation is quite tenable for the experiments cited because each one is dependent upon homeostatic need as a source of motivation.

In the case of information processing, the adaptation levels and expectations deriving from previous experience provide the standards for the incongruity or congruity of new inputs through the eyes and ears. Thus, any arousal that may occur with incongruous inputs can hardly be attributed to drive-stimuli; this is especially true when, as in William James's (1890) case of hearing the clock only when it stops ticking, the incongruity consists of a reduction in the intensity of input. Closely related is the work of the Russian investigators on the orienting reflex already mentioned. On the side of overt response, the orienting reflex consists of such changes in the sense organs as dilation of the pupil, photochemical changes in the retina, changes in such skeletal muscles as those directing the sense organs, arrest of ongoing actions, and increases in muscle tonus. Along with these relatively overt changes are the relatively covert evidences of arousal indicated by increases in palmar conductance (GSR), vascular changes (plethysmograph), changes in heart rate (EKG), and changes in brain waves (EEG) (see Berlyne, 1960; Razran, 1961). Repeated encounters with any given change of input lead to an adaptation in the course of which evidences of attention and arousal disappear. Thereafter, alterations of the pattern to produce incongruity between input and the expectation standard typically reinstate the arousal reaction.

In one dramatic experimental demonstration of this principle, Sharpless and Jasper (1956) repeatedly presented their cat-subjects (with needle electrodes implanted) with loud sounds lasting for some three seconds. At first, each presentation evoked a burst of irregular, high-frequency EEG waves of low magnitude like those commonly associated with anxiety or great effort. For each succeeding presentation, the EEG arousal reaction became shorter, and the changes in frequency and magnitude became less in degree. After some thirty trials, this arousal reaction had essentially disappeared. When the experiment was repeated on the same cats day after day, the arousal reaction tended to recover spontaneously on each successive day, but the adaptation to it became more and more rapid. Following adaptation, however, a change in *any characteristic* of the stimulus brought back the fast EEG waves of low magnitude. A reduction in loudness was as effective in restoring the arousal reaction as an increase in loudness. Moreover, changes in pitch were as effective as changes in loudness.

Even more dramatic for theoretical import is a 1958 study by Vinogradova. Unfortunately, I know this work only from the secondary accounts of Berlyne (1960) and Razran (1961). According to these reports, I glean that Vinogradova presented repeatedly a tone, paired in sequence with an electric shock, to her human subjects. The vascular changes contingent with these presentations were recorded with a plethysmograph. As the presentations were repeated, the vascular response decreased and was finally extinguished. Then, by omitting the shock, which by traditional theoretical beliefs would certainly be considered the noxious and painful portion of the stimulus complex, the presentation of the tone alone evoked the vascular indication of arousal. It is exceedingly difficult to see how the return of the vascular indication of arousal with the omission of the accustomed noxious electric shock can be anything other than evidence of arousal evoked simply by what I am calling incongruity.

Fundamental in the experience of providing a basis for such arousal reactions is this tendency of organisms to adapt to any particular change of input or pattern of input or character of input with repeated encounters. Thus, the adaptation level, of which Helson (1964) has made so much in psychological theory, constitutes one very important basis for the standards determining the incongruity or congruity of new inputs.

There are undoubtedly limits to the intensity of input and to the suddenness of change to which human beings can adapt. Evidence of such limits comes from the studies of the startle pattern by Landis and Hunt (1939). Moreover, marked species differences exist in the readiness for adaptation in the various kinds of changes of input (see Razran, 1961). For instance, the orienting response to a rustle sound like that produced by grass rubbing grass readily adapts in the dog but is extremely persistent in the rabbit, as the Russian investigators have found. The existence of such species differences on the limits to adaptability for various kinds of inputs suggest that innate reactions to various inputs exist. Such a suggestion is corroborated, moreover, by the fact that such receptor inputs as bitter tastes (Warren & Pfaffmann, 1958), flicker in the intensity of light (Meier *et al.*, 1960), and vibration contact (Hunt & Quay, 1961) fail to become neutral even with a lifetime of continual encounters unless, as in the case of Pavlov's (1927) use of faradic shock as a signal for food coming, they become sequentially organized with consummatory acts. Such facts hint that there may well also be individual differences in reaction to various kinds of receptor inputs that would help substantially to determine the variations in the outcome of repeated encounters with given kinds of input. Although such considerations go well beyond the point that incongruity in information processing provides a source of arousal that can both energize and instigate responses, they indicate a domain needing investigation which I feel it is important to note.[6]

It is also worth recalling that two of the theories of anxiety based on clinical observations are highly consonant with this notion of emotional arousal inherent within organisms' informational interaction with their circumstances. Rogers (1951) has presented a theory that anxiety, which he terms "psychological tension" or "maladjustment," arises out of an "inconsistency" between the self-concept and various concrete perceptions. His notion of the self-concept may be seen to correspond to what I am calling a standard. It is presumably a standard based upon information about the self in the storage. This information presumably derives from both idiosyncratic perceptual interaction with circumstances—physical and social—and from communicated evaluations (information) "taken over from others, and perceived in distorted fashion as if they had been experienced directly" (Rogers, 1951, p. 498). Rogers' "inconsistency" is operationally defined as the discrepancy between the self and the ideal self, each described with inventories or adjective checklists. Such operations make this "inconsistency" a special case of what is here called "incongruity."

The second of these formulations comes from Kelly (1955). In Kelly's theory, what he terms "personal constructs" constitute the standards. These constructs represent active efforts on the part of an individual to make sense out of his observations and out of what he is taught in the course of his communications with other people. Thus, an individual may be led by communications so to construe the world that the information coming by way of his idiosyncratic perceptions is incongruous with his constructions. This incongruity is seen by Kelly to be the major basis for emotional distress or anxiety.

Elsewhere I have suggested that this line of conceptualization has still largely unexamined implications of personality dynamics (Hunt, 1965). Both Sigmund Freud (1926) and Anna Freud

[6] It may well be that a major source of genotypic influence on psychological development derives from innate individual differences in the hedonic value of various receptor inputs.

(1936) conceived of the mechanisms of defense as serving to protect an individual from anxiety. Sigmund Freud, at least in his later days, when he came to see repression as a consequence of anxiety rather than as its source, saw anxiety originating out of such painful experiences as castration threats, Oedipal anxiety, and other overwhelmingly intense emotions. The fact that Festinger (1957) and his students have found human subjects utilizing various strategies to avoid information dissonant (incongruous) with their beliefs and commitments suggests that these mechanisms of defense may function chiefly to protect individuals from information incongruous with that already stored or involved in various plans. Probably the most important category of stored information in this context is that concerning the self, and the self-concept constitutes a very highly important category of standards.

Incongruity and the Direction-Hedonic Question

The part of intrinsic motivation in answering the direction-hedonic question is both interesting and problematic. It is interesting because it promises ultimately to help in the explanation of what has been given various characterizations such as "thirst for knowledge," "growth motivation," "spontaneous interest in learning," and "self-actualization." It is problematic because the attractive notion of incongruity is operationally slippery. It is difficult to formulate the conception in a fashion that will guide measurement operations into successive approximations of clarification. (For another approach to this issue, see Schneirla, 1959, 1964.)

In his theory of cognitive dissonance, which I would include within the domain of the generic notion of incongruity, Festinger (1957) assumes that dissonance is always a source of psychological discomfort. He has written: "The basic hypotheses I wish to state are as follows: 1. The existence of dissonance, being psychologically uncomfortable, will motivate a person to try to reduce the dissonance and achieve consonance. 2. When dissonance is present, in addition to trying to reduce it, the person will actively avoid the situations and information which would likely increase the dissonance" (Festinger, 1957, p. 3). These propositions cannot be universally true. They may be true for those instances in which the standards involved are either plans or wholehearted commitments, but they cannot be true for all kinds of standards, because organisms not only withdraw from and avoid situations yielding inputs that are incongruous, but they also seek situations yielding incongruous inputs.

Withdrawal, avoidance, and a negative hedonic evaluation of incongruity are illustrated by the experiments of Hebb and Riesen (1943) and of Hebb (1946). These investigations were prompted by the Watson-Rayner (1920) conception of emotional disturbances as conditional responses. The observations of Hebb and Riesen that the infant chimpanzee's fear of strangers does not appear until the infant approaches about four months of age is highly incongruous with the conception of fear as a conditioned response because, in the case of those reared in the Yerkes Primate Laboratory, where their histories are known, any opportunity for strangers to become signals for painful stimulation from strangers was completely eliminated. Hebb (1946) later found that even intense panic reactions could be induced in laboratory-reared chimpanzees by showing them the sculptured head of a chimp, where the expected remainder of the body was absent, and by showing them an anesthetized infant chimpanzee, where the customary postures and motions were absent. Near-panic could also be induced in young chimpanzees merely by having the familiar experimenter appear in a Halloween mask or even in the coat of the also familiar animal keeper. Such observations have been interpreted to mean that emotional reactions arise in predetermined fashion directly out of organismic maturation (Jones & Jones, 1928; Jersild & Holmes, 1935). When such observations are coupled with the observations of Riesen (1947) that chimpanzees reared in darkness show no fear of strange people or objects even when much older than the "normal" four months, however, the notion of maturation as an explanation breaks down. As Hebb (1946, 1949) pointed out, the role of experience, *i.e.*, the "primary learning," is to establish the "cell assemblies" and "phase sequences" that he presumed to be disrupted by incongruous inputs. Here, residues of past perceptual encounters functionally equivalent to cell assemblies and phase sequences may be seen to constitute the standard of the TOTE unit against which the incongruity of "the familiar in an unfamiliar guise" is detected.

Fear-like emotional disturbances in children and pets, which have long been puzzling, become understandable in these terms. Fears of the dark and of solitude in the human child, which puzzled Freud (1926), and in the chimpanzee, which puzzled Köhler (1924, p. 251), can be seen as the incongruity which results from the absence of accustomed receptor inputs within any familiar context. Other examples appear in the young child who becomes disturbed when a familiar nursery rhyme is altered in the reading, the pet dog that whines and barks excitedly when his young master walks on his hands, the pet cat that loves to be petted by his child mistress and by a familiar neighbor (in whose house he was raised) but runs frantically to hide at the sight of the neighbor carrying that child on his shoulders. Although he made little of the matter, Piaget (1936) noted that his children showed emotional distress upon encountering radically altered versions of things they had come to recognize. In the domain of aesthetics, moreover, the dissonances of some modern music, the unfamiliarity of form and organization in some modern painting and in some modern statuary, may serve to repel if not to frighten beholders. All such observations are consonant with Festinger's (1957) formulation of dissonance, or incongruity, as a source of psychological discomfort.

On the other hand, a variety of observations attest that incongruous inputs may also elicit approach responses and have positive hedonic value. Berlyne (1960) found that both rats and human beings will remain oriented toward objects which are novel (incongruous) longer than toward objects which, through repeated encounters, have lost their novelty. Thus, rats sniff longer at novel objects than at familiar objects, and human beings look longer at complex and novel objects than at simple or common objects (Charlesworth, 1964). The principle that incongruity can be attractive covers Montgomery's (1952) finding that the spontaneous alternation of rats in a T maze is more a matter of the animals' choosing the relatively more novel (incongruous) goal-box than it is a matter of fatigue of the turning-response used in the previous trial. This principle also covers the fact that monkeys will peep more often at a changing scene, where the incongruity is relatively greater, than at an unchanging scene (Butler, 1954). Similarly, this principle includes the findings of Bexton, Heron, and Scott (1954), Heron, Doane, and Scott (1956), and Lilly (1956) that after human beings have been faced for considerable time with homogeneous, unchanging, and therefore completely congruous circumstances, they actively seek the relative incongruity of new situations of almost any kind. The urgent incentive value of incongruity under such conditions is dramatized by the behavior of a young man of "high brow" musical tastes who, during his third afternoon of homogeneous input in the stimulus-deprivation chamber at McGill, repeatedly pressed a key that brought him some two minutes of "country music" from a scratchy record (Hebb, personal communication).

The fact that situations giving rise to incongruous inputs can sometimes be distressing and repelling and can sometimes be pleasing and attractive to a given animal or person is puzzling until one hits upon the notion that there must be an optimum level of incongruity, another kind of standard, which, at any given time, divides attraction from repulsion. The optimum hypothesis has been suggested by several theorists. Such a hypothesis was implicit in Hebb's (1949) discussions of fear and pleasure, and it was made explicit by Hebb and Thompson (1954, p. 551). Helson's (1947, 1964) conception of the *adaptation level* (AL) constitutes just such an optimum, one based upon experience, for the AL is defined quantitatively as a weighted log-mean of the intensities of input encountered. McClelland, Atkinson, Clark, and Lowell (1953) have proposed the notion that the affective arousal, which they conceive to be crucial in motivation, is attractive and pleasurable for small discrepancies between a characteristic of input and the AL of the organism for that particular characteristic and modality of input. Contrariwise, this affective arousal is distressing for large discrepan-

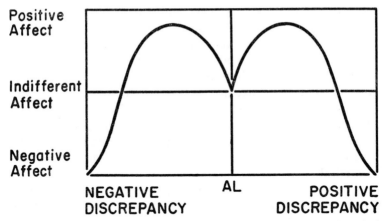

FIG. 3. Affective value as a theoretical function of discrepancy of level of stimulation from the adaptation level (AL) (after Haber, 1958).

cies between the input and the AL. Haber (1958) has depicted this relationship in the bilaterally symmetrical curve pictured in Figure 3.

The largest body of experimental evidence relevant to the hypothesis of an optimal standard in the form of an AL for the intensity of a given modality of input is to be found in those studies of the reinforcing effects of light upon bar pressing. Reviewing these studies, Lockard (1963) concluded that changes in the intensity of light could not account for these reinforcing effects and that the effects must be found in the intensity characteristics of the light stimulation. Since then, Kiernan (1964) has criticized Lockard's conclusion. Bringing in new evidence from the investigations of Leaton, Symmes, and Barry (1963), Kiernan notes that changes in the intensity of light, when the ongoing intensity is the standard, do have reinforcing effects and that decrements as well as increments of intensity reinforce. Even more recently, McCall (1965), a student of mine, has devised an ingenious experiment measuring levels of intensity antecedent and consequent to a bar press; he found a highly significant interaction between the antecedent, or the standard, and the consequent levels. Of this interaction variance, 86 per cent can be attributed to stimulus change, and decrements have reinforcing effects approximately equivalent to increments of equal amount. While such findings may hold over a wide range of intensities for auditory and visual inputs, there are limitations to the principle. Such effects cannot be expected to hold for levels of intensity so high that they produce pain. Nor, as Hunt and Quay (1961) have pointed out, will they hold for painless inputs which typically evoke withdrawal. This fact suggests that various modalities of stimulation probably have gene-determined hedonic values that would destroy the bilateral symmetricality of Haber's theoretical curve.

The hypothesis of an optimal standard has also taken other forms. Some of these assume an optimum of something within the organism's informational interaction with its circumstances. One form assumes an optimum of "uncertainty." In a very interesting series of experiments, Munsinger and Kessen (1964, 1965) have used sets of random shapes containing figures of 5, 6, 8, 10, 13, 20, 31, and 40 independent turns. They have given their subjects an opportunity to express their preference for each shape in comparison with every other by means of the psychometric method of paired comparisons. They term the variable that increases with the number of turns *uncertainty,* as it was called in the Attneave (1954) application of information theory to perception, which suggested their approach. Munsinger and Kessen have found repeatedly that preference typically goes to those shapes with an intermediate number of turns, as would be expected from the optimum hypothesis.

Another form of this hypothesis assumes an optimum of "complexity." In another very interesting series of experiments, splendidly summarized and integrated by Walker (1964) in the Nebraska Symposium on Motivation, the organism was described as selecting "successive events in terms of the psychological complexity of the alternatives. It chooses as a next event that one of the available next events which is nearest its optimal 'psychological complexity.'" Walker describes "psychological complexity" as depending on "(1) the complexity of the stimulus, if there is one, that initiates the event; (2) the arousal properties of the event; (3) the frequency and recency of past occurrences of the event; and (4) selective readiness for that class of events." As does mine, Walker's formulation employs the principle of adaptation to repeatedly encountered events or inputs. By virtue of this principle, each level of complexity repeatedly encountered comes to fall below the optimal level, and the organism seeks, therefore, an increasing level of complexity. This formulation has built into it a basis for behavior change and psychological growth, to which the discussion will shortly return. Walker's formulation of optimal complexity also has the merit of incorporating both complexity (incongruity) and arousal, whereas most other theorists have attempted a choice between them.[7]

Incongruity or arousal.—Whether it is an optimal standard of incongruity or an optimal standard of arousal which dictates the direction of behavior with respect to the source of input and to its hedonic value has become an issue. McClelland, *et al.* (1953) explicitly made affective arousal the crucial factor in their motivation theory. Yet, implicitly, they also made affective arousal consequent to the incongruity of the ongoing input with the adaptation level (AL) for the input concerned. Thus, they left the matter at issue, as have others since.

Hebb (1949) interpreted pleasure to be the consequence of a little frustration or a little disruption of phase sequences by what is new in a familiar situation; he interpreted fear to be the consequence of too much disruption of phase sequences by the absence of accustomed receptor support or by the familiar in an altered guise. This combination had the effect of making incongruity the central causal factor. Later, however, Hebb changed his view. From the empirical finding that maximal capacity to discriminate between paired flashes of light comes with

---

[7] I believe it is justifiable to consider *complexity* as a special case of *incongruity*, generically defined, because it is presumably the differentiated character of the complex *situation* (a term I much prefer to *stimulus* for a variety of reasons beyond the concerns of this paper) that makes it impossible for the organism to code and process all the various parts and aspects. Thus, with each new encounter, these still uncoded and unprocessed parts and aspects provide a basis for incongruity between the input and what is already in the storage.

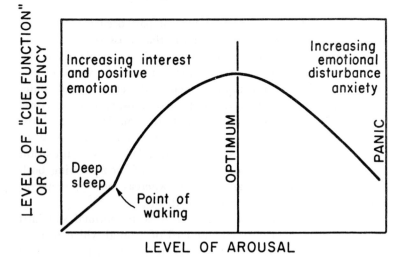

FIG. 4. The level of "cue function" and efficiency as functions of the level of arousal, with theoretical implications for incentive or reinforcement value (after Hebb, 1955, with modifications).

intermediate levels of arousal (see Lindsley, 1957), Hebb (1955) inferred that there must be an optimal standard of arousal. McGill students left situations of homogeneous input after some three days, even though they were paid twenty dollars a day (see Bexton, Heron, & Scott, 1954; Heron, Doane, & Scott, 1956); Hebb inferred therefrom that too low a level of arousal must be as aversive as too high a level and, thus, that an optimal standard of arousal is crucial in determining the direction of behavior with respect to a source of input. Leuba (1955) made a similar inference based on somewhat different facts, namely, on the curvilinear relationship between efficiency as measured in reaction time (Freeman, 1940) and pursuit performance (Schlosberg & Stanley, 1953), on the one hand, and level of arousal, on the other. The resulting relationships have been depicted by Hebb (1955) as shown in Figure 4.

It should be noted here that the curvilinear relationship of neither the level of cue function nor the level of efficiency with the level of arousal holds any necessary implication that an optimal standard of arousal exists below which situations that increase arousal have incentive value and above which situations that reduce arousal have incentive value. To be sure, the finding of EEG waves of lower than average frequency and of larger than average amplitude in the records of student-subjects encountering nearly homogeneous inputs in the McGill experiments would seem to support such a position. Yet Berlyne (1960) has made another tenable interpretation, corresponding to one made earlier by Myres and Miller (1954).

While this alternative interpretation is consonant with the principle of drive-reduction, it is ironic that it was made by Myres and Miller (1954) and Berlyne (1960, pp. 188 ff.), who have been concerned to preserve drive-reduction theory, because, in effect, the alternative interpretation makes incongruity central in the causal relationships. It was when Myres and Miller found that well-satiated and comfortable rats would press a bar or turn a wheel for an opportunity to explore the differently colored opposite end of a Miller-Mowrer box that they assumed homogeneous inputs would produce a monotony or "boredom drive." Such a drive, they assumed further, could be reduced by the variation of receptor inputs (incongruity) that an animal obtains by changing its position in exploratory behavior. The Myres-Miller conception is depicted graphically in Figure 5, although they were concerned only with the left-hand portion of the curve, relating arousal to stimulus change.

Berlyne too assumed that circumstances providing only homogeneous input produce a "boredom drive" which presumes an increase in arousal. Berlyne was led to the optimum hypothesis by assuming what he calls an optimum of "arousal potential." I have drawn Figure 5 to depict the Berlyne conception. In it, the ordinate represents arousal and the abscissa represents "arousal potential." According to Berlyne's argument, "arousal potential" inheres in what he calls "collative variables." These are "stimulus change," "novelty," "incongruity," and "complex-

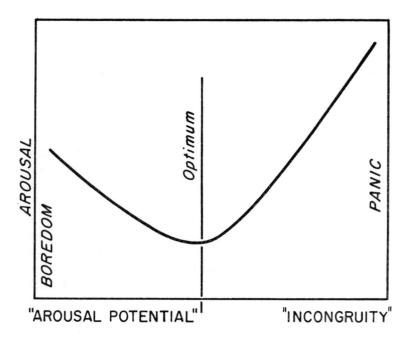

FIG. 5. Arousal as a theoretical function of "arousal potential" (Berlyne, 1960) or "incongruity" (after Hunt, 1963b).

ity." They are "collative variables" precisely because they derive from the relationship between the receptor inputs of the moment and the residues of past experience. Although Berlyne (1960, chaps. 7 & 8) believes that these collative variables have in common some degree of conflict, defined as competition for the final motor path, this is still a matter of opinion. His definition of "arousal potential" puts it into the domain of informational interaction and makes it a special case of, if not an equivalent of, what I am terming, generically, *incongruity*. Thus, the abscissa of the graph in Figure 5 properly represents "incongruity" as well as "arousal potential."

Defending the notion that homogeneity of input produces a

boredom drive, Berlyne, like Hebb, has appealed to the results of the McGill studies of Bexton *et al.* (1954) and Heron *et al.* (1956). Hebb, on the one hand, accepted the low average frequency of brain waves with their high average amplitude as evidence of lower than optimal arousal during homogeneous input; Berlyne (1960), on the other hand, argued that the low averages may well not have been the basis for the withdrawal of the McGill students from the situation. Moreover, Berlyne cites personal correspondence with Heron for the fact that at times the subjects of this experiment showed irritation, and he suggests, therefore, that their withdrawal may well have been instigated by the heightened arousal of a boredom drive. Still another interpretation of this behavior is possible. Heron, Doane, and Scott (1956) report that their subjects experienced hallucinations and showed fear during the third day of homogeneous input. Fear of the implications of self-hallucinating might also have instigated the withdrawal of the students from the experiment.

The Hebb-Leuba and the Berlyne (including my own version of it) theoretical positions have quite different empirical implications. First, they imply different levels of physiologically indexed arousal at the time of seeking stimulus change. If it be true that an optimum of arousal determines the direction of behavior with respect to the source of input and that an arousal level below the optimal standard is aversive, then one would expect monkeys in a Butler-type experiment to time their openings of the window for a peek outside with levels of arousal below average. Contrariwise, if the conditions of homogeneous input produce a boredom drive, one would expect the monkeys to time their peeking behavior with higher than average levels of arousal. In a series of experiments that were prompted by other theoretical considerations, Fox (1962) placed monkeys in dark cages equipped with a bar press that illuminated a 60-watt lamp overhead for 0.5 sec. As the monkeys remained in the dark, EEG recordings from deep electrodes showed increases of slow waves of high amplitude for at least an hour or two. Remaining in the dark apparently reduced arousal. This predominance of slow waves of high amplitude in the EEG record increased during each period in which the monkeys were not responding. Whenever such waves came to occupy 80 per cent to 95 per cent of the total record for a period of 20 sec., Fox reports that a burst of bar pressing for light could safely be predicted to occur within the ensuing 20 sec. These results lend support to the Hebb-Leuba position that arousal levels below the optimum are aversive, that they motivate the organism to seek change of receptor input. Fox (1962) himself interpreted his results to mean that the monkey has a need for light to maintain an optimum level of arousal in the brain-stem reticular-formation. The fact, already noted, that rats will press a bar for either increments or decrements of light intensity suggests that Fox's monkeys might well have done so too if his experiment had been designed to permit such a possibility. That the results are congruent with an interpretation of a need for light may well be an artifact of the experimental design.

Second, drugs that tranquilize and excite should have differing effects upon preferences for high and low levels of incongruity. If it is an optimal standard of arousal that determines the direction of behavior, pharmacological exciters should reduce the preference for novel presentations (high incongruity) over banal ones, according to either position. On the other hand, if the Hebb-Leuba position is correct, tranquilizers should increase preference for novel presentations, and if the Myres-Miller-Berlyne position is correct, they should either decrease preference for the novel or, if one accepts the point that it is incongruity rather than arousal that is crucial, they need not affect preference.

Haywood and Hunt (1963) have compared the effects of injections of epinephrine and of sterile isotonic saline on novelty preference. They found no difference. The theoretical significance of this finding was marred, however, by failure of the injections of epinephrine to increase palmar sweating, for this is the physiological indication of arousal most consistently manifested in encounters with incongruous inputs (Haywood, 1961, 1962). In perhaps the clearest of studies showing this, Haywood (1963) has found that delayed auditory feedback, a nice example of incongruity, produces marked increases in palmar sweating without altering either heart rate or pulse pressure.

In another such study, Schulte (1964) employed a measure of preference for differing levels of incongruity ("uncertainty") developed by Munsinger and Kessen (1964) and compared the effects of injections of metamphetamine, which should increase arousal, with the effects of sodium amytal, which should decrease arousal, and of sterile isotonic saline, which should not alter arousal. As already noted, the Munsinger-Kessen measure is based on sets of random shapes containing figures of 5, 6, 8, 10, 13, 20, 31, and 40 independent turns. When each of these is paired with every other in the method of paired comparisons, Munsinger and Kessen have found that preference typically goes to those shapes with intermediate numbers of turns. If arousal is crucial in determining such preferences, metamphetamine and sodium amytal should have opposite effects. Schulte, however, found no effects of either drug on the number of independent turns preferred. On the other hand, Munsinger and Kessen (1965) have found that repeated encounters with shapes of many turns increases preference for those with many turns. The absence of effects on preference from drugs altering arousal combined with the presence of effects on preference from such informational interactions suggests, at least tentatively, that even though incongruous inputs will alter arousal, arousal *per se*, as induced pharmacologically and indexed physiologically, does not affect preference for differing levels of incongruity.

On the other hand, when Fox (1962) measured monkeys' rates of bar pressing for light after injections of amphetamine, he found marked increase in the response rate when each press resulted in a half-second flash of light. When no flash of light resulted from pressing the bar, the result was a slight increase during the first hour of testing and then a decline to a very low level of responding. These results are puzzling, but perhaps they can be illuminated by some findings of Schachter and Singer (1962) and of Schachter and Wheeler (1962); see also the paper given by Schachter & Latané (1964) in the Nebraska Symposium of last year. In the Schachter-Singer study, injections of epinephrine, especially when unexplained, produced either marked increases in hostile behavior or marked increases in the vigor of whimsical behavior, which depended upon the behavior of a stooge in the same situation. In the Schachter-Wheeler study, injections of epinephrine increased both the frequency and the vigor of laughs at a slapstick comic movie over the vigor of such behavior following injections of sterile isotonic saline. Perhaps the arousal induced by such pharmacological agents acts on the vigor of any motor system, even bar pressing. Thus, so long as bar pressing brought changes in light intensity, the amphetamine energized the pressing instigated by them; when these contingent changes in light intensity were absent, the amphetamine had little or no effect. Were it not for the fact that cue function, as indexed by such measures as thresholds for flicker-fusion, is maximal with intermediate levels of arousal, one could say with some confidence that the chain of effect is from perception of incongruity to arousal to energization of motor action. Pharmacologically induced increases and decreases of arousal by the drugs studied do affect motor action, but they have not affected preference. The issue, however, is far from settled.

Intrinsic Motivation and Behavior Change

The part played by intrinsic motivation in answers to the remaining motivation questions is probably best seen in connection with the role of intrinsic motivation in psychological development. Yet the role of such motivation in behavior change, or learning, deserves special comment here. The hypothesis of an optimal standard suggests a conception of learning and of behavioral or conceptual change which differs markedly from those traditional in learning theory.

In the dominant theory of drive-reduction, behavior changes have been seen to be motivated by frustration (Freud, 1933, p. 166; Melton, 1941) or by fatigue (Hull, 1943; Miller & Dollard, 1941). When in such problem situations as those posed by Thorndike's (1898) problem boxes the ready-made responses of animals fail to achieve the animal's goal of escaping the enclosure to get the food outside, animals typically manifest a variety of responses.

These responses constitute what Hull (1943) called the "response hierarchy." The unrewarded repetition of a response at the top of the hierarchy was conceived gradually to weaken the response and to permit the appearance of others originally below it in the hierarchy. Such substitution has been supposed to continue until a response or a combination of responses appeared that, by obtaining reward, survived as the fittest for the situation. While hundreds, perhaps thousands, of studies of animal learning attest that behavior will change in this fashion, weakening dominant responses by means of frustration or fatigue does not constitute the only motivation for behavior change, nor does it provide efficient control of behavior. Skinner (1953, 1957) and his colleagues have demonstrated that given response patterns can be obtained much more quickly and efficiently through the technique of progressive shaping with reward. Because of his bias against theory, Skinner (1950) has defined reward as anything which will reinforce such behavior change, but, for the most part, he has actually used extrinsic rewards such as food for hungry pigeons. The result has been a highly efficient technique for controlling behavior and getting animals to do what a trainer wants them to do.

The hypothesis of an optimal standard of incongruity supplies a motivation for behavior change and learning that is inherent within the organism's informational interaction with its circumstances; inherent within seeing and hearing. Repeated encounters with given, static organizations of input lead to adaptation. In the investigations of the orienting response, this adaptation shows as a loss of attention value and of arousal reaction. One can readily demonstrate this kind of adaptation for himself by prolonged staring at a word typed on a page. The word shortly gives way to a jumble of black and white shapes, a trick once used by Titchener to eliminate meaning. This fact that repeatedly encountered static organizations of input become subjectively passé prompts organisms to turn away from unchanging circumstances to those providing moderate degrees of incongruity. This supplies an explanatory interpretation of both exploratory and manipulative behavior.

The principle of adaptation applies to sequential organizations of input as well as to static organizations. As Hebb (1949) put the matter in the terms of his psychoneurologizing, "the phase sequence continually needs new content to maintain its organization and persistence [p. 228]. . . . The thoroughly familiar arouses a well-organized phase sequence; the very fact that it is well organized means that it runs its course promptly, leaving the field for less well-established sequences: and so, from this theoretical point of view, one would find behavior dominated always by the thought process that is not *fully* organized—one that is achieving new organizations or one in which synaptic decay makes it necessary that organization be reachieved" (p. 229). Whether the neurologizing here be ultimately correct or not, it acknowledges and dramatizes the principle of adaptation that is so evident psychologically in a person's informational interaction with sequentially organized circumstances.

The operation of such psychological growth can easily be illustrated in the aesthetic domain. What determines the consonance or dissonance of tonal combinations has long been at issue; Benjamin Franklin commented on the matter in his autobiography. Helmholtz saw consonance as continuous tonal sensation and dissonance as intermittent sensation, but Stumpf noted that dissonance could appear in the absence of beat-like intermittence and offered the interpretation that consonance is a matter of fusion, while dissonance is a matter of failure of tones to fuse, which, in turn, is due to their vibration ratios (see Lundin, 1953). It was H. T. Moore (1914) who offered the view that consonance is a matter of fusion that comes with repeated encounters or hearings. Thus, he noted that a rise in both the consonance and pleasantness of a combination of tones with a given vibration interval occurs with repeated hearings, but the pleasantness later declines with further hearings. Moore noted also that the octave, which is the most consonant of intervals, is typically not the most pleasant, that the fifth gives way to the third, and the third to the fourth, with repeated hearings. He suggested, moreover, that with more frequent hearing, the minor seventh may ultimately rank as the most pleasurable of all intervals because it makes more demands on the mind than any other.

The same principle is manifest in the case of sequential organizations of music. Simple melodies without orchestration lose their appeal with fewer hearings than do those same melodies with orchestration. Moreover, on first hearing, complex melodies may be less appealing than simple melodies, but with repeated hearings, the complex melodies gain pleasantness and retain it through a larger number of hearings.[8]

Experimental demonstrations of intrinsically motivated behavioral change are extremely few. We have the evidence, summarized above, of the interest various animals show in the incongruity produced by changing or novel circumstances. We have such studies as that of Charlesworth (1964), showing that children repeat a "game" resulting in a surprising outcome more than they repeat "games" resulting in expected outcomes. But studies of behavior change based on this principle are exceedingly rare. Those known to me have been done by Walker's students at Michigan. In two experiments, Dember, Earl, and Paradise (1957) presented rats with a choice between two levels of visual complexity in a figure-8 maze. In one experiment, the walls of one loop were painted solidly black and white, the walls of the other loop in black and white horizontal stripes. In the second experiment, the walls of one loop were in horizontal stripes, the walls of the other in vertical stripes. Horizontal stripes are more complex than solid colors in the sense that the eye encounters more changes in the level of illumination per unit of time in the striped setting than in the one of solid color, and vertical stripes are similarly more complex than horizontal stripes. From theoriz-

---

[8] This view is very close to that formulated last year by Walker (1964) for the Nebraska Symposium. In the case of these musical illustrations, Walker's term *complexity* may seem more apt than my term *incongruity*, yet the choices made by the organism are based upon a comparison of the inputs of the moment with some neurally coded standard within it. Moreover, reversals in aesthetic taste from the objectively complex to the simple are common, and their desirability may well be a matter of seeking incongruity wherein objective simplicity offers incongruity with an internal standard of high objective complexity. Perhaps the variations in the complexity of themes and of orchestration in symphonic compositions exemplify such a principle.

ing somewhat similar to that presented here, Dember, Earl, and Paradise accepted the fact that they could make no prediction about which loop would be preferred on the first encounter by any animal because they lacked knowledge of the complexity to which the animal had already become adapted, but suggested that they could predict that those animals changing their preference—defined as spending more time in one loop than the other —of loop from one encounter to a second of the same duration would change from the less to the more complex one. This suggestion was confirmed. Of a total of 13 animals making spontaneous changes of preference in the course of repeated encounters with the two pairs of mazes in these experiments, 12 were in the predicted direction.

Perhaps this same principle may account for what Ives Hendrick (1943) has termed the "urge for mastery" and White (1959, 1960) has termed "competence motivation" within the domain of action and skill acquisition. The tendency of children to progress, for instance, from buttoning with large buttons to buttoning with smaller and smaller buttons among the Montessori materials is highly consonant with such a view. Moreover, Earl (1957) has obtained results with block-design problems for children aged 10 to 12 years like those obtained by Dember, Earl, and Paradise (1957) with maze walls of differing complexity for rats. Children spend more and more time with the more complex problems. While exploratory behavior and manipulative behavior appear to be adequately explained in terms of an optimal incongruity within the auditory and visual systems, within the domain of action, the inputs come not only through the eyes and ears but as feedback from the muscles. Moreover, the role of autonomic functioning appears to amplify the operation of the mechanism in a fashion not yet clear to me.

In the context of intellectual development (Hunt, 1961, pp. 267–286), I have called attention to what I termed the "problem of the match," *i.e.*, the problem of arranging a proper relationship between circumstances and existing schemata to produce accommodative modification in the structure of schemata for intellectual growth. The optimum hypothesis and one's inability to predict such matters as an individual animal's choice of loop for an initial encounter raises this same "problem of the match" from a motivational standpoint. In fact, the problem is perhaps more one of motivation than one of intellect.

The hypothesis of an optimal standard of incongruity, combined with observational evidence from aesthetics and infant education and with experimental evidence such as that from the Michigan studies, suggests at least the existence and the gross outlines of a mechanism for the "growth motivation" assumed by Froebel (1826), for the spontaneous interest in learning upon which Montessori (1909) built her "scientific pedagogy" (see Hunt, 1964), and perhaps for the "becoming" of Allport (1955) and the self-actualizing motivation of Maslow (1954). Moreover, if one reinterprets the ancient notion of the rational to mean choices based on informational interaction of the organism with its circumstances, one can also say, with Aristotle, St. Thomas Aquinas, and John Locke, that a rational basis for motivational choice is built into human nature, and that perhaps the founding fathers of our political structures were less far wrong in their assumptions about the nature of human nature than have been the theories from behavioral science that have dominated this century thus far. One can also say from this standpoint that something of the rational exists as well in animals, especially in mammals, and that Descartes unduly exaggerated the difference between human beings and animals. Perhaps the role of intrinsic motivation, this motivation inherent within information processing and action, shows in even more interesting fashion in psychological development.

Developmental Epigenesis of Intrinsic Motivation

Piaget's observations of the psychological development of his own three children suggest the outlines of a developmental epigenesis of intrinsic motivation, even though his concern was with the development of intelligence and construction of reality rather than with motivation. Reading and rereading his accounts of his actual observations, I have gleaned that there are roughly three stages of intrinsic motivation during the first two years

of the human infant's life. The stages may well be artifacts in
the sense that after the child is born, his life consists of repeatedly
encountering objects, persons, and places at approximately the
same rate of repetition. Perhaps these stages are more properly
phases in the course of the infant's encounters with any given
kind of change in or pattern of receptor input. At any rate,
during the first stage, the infant can be said to be attentive and
responsive to changes in ongoing input. During the second phase,
he shows the beginning of intentions directed toward keeping
or gaining perceptual contact with sources of input which have
just become recognizable through repeated encounters. At the
third stage, the child becomes interested in novelty; it is now
that the principle of optimal incongruity becomes clearly operative.

Stage One of Intrinsic Motivation

Stage One in my scheme encompasses both the first and second of Piaget's stages of intellectual development. According to
his observations, it would appear to endure from birth to roughly
four or five months of age, but the age of transition may vary
greatly with the circumstances encountered. During this first
stage, the human child may be said to be responsive. He is
responsive not only to painful stimuli and to such homeostatic
needs as hunger, but also to such changes in ongoing input as
increments or decrements of illumination and sound. Even the
newborn infant appears to respond to such changes: his response
is indicated by cessation of activity and by a tendency to turn his
head toward the source of the change in receptor input.

In this first stage of intrinsic motivation, the standard of
reference against which new receptor inputs become incongruous
is the ongoing input of the moment. This standard, unlike those
of later stages, is outside the organism rather than inside. Thus,
incongruity becomes a matter of change in some characteristic
of ongoing inputs. This responsiveness to change in input,
especially through the eyes and ears, indicates that a basis for
motivation inherent in the infant's informational interaction
with his circumstances exists, ready-made, even at birth.

Piaget's observations suggest that infants' reactions to changes in ongoing input, reactions consisting of cessations of activity and orienting of receptors toward the change, are comparable to the "orienting reflexes" studied by the Russians, although I know of no instances of arousal having been obtained. Orienting responses have been found in all species studied (see Berlyne, 1960; Razran, 1961), and I suspect they are present in all mammals at birth, or as soon as the eyes and the ears are open. In the Russian investigations, marked differences have been found in the readiness with which animals of the various species show adaptation to specific kinds or patterns of change in input. As noted above, these differences suggest that responsiveness and, probably, the direction of response to various modalities of input have, in part, an innate, gene-determined basis.

At birth, sucking, grasping, looking, listening, vocalizing, and wiggling appear to be relatively independent systems or sensorimotor schemata. The orienting reflex appears to be the motivational basis for the coordination of these systems that Piaget (1936) observed during what he called the second stage of sensorimotor development. A coordination between the ears and the eyes appears when "things heard repeatedly become things to look at." Such a coordination appears to be motivated by a repeatedly encountered change in auditory input, of such degree and suddenness as to evoke the orienting response, that is followed, also repeatedly, by a change in visual input, also of such degree and suddenness as to evoke the orienting response. A coordination between looking and grasping appears when "things seen become something to reach for and grasp," and such a coordination presumably has a basis similar to that for ear-eye coordination. A coordination between grasping and sucking appears when "things grasped become something to suck."

The mode of acquiring the coordination between the ears and the eyes looks very much like the classical conditioning of Pavlov (1927): changes in sound become conditional stimuli for the looking that could originally be evoked only by changes in illumination. On the other hand, while looking may involve some motor output, it is minimal, and the coordination of listening and looking more nearly constitutes what Hebb (1949) has termed a sensori-sensory association or what Riesen (1958) has called a stimulus-stimulus relationship than the traditional stimulus-response relationship.

While circumstances that yield only homogeneous receptor input may produce unpleasant boredom, decrement in performance, and even hallucinations in adults, in the neonate their effects appear to be apathy and retardation. It has long been noted that infants who have lived in orphanages from birth typically show both apathy and retardation. For years, it was assumed that this retardation was genotypic; only those genotypically inferior infants were supposed to have got into and to have remained in the orphanage. Spitz (1945, 1946) helped depose this interpretation with the finding that the developmental quotients (DQs) of infants dropped progressively in one orphanage ("Foundling Home"), where the infants were deprived of maternal contact, whereas the DQs of infants actually increased with time in another institution ("Nursery"), where the mothers had daily contact with their infants. Because the condition associated with retardation was absence of maternal contact, Spitz inferred that the retardation he found in the "Foundling Home" was attributable to an absence of mothering. But there is another inference possible. One of the important consequences of "mothering" is probably the opportunity to encounter many variations in receptor input. Another is probably an opportunity to encounter sequentially organized receptor inputs. Still another is the opportunity of the infant to get change of input from his own actions. Although hunger and thirst are of the essence for survival, opportunities for such informational interaction are very likely of the essence for interest in objects, persons, and places. Without such opportunities during the earliest weeks and months, the infant remains apathetic. Since the neonate's only standard for informational interaction is that of ongoing input, the absence of change presumably means the absence of motivation and responsiveness. This, by definition, is apathy.

The consequence of prolonged apathy is retardation. The degree of retardation that can result from orphanage rearing has been dramatized by the findings of Dennis (1960) for an orphanage in Teheran. Of those infants in their second year, 65 per cent were not yet sitting up, and of those in their fourth year, 85 per cent were not yet walking. When one considers that nearly all family-reared infants are sitting by age 10 months and that nearly all family-reared infants are walking by age 2 years, the extent of the retardation becomes dramatic, and it becomes clear that the genotype does not guarantee or predetermine the rate of development. This rate is in large part a function of the quality of infant-environment interaction. This Dennis study does not specify the conditions responsible for the retardation. Dennis attributed it to lack of opportunity to learn locomotor skills. It seems more likely to me, however, that the chief factor was the restriction in the variation in perceptual inputs. While the infants in this Teheran orphanage had adequate light, their view was that of homogeneous off-whiteness of the ceiling and the sheets around their cribs. While they heard a great deal of noise, because the orphanage was located in a portion of the city where the intensity of auditory input was high, changes in auditory input, and particularly changes in such input sequentially organized with changes in visual input, were absent.[9]

[9] Although the permanence and irreversibility of such marked retardation is not immediately pertinent to my discussion of the role of changes in ongoing input for the motivation of early infantile psychological development, I do not want to seem an alarmist in citing the Dennis findings to dramatize the importance of experience in early development. Dennis (1965) recently found that supplementary experiences can quite quickly overcome much of such retardation as that he observed in the Teheran orphanage, although this latter study was made at The Creche in Beirut. Burton White (White & Castle, 1964; White, Castle, & Held, 1964) has found that the development of visual exploration and of visually directed reaching can be quite readily speeded by handling infants. It is likely that duration is the most important factor in determining the degree and permanence of the effects of encountering any set of circumstances in the course of development. This principle is attested by evidence from a variety of studies, of which the following are but illustrative. While Carmichael (1926) detected no influence of chloretone for 8 days on the development of swimming by tadpoles, Matthews and Detwiler (1926) found swimming permanently impaired when the tadpoles remained in chloretone solution for 13 days. While Cruze (1935) found the capacity to learn pecking undamaged by keeping newly hatched chicks in the dark for as

When infants do encounter the changes of receptor inputs that keep them alert, they develop psychologically, and the nature of their motivation changes.

Stage Two of Intrinsic Motivation

The second stage in the developmental epigenesis of intrinsic motivation appears when infants begin acting to regain perceptual contact with various kinds of receptor input. Such activity contains within it the element of anticipation of the outcome. Anyone who has ever dandled an infant on his knee is familiar with this behavioral phenomenon. When the dandler stops his jouncing motion, the infant takes it up in what appears to be an effort to resume the game. Piaget (1936) observed such activity in a variety of situations: Lucienne shaking her legs to set in motion the dolls hanging from the hood of her bassinet; Laurent waving his arms against strings to move the celluloid balls

---

long as 5 days, Padilla (1935) found that keeping such chicks in the dark for 8 days or longer left them unable to learn to peck at all—they would starve in the midst of plenty. At the level of human beings, Skeels and Dye (1939) found that retarded infants who were transferred from an orphanage to a school for the retarded, where they received abundant attention from both adolescent and adult female "students," showed rapid increases in IQ. Controls of originally higher IQs who remained in the orphanage, however, showed progressive decreases in IQ. Such data agree with those of Dennis that the retardation of orphanage rearing is readily reversible if conditions are altered after only a short duration. On the other hand, when conditions producing retardation have been allowed to endure unaltered, the consequences apparently become irreversible. Skeels (1965) has conducted a follow-up of the individuals in this orphanage study. Of the 13 who were transported from the orphanage to the school for the retarded (where they got a corrective experience), all are self-supporting; none is a ward of an institution; the median school grade completed is the twelfth; 11 of the 13 are married; and 9 have children of their own. Of the 12 who remained in the orphanage, 4 are still wards of state institutions, and one died in a psychiatric hospital; the median school grade completed is the third; half are unemployed and those employed are, with one exception only, unskilled laborers; only 2 have married, and one of these has been divorced. The effects of early experiential deficits are always subject to some corrective influence, but the longer they endure, the less the recovery. Whether living in conditions that produce retardation inevitably results in some reduction of developmental potential is an unsettled issue. It is likely that functions differ in their capacity for recovery, and it seems likely that intellectual functions may recover less completely than locomotor functions, but these are only suspicions. The evidence is not in.

attached to them and to the hood of his bassinet; Laurent again, at first surprised by the noise from his new rattle, shaking it and getting the noise several times, then devoting himself with delight to the shaking—with each cessation of the noise looking at the rattle as if in anticipation as he resumes the shaking; Jacqueline shaking a little bell to get Pappa Jean to continue his imitation of the mewing of a cat; and Laurent shaking his legs to get Pappa Jean back to the business of blowing smoke rings. Such activities typically made their initial appearance when Piaget's children were between four and five months of age, but again, the age may vary.

When such activities appear, the infant is no longer merely responsive. The fact that the infant appears to anticipate the goal of his action and to act in the absence of some event that he has experienced implies more than the mere attention going to the changes in ongoing input during the first stage of intrinsic motivation. It is "intention" in the sense that the instigation of the action is based on incongruity with a standard within the infant. I gather from Piaget's observations that the earliest of these "intentional" activities occur in an effort to regain perceptual contact with newly familiar inputs that have stopped. Piaget speaks of activity "to make interesting spectacles last," yet the instigation of the child's activity is the momentary loss of the interesting input. While later, as in the case of Laurent discovering that he can make a noise with the rattle, relatively unfamiliar inputs can become "interesting spectacles," the earliest spectacles appear to be interesting because they have been encountered repeatedly. It would appear that objects, persons, and places become attractive with repeated encounters. From this I have gleaned that emerging recognitive familiarity is a basis for cathexis or emotional attachment.[10]

---

[10] Although I make a great deal of this hypothesis, I mean nevertheless to be tentative about it. I want to be tentative because it may well be that the infant becomes attached to the sources of changes in input that are contingent upon his actions. I have already touched on this possibility in accounting for the deficit found by Dennis in the Teheran orphanage, and I shall return to it again in connection with our own investigations suggested by this hypothesis that emotional attachment comes with recognitive familiarity.

This attachment to objects with new-found recognitive familiarity leads not only to efforts to regain or obtain perceptual contact, but also to such expressions of delight as the smile and to expressions of distress when the perceptual contact cannot be regained. Spitz and Wolf (1946) have contended that smiling is strictly a social response, one which registers the infant's delight at witnessing the facial constellation which has been associated with his previous satisfactions of hunger and discomfort. Piaget, however, reports a variety of instances in which his children smiled at things other than faces. They smiled when the dolls hanging from the hood of the bassinet moved, even though no person was in view. They smiled when familiar objects were hung from the hood. They smiled at the sight of their own hands coming before their eyes, and Laurent smiled on finding his nose with his fingers after repeatedly having made such contact. In these various instances the smile appeared only after the infant had encountered the circumstance repeatedly. From such evidence, Piaget gathered that a smile is a sign of recognition. Presumably, once an infant has encountered a circumstance enough times to have established within his brain a central process which provides a coded representation of that circumstance, this representative central process can provide a basis for recognition of the circumstance through the coded pattern of input deriving from perceptual contact with it. Such observations suggest that recognition is a source of (recognitive) joy and cathexis of the recognized object, person, or place.

It is only at or after this second stage of intrinsic motivation that a human infant begins to show fear of strange objects, persons, and places or to show distress at the absence of familiar ones. These emotional reactions presumably make their appearance because the infant has acquired, through repeated encounters with familiar objects, persons, and places, central processes representative of them. The central processes constitute standards with which the inputs from the strange are incongruous. With these new informational standards, the infant acquires new ways, well beyond those of painful stimulation and homeostatic need, to become disturbed. Not only does the strange frighten him, but, also, loss of perceptual contact with cathected objects, persons, and places can be a source of what has been called "separation anxiety," although it might better be called "separation grief." In psychoanalytic theory, this separation anxiety has been considered to be a matter of rupture at birth of the infant's symbiotic relationship to its mother (see Ribble, 1944), but actually neither fear of strangers nor separation distress is present at birth in either human beings (Freud & Burlingham, 1944) or chimpanzees (Riesen, 1958). Anna Freud and Dorothy Burlingham were surprised during the London blitz to find such distress absent in the children removed from home before they were between six and nine months of age. For children in the last quarter of their first year and in their second year, when Piaget (1936) found objects to be acquiring permanence, this separation grief progressively increased in both intensity and duration. For children of three and older, with language permitting them to understand that parents would return, the severity and duration of separation grief abated. Observations consonant with these have also been reported by Schaffer and Emerson (1964). On the side of action, moreover, once the infant has intentions and plans, not only can he be disturbed by being deprived of expected nourishment, but he can also be frustrated in fashions that may have no connection with either painful stimulation or homeostatic need.

It is instructive to note the similarities between the human infant's efforts to maintain or regain perceptual contact with objects acquiring recognitive familiarity and the "following response" of animals which constitutes evidence of imprinting in their infancy. The human infant's efforts appear to be functionally equivalent to the "following response." Heinroth (1910) and, later, Lorenz (1935) observed that in such fowls as geese an hour or two of perceptual encounter with the maternal goose serves to establish a kind of attachment which ensures that the gosling will follow her. Although a wired-in preference appears to exist in newly hatched fowls for the pattern which corresponds to the female adult of the species, goslings readily become attached to and follow adult females of other species or even human beings. Ramsay (1951) has even imprinted young fowls on such diverse objects as a football and a green box. Moreover, Hess (1962) reports that such following responses after a period of perceptual contact have been shown to occur in a variety of birds, fish, and in mammalian species where the young are mobile shortly after birth. I should like to suggest that this following response in imprinting may be a special case of the principle that cathexis occurs with recognitive familiarity.

In this same connection, it would appear also that the duration of perceptual contact required to produce recognitive cathexis increases up the phylogenetic scale. For instance, in ducks and geese, the duration of perceptual contact required to produce the following response is apparently a matter of no more than minutes or at most two or three hours (Thorpe, 1956, pp. 357 ff.). In sheep and goats, the required duration of contact appears to be a matter of but two or three days; and lambs prevented from establishing such perceptual contacts with an adult sheep for so long as two weeks become loners, without that gregarious attachment to the herd by which ungulates survive in the wild (Scott, 1945). In such ungulates as deer (Darling, 1938) and buffalo (Hediger, 1950), the required time of contact is also a matter of but two or three days to establish the following response.

Now compare these times of perceptual contact with those required by infant primates and human beings to discriminate their own mothers from others—a discrimination evidenced by approaches to the mother, fear of strangers, and separation distress.[11] In the monkey, some ten days or two weeks of contact are required (Harlow, personal communication); in the chimpanzee, about two months (Riesen, 1958); in the human infant, as already noted, five or six months. Thus, up the phylogenetic scale, with the increasing ratio of intrinsic portions of the brain to extrinsic portions, there is an appreciable increase in the dura-

[11] Presumably, young ducklings and young ungulates learn to discriminate their own mothers from other females of the same species during this period that produces the cathexis indicated by the following response, but the reports do not describe explicit tests of such discrimination.

tion of perceptual contact required to establish the behavioral evidences of emotional attachment to such objects as the mother figure. This suggests that the time required to develop central processes to mediate such discriminative attachment takes substantially longer in brains where the intrinsic portion is large than in brains where the intrinsic portion is small.

Functions of recognitive cathexis in psychological development.—This attractiveness of objects with emerging recognitive familiarity may well be the motivation for those responses which Dennis (1941) has characterized as autogenic. One of these is babbling. Babbling appears to consist of an ear-vocal coordination in which the child manages to gain auditory control of his own voice by making the sounds he hears when he vocalizes. The repetitive element in this behavior has been puzzling, and various attempts have been made to explain it. The notion that an often-encountered sound becomes attractive as recognition dawns could account for this repetition, first remarked upon by J. M. Baldwin (1895). Observations of children in the second motivational stage suggest that they do not repeat sounds that they have heard but once. Rather, the repetitiveness of their babbling probably derives from the attractiveness of sounds made recognizable through repetitive encounters. This is a conception much like that advanced by Mowrer (1950) for the motivation of talking in birds, except that the attractiveness of voice sounds, in Mowrer's theory, was presumed to come from their association with satisfaction of hunger. Mowrer's method of training, however, consisted in keeping the bird's cage covered except for the period of vocal contact when he gave the bird its only food. The fact that the cage was covered may have been highly important. It is likely that the opportunity to hear vocalizing in such a situation was as important as the food in producing the cathexis of voice sounds which Mowrer also believed to motivate the bird's attempt to produce them.

The same mechanism may well account for the motivation of the hand-watching and foot-watching which appear as items characteristic of infants four months old in scales of infant psychological development (Bühler & Hetzer, 1927). Movements of the hands may provide the infant both with an attractive sight, once the hands have been recognized visually, and with changes in view contingent upon self-initiated movements. This hand-watching game, moreover, appears to provide practice in eye-hand coordination.

Imitation may have a similar motivational basis. It was the merit of Piaget (1936) to note that an infant's first imitations occur with activities that are already within his repertoire. One can fairly readily demonstrate this with the vocalizations of a child of three, four, or five months. If, for instance, one holds a child, looks at him, and talks in the fashion of adults, one typically gets little attention: the infant's face shows no special interest, although his eyes may seek his holder's. On the other hand, if one takes care to find out what babbling vocalizations the child has been making on his own and then makes an approximation of those sounds, the infant's response usually changes radically. His eyes widen as he hears the familiar vocalization. He is likely to make his mouth go. Sometimes he will vocalize the sound in return. This is the pseudo-imitation of the familiar, and it too appears to be motivated, at least in part, by the interested delight that the infant appears to get from hearing an adult make the sounds of his own repertoire. In our attempts to develop ordinal scales of psychological development for young infants, Dr. Uzgiris and I had hoped to utilize this pseudo-imitation of the familiar, but it appears to be turning out to be too undependable for such a purpose. On the other hand, as a demonstration to oneself that familiar schemata do interest infants and will sometimes induce them to vocalize in return, it is quite useful. Moreover, the importance of the familiarity can readily be demonstrated simply by making distinct variations of those vocalizations already familiar to the child. These are typically followed, in an infant at this stage of development, by an obvious drop in interest.

Finally, I suspect that repeated encounters with a variety of different objects, persons, and places leads gradually to something akin to one of Harlow's (1949) "learning sets." This "learning set" may be described as a kind of generalization that "things heard and seen should be recognizable." Such a learning set may come to operate in the fashion of a "plan," to use the term of Miller, Galanter, and Pribram (1960), or of an habitual set to get inputs to come clear, as Woodworth (1947) has described as the goal of perception. Woodworth wrote of this as the "will to perceive," manifested, for example, in movements of fixation, focusing, and convergence to get clear vision. "Clear vision" or "clear hearing," however, may be a less accurate statement of the goal than recognition, *i.e.*, to find out "what is there."

Years ago, Marjorie Drury (1933) made a study of the effect of repeated tachistoscopic encounters with various patterns in peripheral vision. I served as a subject in her experiment. I can still recall the irritating frustration of having unrecognizable blobs appear for but an instant. The brevity of the exposure interrupted the "plan" for recognition. Gradually, however, with a number of viewings each day over several weeks, these figures took on distinguishing characteristics. When they did, the irritation disappeared, and a mild sense of triumph took its place. What seems to be necessary for such recognition is a central process, the coded characteristics of which constitute a standard that will match the coded characteristics of the input from the recognized object. Under ordinary circumstances, when the quality of the incoming information is poor, a sophisticated perceiver may well call up a series of representative processes, or images, in his struggle for recognition. If he accepts one that matches badly the object with which he has perceptual contact, it may well interfere with the retrieval of the proper image when the quality of perceptual input has been cleared. Evidence of such a state of affairs comes from the work of Bruner and his collaborators with the "ambiguiter" (see Bruner & Potter, 1964).

At this stage emerges, perhaps, a second "learning set," this one clearly involving action rather than information processing. Repeated efforts to regain perceptual contact with interesting spectacles may lead to a generalized attitude which one might verbalize: "If you act, you can get interesting experiences." Such a learning set would also operate as a standard, congruency with it stopping the activity at least temporarily. This is admittedly a highly tentative formulation. Alternatively, one may interpret the phenomena to consist in simple coordinations of specific schemas of action with looking and listening, during which changes of visual and auditory input reinforce the schema of action. It is hard to escape the impression of initiative and intentionality in these activities, however, for the attitudes of infants seem to telegraph what they anticipate. Moreover, Piaget's observations of his own children during the ages from roughly four or five months to eight or nine months uncovered a progressive separation in their activities of ends from means; a progressively increasing proportion of the activities appeared to arise from intentions in which the children's attitudes implied anticipation of the outcome.[12]

If it be a fact that the earliest of these action goal-standards concern regaining familiar receptor inputs, it has important implications for our theorizing about psychological development. It calls into question the notion that those semi-autonomous processes that come to mediate behavioral organization and to constitute thought are primarily the residues of motor action. This motor primacy notion has been traditional from James (1890), Hall (*e.g.*, his aphorism that "the mind of man is handmade"), and Dewey (who saw knowledge as the by-product of action), through Watson (for whom thought was sub-vocal speech), to Osgood (1952, for whom the mediating responses are the light portions of the total responses to situations) and Skinner

---

[12] Piaget's distinction between ends and means is not equivalent to that of the functional school between need and action to meet the need (Dewey, 1896; Angell, 1907). Neither is it equivalent to Freud's (1915) differentiation of the aim of a *Trieb* (or instinct, as Brill translated it) from its mode, nor to the differentiation of a goal from the instrumental act to achieve it (Hull, 1943; Miller & Dollard, 1941). According to Piaget's description, only the means remain within the infant's action system; the end lies quite outside the system in the sense that it involves either getting receptor input from object and person sources in the situation or acting upon some object or person. Most distinctive in Piaget's interpretations of what he saw in the psychological development of his children is the notion that either getting mere auditory or perceptual inputs or acting in a specific way on outside objects or persons may constitute goals. It is thus that one schema, like grasping something, can become the end, while pushing or striking things in the way can become means.

(1957). Piaget (1936, pp. 159 ff.) appears to have missed this implication of his own observations. His interpretations stress the element of outlined acts as the basis of recognition, and he did observe such evidence of recognition. Bruner (1964) apparently has used Piaget's interpretation as the basis for the generalization that representational processes are first "enactive," then "iconic," and finally "symbolic." It would appear, rather, that they are first crudely iconic. This is to say that they are first iconic after the fashion of, if not actually in the nature of, Hebb's (1949) "cell assemblies," which are acquired through looking and listening. Later, then, they are probably iconic and enactive in combination. The differentiation of actions—based on goal-standards deriving from information processing—from information processing *per se* very likely occurs in this second stage in the developmental epigenesis of intrinsic motivation.

In Piaget's observations, the first action schemata to become a goal-standard is prehension. Here it is the attractiveness of the seen object that motivates the reaching and attempts at prehension. As a consequence, in the aphorism of Piaget, "something to look at becomes something to grasp." Yet it appears to be correct that in this active interaction with the desired object, the infant anticipates the goal of grasping the object. This appears to be correct because if the object remains beyond his grasp, he resorts to other schemata. He may wave his arms, shake himself, shake his legs, roll, or vocalize in a complaining fashion. All such alternative activities cease, however, once he grasps the object. This indicates that indeed grasping the object was the infant's goal-standard, and congruity with it stops the striving. It should be noted that, except for the feeding bottle, these prehensive goals typically have had no association with relief from pain or hunger. At first the interesting objects are apparently those which have acquired attractiveness through perceptual recognition from repeated encounters, but there may also be objects giving rise to auditory and visual inputs that are innately attractive. Later the interesting objects come to be those which are novel.

Such a conception of this second stage in the development

of intrinsic motivation provides a hypothetical explanation of Piaget's descriptive aphorism that "the more a child has seen [and heard], the more he wants to see [and hear]."

Stage Three of Intrinsic Motivation

The third stage in the developmental epigenesis of intrinsic motivation emerges with an infant's interest in things novel. Piaget observed that this "reversal transformation" from interest in the familiar to interest in the novel began in the latter portion of the fourth stage of sensorimotor development with interest in and attempts to imitate novel vocalizations. When nine months old, Jacqueline, for instance, reacted for the first time to a vocalization new to her: "gaga." Her reaction, as reported by Piaget (and I have personally observed similar instances), consisted of sustained and varied vocalizing: "mama," then "aha," then "dada," then "vava," and finally "papa" (Piaget, 1945, p. 46). Piaget conceived this interest in the novel to arise out of a conflict between the attractiveness of the familiar aspect of the new pattern, which prompted Jacqueline's effort at imitative reproduction, and the discrepancy which blocked her imitative effort at reproduction. He speaks of imagery as internalized imitation. He contends that "the image is the result of a construction akin to that which produces the schemata of intelligence, but which takes its material from the 'world of sensation.' But we must add that this material is motor as well as sensorial . . . the image is as it were the draft of words to come in the interiorization of acquired exterior language" (1945, p. 70). Again appears the issue of the primacy of receptor inputs and information processing, on the one hand, and of motor schemata, on the other, but this time after the separation of ends from means within intrinsic motivation.

The primacy of receptor inputs and information processing shows in two ways, I believe. First, the interest in the novel appears to derive from the attractiveness of the familiar aspects of the vocal pattern perceived. Note that the rhythm of a double *ah* is common to the instigating pattern and to each of Jacqueline's efforts at reproduction. This looks like a special case of what is termed *stimulus generalization* in behavior theory. Second, the discrepancy between the infant's effort to reproduce the "gaga" pattern is a matter of comparing her perception of her own vocalizations with her immediate memory of the model. It is this perceptual discrepancy which presumably frustrated Jacqueline's intention of reproducing the model, and thus her search through a series of double *ah*s in combination with her repertoire of consonants.

At the same time, repeated encounters with thoroughly familiar objects become "old stuff," as is attested by the various evidences of perceptual adaptation. Moreover, another kind of adaptation may be involved. Infants who are exposed to a variety of inputs each day may develop a kind of standard for change. This may be conceived as a kind of "addiction to change." This sort of motivation appears to have implications for cathexis and emotional attachment which contrast with attachment to the familiar.

Significant persons and familiar places.—Parenthetically, it is interesting to note in this connection that it is precisely at this stage of development when interest in novel inputs appears that both chimpanzee and human infants also begin to manifest serious and persistent attachment to familiar persons and places, attachment marked by "separation grief" (Freud & Burlingham, 1944) and "fear of the strange" (Hebb & Riesen, 1943). Again, the primacy of information processing is important, for such grief and fear depend upon substantial ability for recognitive differentiation and upon the existence of stable representations of objects, persons, and places in the storage.

This is a highly important and puzzling matter. The optimum of incongruity may be a factor, but it can hardly be the whole story: infants, on the one hand, are attracted by new toys quite different perceptually from familiar toys, while, on the other hand, they withdraw from strangers who are very little different perceptually from familiar persons. The infant's strong cathexis of significant persons and familiar places probably represents an instance in which the effects of intrinsic motivation are combined with those from other motivation systems. The traditional notion that objects are cathected through association with homeostatic gratification contains some truth, as shown by the finding of Igel and Calvin (1960) that puppies prefer surrogate mothers providing both lactation and contact comfort to surrogates providing only contact comfort. Experiences of contact comfort also constitute an important basis for cathexis, as indicated by the turning of Harlow's (1950, 1953) monkeys to padded surrogate mothers for various kinds of solace. Moreover, the participation of familiar persons and places in an infant's idiosyncratic efforts to get recognized forms of reaction probably strengthens cathexis. Evidence for such a statement comes from the recent longitudinal studies of Schaffer and Emerson (1964). During the latter portions of the first seven months, infants protest about equally the withdrawal of any responsive adult, strange or familiar; even after the seventh month, multiple attachments are common, and the strongest attachments do not necessarily go to the caretaking adult but rather to the person who interacts most intensely with him and is most responsive to his demands for attention. Apparently, either the absence of responsive persons and places—after cathexis from such combined motivational sources—or the presence of strange persons and places may underlie the separation grief and fear of the strange which become manifest at the very time that interest in novel objects becomes manifest. The new-found interest in the novel is probably limited to those sounds, sights, and action schemata for which the infant has cathexis from recognitive familiarity only.

Some developmental consequences of interest in novelty.—In the process of psychological development this emerging interest in novelty appears to provide motivation both (1) for a number of the developmental transitions that typically take place toward the end of the first year and through the second—in the fifth and sixth stages of sensorimotor development—and (2) for the continuing process of psychological growth and self-realization already noted.

One of these transitions is the shift of attention from spectacles and action schemas *per se* to objects and what objects do as the infant drops them, throws them, and manipulates them. This takes place in the familiar throwing schema so distressing to mothers who take pride in the orderliness of their homes.[13] This throwing schema begins with the emergence of the new means, "letting go." "Letting go" demands an inhibition of the grasping reflex. In the traditional conception of development, "letting go" has been seen as a matter of maturation which is supposed to be predetermined by an infant's genotype. To what degree the onset of "letting go" can be speeded or slowed by deprivation or enrichment of previous perceptual and manipulative encounters with objects has not been studied.

Children do appear to discover the schema of "letting go." When they do, they use it; they take delight in dropping things. At this point, Piaget found their attention shifting from the new-found action schema, the "letting go" and the spectacle of something falling, to the object that drops. This shift of attention appears to bring about a transition from relatively passive "dropping" to active, intentional throwing with attention to the trajectory of the object. From this the infant appears to learn something about the relationship between the trajectory of the object and the effort of his own action. Dropping and throwing, of course, constitute but two of the infant's various manipulative schemata. Others include the rolling, striking, sliding, pressing, and mauling of objects. The representative central processes that mediate object-permanency show rapid growth as the variations of acting-on-objects increase. Presumably, the rate at which information gets into the storage increases markedly with motivation to pursue the novel through manipulation; and increasing stability of representative central processes begins to show in the

---

[13] Piaget apparently had various theoretical interpretations of his observations at various stages of his writing. In his *Origins of Intelligence* (1936), Piaget interpreted the shift of attention from the spectacle to the object as a discovery leading to the interest in novelty. Nearly a decade later in *La Formation du Symbole* (1945), he cited the instances of interest in novelty by his children's attempts to imitate novel phenomic patterns and gestures which took place considerably earlier in the latter portion of Sensorimotor Stage Four.

infant's ability to follow an object through sequential displacements instead of returning with its disappearance to the place where it was found before (see Hunt, 1961, pp. 154 ff.).

While information processing may have primacy and may continue to be of central importance in the development of imagery, Piaget is correct that action is highly important. The role of action, however, appears to be one of increasing the variety of angles from which an object or a scene is viewed, or increasing the variety of impressions through various modalities obtained per unit of time.

Second, the interest in novelty appears to motivate what Piaget has called the "discovery of new means through active experimentation." With the development of interest in novelty, the action schemata cease to be merely repetitive. They come to show modification with each repetition. The resulting modifications in the structure of a given schema appear to imply a constructive, original, and even creative element within the infant's activity. Thus, whereas during the second motivational stage, the effort to achieve intentional ends consists simply of repetitive use of each schemata in the infant's repertoire, during the third stage, action schemata or responses irrelevant to the intentional goal are relatively quickly eliminated, while those relevant are progressively modified in their structure.

One of the earliest examples of this original, constructive, creative approach to achievement of an intentional end was observed by Piaget in connection with what he calls "the behavior pattern of the support." Laurent had not "understood" the relation "placed upon." Only occasionally and accidentally had he drawn a cushion toward him in order to grasp from it a box with which he had previously played. At age 11 months and 16 days, however, Laurent appeared to discover the relation between support and box. Pappa Jean immediately followed this with other tests of the generality of Laurent's comprehension. He put his watch out of Laurent's reach, on a red cushion directly in front of him. After trying to reach the watch directly, and after shaking his legs, Laurent grabbed the cushion and drew it toward him as before. Pappa Jean tried this with several other objects which interested Laurent and with several other kinds of support; Laurent immediately grasped each support and drew it toward him. Apparently, Laurent had solved this problem, or, let us say, he had acquired a new "learning set" for this category of problems.

Other instances of original, constructive creativity were observed in accommodative groping to bring an object within reach with a stick or to bring a stick through the bars of the play pen. Each led to similar solutions. The opportunity to encounter repetitively a wide variety of such problems very likely constitutes an essential kind of experience leading to "competence," the term White (1959) has used for the motivation involved. This seems especially true if the problems encountered are such that the infant must persist in his accommodative groping to achieve his ends but can ultimately succeed, such experiences fostering his confidence in his capacities. With repetition, such experiences probably lead to a trait-like, second-order "learning set" that is perceived by adults as independence, confidence, and/or competence.

Third, an infant's interest in novelty appears also to motivate imitation, especially imitation of actions, gestures, and vocalizations new to him.

Imitation, along with sympathy and suggestion, has long been seen to have a central role in socialization (see G. W. Allport, 1954). It has been used to account, in part, for behavioral conformity in savage societies, for fads, fashions, and cultural diffusion, for the mental development of children (Baldwin, 1895), for empathy (Mead, 1934), and for role theory. Imitation has been regarded and defined as many kinds of things. It has been seen as an instinct (James, 1890), as a "nonspecific innate tendency" (McDougall, 1908), as an "echo" of action in progress (F. H. Allport, 1924; Holt, 1931), as a generalized instrumental habit of matching one's behavior to that of a model in order to get extrinsic rewards, or as a case in which being different acquires drive-value (Miller & Dollard, 1941), and as behavior based on comprehension of the means-end relationship (Köhler, 1924; Ashby, 1952, chap. 16).

Baldwin (1895) based his conception of the role of imitation in the mental development of children on careful observations of his own children, as did Piaget. He noted that in children and adults, but not in infants, he could distinguish both automatic (nondeliberate) and deliberate imitation. In the course of infant development, he, like Piaget, found stages. In the first, which Baldwin called the *projective* stage, receptive perception predominates and the infant appears to receive impressions of the model as a photographic plate receives an image. In the second, or *subjective* stage, the infant appears to assume the movements, strains, and attitudes of the model, and he becomes a "veritable copying machine." In the third, which Baldwin called the *ejective* stage, the infant recognizes that he is acting like another person, and he gleans from the way he feels about his own imitative action how the other individual must feel about his own situation. In this ejective stage of imitation, Baldwin saw the basis for empathy that George Herbert Mead (1934) later elaborated into the first formulation of the role theory that has become dominant in social psychology.

Baldwin's (1895) descriptions of his observations are not so clear as Piaget's, but one gleans that Baldwin's *projective* stage corresponds roughly to the pseudo-imitation of familiar models during the third and fourth of Piaget's stages of sensorimotor development and to what I here term the second stage of intrinsic motivation. Also, one gleans from the fact that the models can hardly have been familiar and from the prominence of motor patterns as models that Baldwin's *subjective* stage corresponds to the imitation of novel patterns that Piaget found in his fifth stage of sensorimotor development and to what is here the third stage of the development of intrinsic motivation.

Perhaps it is worth noting too that this imitation of novel actions, gestures, and verbal phones corresponds descriptively to the psychoanalytic concept of "incorporation" in which motivation is conceived to be based upon defensive "identification" with the threatening Oedipal father figure or mother figure (Fenichel, 1945, pp. 147 ff. & 164 ff.).

Language development.—Because of its tremendous importance in socialization, language development and the roles therein of interest in novelty and of imitation deserve special comment.

The onset of imitative interest in novel vocal phones appears to motivate a rapid increase in an infant's repertoire of vocal phones. Such a concept of development in vocal repertoire differs sharply from traditional theory. In the traditional view, vocal development was supposed to be representative of motor development in general, proceeding from mass activity through differentiation to finer muscular coordination. Thus, the repertoire of vocal phones was presumed to unfold automatically with anatomical and physiological maturation. Results of observational studies appeared consonant with such a notion (see McCarthy, 1954). Vowel sounds, which require little if any articulation, predominate at first, occurring five times more frequently than consonants during early infancy, with consonant frequency failing to equal vowel frequency until children are about two and a half years of age. According to Irwin's (1941) observational findings, vowel development proceeds from the front to the back of the oral cavity, *i.e.*, from the *e*-sound of the word *lea*, through the long *a* of *take*, the short *a* of *at*, the short *o* of *cot*, the long *o* of *coat*, the short *u* of *cut*, to the long *u*-sound of *true*. Contrariwise, the consonants, which result from fine control of tongue, throat, and lip movements, progress from the gutterals at the back of the oral cavity toward the front. In the course of this maturation, each child is presumed to unfold within his own vocal repertoire all of the phones of all languages (see Bean, 1932; Grégoire, 1937, 1947; Irwin, 1947; Latif, 1934; Lewis, 1951). Thus, according to this traditionally dominant view, socialization consists in a selection of those phones from the infant's presumably abundant repertoire. This selection is achieved, albeit unwittingly, by the adult culture-bearers through reinforcement of those phones which sound like language with vocalizations and facial expressions of approval and interest.

Not all investigators of language development have approved of this traditionally dominant view. Lynip (1951) has argued that the early cooing and crying utterances of infants cannot properly be represented with phonetic symbols. Moreover, from Champneys in 1881 to Charlotte Bühler (1930) and Mary Shirley (1933), investigators have observed infants to imitate phones made by adults. I have also observed such imitation. The notion that an interest in novel vocal sounds motivates an infant's attempt to make what are to him new phones is more nearly consonant with such observations. Moreover, it makes unnecessary the presumption that the child must unfold a vocal repertoire of all of the phones of all languages. The acquisition of phones may rather be motivated by that interest in novelty emerging in the developmental epigenesis of each infant's informational interaction with his circumstances.

This motor side of language has, at first, little or no meaning. Moreover, the primacy of information processing is further supported by evidence that meaning comes as phonemic combinations come to stand for, or symbolize, idiosyncratic images that the infant has already developed through perceptual contact with objects, persons, and places. In Piaget's (1945) observations, even those pseudo-words, whose meanings are highly individual, came only after his children had shown such evidence of established imagery as following objects through hidden displacements, imitative play with models no longer present, and invention of new means through mental combination. Moreover, Hebb and Thompson (1954) have noted that chimpanzees have imagery, as shown by their skill in dissembling a purpose by acting attractive and friendly, only to spit a mouthful of water on the human being who succumbs to the attraction. Yet chimpanzees have no symbolic language.

First pseudo-words consist typically of somewhat garbled phonemic combinations, on the vocal-symbol side, that stand for highly idiosyncratic images, on the side of the symbolized. Thus, one of the first words spoken by one of our children was, "maia-ma," a corruption of "mailman." When she was learning to walk at about eleven months of age, her mother permitted her to go through the living room to the front door when, in midmorning, the mailman rang. "Maia-ma" came to signify the following: the doorbell ringing, a noise on the front porch, a piece of white paper, a newspaper or a magazine, and the goal of being walked to the front door. She would raise her hands to me and say excitedly, "Maia-ma, maia-ma." This meant: "Take my hands and walk me to the door and back."

Following the acquisition of a number of such pseudo-words, each of which goes through a process of correction from the culture-bearing adults, an abrupt change typically takes place in language development. This change is marked by the child's beginning to ask, "What's that?" This question may be asked *ad nauseum* for one thing after another. It appears that the acquisition of few pseudo-words combines with the corrections to lead the child to the highly important "learning set" that "things have names." This learning set appears to provide another kind of habituated task which is interesting and absorbing. The name of an object becomes a task-standard, and the lack of a name becomes a question-instigating incongruity. One consequence of acquiring this task-standard is a rapid increase in the rate of acquiring vocabulary.

Probably this learning set that "things have names" has been one of the most widely recognized in psychological development since it was brought to light in the course of Helen Keller's (1903) learning to speak. Helen, as is well known, had been both blind and deaf for several years following an illness in her second year of life. Teacher (Anne Sullivan) took over, but Helen failed to hit upon the learning set that "things have names" until the critical water-pump incident that came in her eighth year. It came only after tedious months of training during which Teacher repeatedly associated the forms of the touch alphabet with objects. One day while getting a drink, however, Helen suddenly discriminated, with Teacher's help, the signs for the pump's water flowing onto her hand from the signs for the cup held in her hand. At this same time she discriminated the signs for both of these from the signs for the act of drinking. The result was the "learning set" that prompted Helen almost immediately to touch object after object and to request Teacher to spell out the signs into her hand. Since this discovery, the sudden increment commonly observed in the rate of vocabulary acquisition has been related to the "what's that" questioning.

Along with this task-set, or standard, that "things have names" come the task-sets that "actions have names" and, later, that "things come in sets or classes." Along with these comes the discovery that one can control some of the behavior of others, even grownups, by the use of words. At this point, language becomes instrumental and the motivation for its acquisition ceases to be largely a matter of intrinsic motivation. It is likely, nevertheless, that the child is motivated to acquire his syntactical habits by his interest in novel vocal patterns. This interest leads to the imitation of the models supplied by the adult culture-bearers within his orbit. Syntactical habits, however, also get a great deal of social correction and reinforcement.

When the child has acquired language as a technique not only of control but also of communication, he comes into the existential situation of all older children and adults. He then has two main channels of informational input, one—with which he started—through direct perception of objects, persons, places, and events, the other through linguistic communication. The beliefs and attitudes acquired through these two main channels of input need not be congruent, as Rogers (1951) and Kelly (1955) have pointed out. When information from observation is incongruous with conceptions or information acquired through communication, a variety of behavioral phenomena result. Such incongruity has been found clinically by both Rogers and Kelly to be a source of anxiety. It can also be a source of delight, as, for instance, when the information from an experiment is dissonant with a theory communicated to one by an academic competitor, especially one from another school (or church) of thought. Or it can be a source of distress when the experiment yields information dissonant with a theory one has personally constructed and to which he has publicly committed himself.

Other developmental consequences of interest in novelty.—On the other hand, as noted in detail above, a positive interest in moderate incongruity of novelty persists throughout life. It is commonly termed "curiosity." It leads to interaction with new aspects of the environment and with such cultural products as art and music. Such interaction appears to result in new learning sets and in plans that in turn motivate achievement. Such a cycle appears to go on endlessly, with positive interest and a quiet joy as its emotional concomitants, when such extrinsic motive systems as complying with institutional standards or meeting the demands and expectations of others do not complicate life.

During the preschool period, interest in novelty appears to provide the young with delight in variations of familiar situations and stories, with trying new skills, and with developing new goals. A combination of interest in novelty with the task-standards acquired through repeated encounters with problems appears to lead gradually to those flexible, reversible processes of thought in which Piaget (1947) found the properties of operational logic, and the childish conceptions of causality, quantity, number, space, time, etc. (Piaget, 1947). Each of these operations and conceptions probably emerges as a generalization from coping with various kinds of concrete situations and kinds of material (Uzgiris, 1964), but they are sharpened when represented in the vocal signs of language. In the period of the primary grades, interest in novelty appears to underlie the child's delight in and preoccupation with phenomena that surprise him and call for explanation (see Suchman, 1960). It is also important in the pleasure of reading about adventure, geographic anomalies, etc. In the years of junior and senior high school, interest in novelty and the learning sets involved in using language to deal with observed phenomena lead gradually to that facility which permits logical operations with propositions; and, instead of observation giving rise to thought, thought comes to direct and dominate observation (Inhelder & Piaget, 1955). Out of this come patterns of interest which participate in the plans of personal ambition and decisions about identity and profession. Through adulthood, and even in old age, interest in novelty is manifest in the artist's experimentation with new forms and in his viewers' appreciation of new techniques, in the musician's play with new techniques and his listeners' fascination with new compositions, and in the bridge expert's captivation with the continual variety of combinations in hands and with new systems of play. As curiosity, interest in novelty and delight in new achievements appear to persist even after professional ambition and sex have waned.

Individuals differ in the degrees of their curiosity and their interest in novelty. Such individual differences in all likelihood have one basis in genotypic constitutions, but they are also likely to be a function of the range of matters on which the individual has cultivated standards of attitude and opinion and in which he has achieved some skill. Again it is appropriate to cite Piaget's aphorism that "the more a child has seen and heard, the more he wants to see and hear"; it is equally true for adolescents, adults, and senior citizens. Individual differences in curiosity or interest in the novel may also be a function of the level of commitment to attitudes and beliefs: the stronger those commitments, the less the curiosity. In turn, commitment may well be a function of the degree to which attitudes and opinions have been strengthened by interaction of intrinsic motivation with such other motive systems as pain avoidance, including disapproval by groups of which the individual is a member, plans or habits of satisfying homeostatic and/or sexual needs, and plans involved in personal ambition.

Summary and Comment

This hypothesis about the developmental epigenesis of that motivation inherent in information processing and action is basically simple, although I have complicated the picture with discussions of corollary implications and issues.

Stage One begins at birth with the orienting response wherein mammalian infants respond with attentional orientation and arousal to changes in ongoing input through the ears and eyes. Repeated encounters with sequences of such changes in auditory input followed by changes in visual input lead to ear-eye coordination whereby "something heard becomes something to look at."

Stage Two begins when repeated encounters with given kinds of input have led to recognition. Objects, persons, and places which have become recognitively familiar also become motivationally attractive, and the attractiveness of the familiar motivates efforts to retain or regain perceptual contact with the recognitively familiar. I have suggested that recognitive familiarity has a part in such autogenic activities as babbling and hand-watching, in pseudo-imitation, and in the learning set that "things should be recognizable." I have suggested further that this learning set probably becomes an habitual task-standard that provides the goal of perceptual activity.

Stage Three begins with the emergence of an interest in what is novel and new in an otherwise recognitively familiar situation. This interest in novelty presumably appears when encounters following the establishment of recognition have led to an adaptation to the inputs from familiar objects and places. The familiar has become "old stuff." The interest in the novel focuses attention on new objects and places and on manipulation of objects and exploration of places. In the course of such enterprises, action, with its task-standards, gradually becomes quite separate from information processing *per se*, and the child appears to acquire a learning set that can be verbalized as "If you act, you can make things happen." The interest in novelty also motivates the imitation of actions, gestures, vocal phonemic patterns, and syntactical habits in speaking. Imitation plays a major role in socialization. In the course of language-learning, the child acquires a number of learning sets such as "things have names" and "things come in sets." These appear to become task-standards that control the child's informational interaction with his circumstances. Finally, the interest in the novel provides a motive for psychological growth that appears to continue throughout life in a variety of forms.

This hypothetical picture of psychological development and of the role of intrinsic motivation in it differs substantially from both the older theories and the more recent ones. In this one, the role of the environment is much less static than that implied in Froebel's (1826) metaphor of "the soil in which the child-plant grows." This picture is more like that in Dewey's (1902) plan for a primary curriculum, but it differs from his by giving primacy to receptor function and less emphasis to extrinsic motives and to the shaping of action. It differs obviously from Freud's (1905) conception of psychosexual development by placing greater emphasis on the child's informational interaction through the distance receptors and less emphasis on sex. This picture differs from that of Gesell *et al.* (1940) by viewing both anatomical maturation and psychological development as less predetermined and inevitable and as more a function of a dynamic epigenetic informational interaction of infants with their environment. The picture presented here differs from that deriving from a combination of psychoanalytic theory with Hull's learning theory (see Miller & Dollard, 1941; Dollard & Miller, 1950; Sears, Maccoby, & Levin, 1957; Sears, Whiting, Nowlis, & Sears, 1953), which has dominated research in personality development and socialization from the 1930s until very recently. Whereas that picture emphasized the role of an acquired dependency drive, presumed to derive chiefly from the feeding relationship between the mother and child, this picture emphasizes what appears to be a largely independent motive system inherent in the infant's informational interaction with things and people. Curiously, the conceptual scheme presented here has much in common with that upon which Maria Montessori (1909) based her system of pedagogy about sixty years ago. Both this one and hers emphasize the receptor side and a spontaneous interest in learning. Perhaps it is not so strange that she, a fine clinical observer, should have hit upon dynamic and practical motivational principles inasmuch as she was among the very few whose observations of children were made in conjunction with attempts to teach them. Moreover, she built upon the earlier observations of such teacher-clinicians as Itard (1801), Séguin (1866), and probably Binet (1909) (see Hunt, 1964). A good clinical observer attempting to teach may have the best vantage point for seeing motivational principles operating in psychological development. He certainly has a better vantage point than the psychotherapist working with troubled adults or a psychologist working in a laboratory of animal behavior.

SOME ISSUES, SOME METHODOLOGICAL SUGGESTIONS, AND A FEW EXPERIMENTAL DATA

Attractive as this conceptual scheme is, at least to me, I fully recognize that, judged by any acceptable standard for scientific theory, the portion concerned with the role of intrinsic motivation in psychological development is little more than a fantasy prompted by some scattered empirical observations. It is hardly surprising, therefore, that I found considerable satisfaction in a prepublication piece by Walters and Parke (1965) entitled "The Role of the Distance Receptors in the Development of Social Responsiveness." This pleasure may merely exemplify the attractiveness of the newly recognized, but it comes not unmixed with the joy of finding others with their necks well out. Although the conceptual scheme I present here is tentative, it has the merit of suggesting investigative issues that are not suggested by other conceptions of motivation and development. It also has the merit of helping to organize findings that might otherwise be lost in the limbo of unconnected facts.

Characteristics of Inputs That Attract Attention in the Neonate

First, this conceptual scheme raises a question about the characteristics of change in visual and auditory input which attract attention and motivate looking and listening in the neonate. Here a few data have already been found which are contrary to the traditional notion that the eye and brain are too immature to permit focusing the eyes and pattern vision at birth (McGraw, 1943; Pratt, 1946): Gorman, Cogan, and Gellis (1957) have found 93 per cent of infants less than five days old responding optokinetically to stripes subtending a visual angle of no more than 33.5 min., and a few responding to stripes of 11 min. By adult standards, this as poor acuity, but it is evidence that a capacity for pattern vision exists very shortly after birth.

Using preference for one of a pair of presentations with time of fixation as the criterion, a method employed by Stirnimann (1944) to study color preference, both Berlyne (1958) and Fantz (1958) have found that infants prefer, *i.e.*, fixate longer, patterned surfaces to homogeneous surfaces. Fantz (1961) has also found that fixation time increases with the complexity of pattern and that preference for complexity increases with age (Fantz, 1958). That is, infants looked longer at horizontal stripes and a bull's-eye than at a cross and a circle, and longer at a checkered pattern than at triangles; and preference for the checkered surface over the plain square increased from 60 per cent in infants less than two months old to 72 per cent in infants more than two months old. Moreover, in the case of the stripes *versus* the bull's-eye, stripes were preferred by 21 of 22 infants less than two months old and the bull's-eye was preferred by 21 of 22 older than two months. Such evidence goes well beyond that from the investigations of the orienting response to show not only that changes of input attract attention, but also that variations in the attractiveness of various colors and patterns of visual input exist almost from birth. It is interesting that Fantz (1965) uses this and other evidence to contend, as I have from the evidence above, that "perception *precedes* [italics his] action and that early perceptual experience is necessary for the development of coordinated and visually-directed behavior."

Auditory input in young infants has been studied even less than visual input. Methodological problems undoubtedly account for this. While one can use preference techniques for simultaneously presented visual patterns, this is hardly feasible for auditory patterns. An approach may be by indicators of autonomic response, as the following considerations would suggest.

Lacey (1959) has put together evidence indicating that the directions of inclination with respect to source of input have counterparts in autonomic patterns. As early as thirty-five years ago, Darrow (1929a, 1929b) reported that simple sensory stimuli (*i.e.*, changes in ongoing input) result in decelerations of heart rate along with decreased resistance of the skin and vascular constriction. Contrariwise, noxious stimulation and/or intellectual concentration (*e.g.*, an arithmetic problem), which presumably call for a withdrawal from or rejection of receptor input, produce *accelerations* of heart rate along with decrease in skin resistance and vascular constriction. These changes in skin resistance and vascular constriction produced by noxious stimulation and concentration were less in degree than those produced by changes in ongoing receptor input. Ruckmick (1936) reports that Wundt once equated pleasant stimuli (*i.e.*, perceptual approach to or acceptance of receptor input) with cardiac deceleration, and unpleasant stimuli (*i.e.*, withdrawal from or rejection of receptor input) with cardiac acceleration. Perhaps the most dramatic evidence comes from the laboratory of the late R. C. Davis (1957; see also Davis & Buchwald, 1957; Davis, Buchwald, & Frankmann, 1955). In these studies, when college students were made to put their feet in cold water and presented with stimuli that had been followed by electric shock (*i.e.*, with inputs which people would be expected to reject or to withdraw from), the pattern of physiological indicators consisted of accelerated heart rates, increased palmar conductance (*i.e.*, decreased palmar resistance), and vascular constriction. On the other hand, young male adults presented with pictures of nude females showed decelerated heart rates, increased palmar conductance, and vascular constriction. Davis called this the P-pattern, and it may imply pleasure and a ready acceptance of the input. Still further support comes from reports by Callaway and Dembo (1958) and Lacey (1959) that increased heart rate or blood pressure is typically associated with inhibitory effects on receptor input and perception. Although Pratt (1946) reports that Canestrini (1912) found even newborn infants showing cardiac deceleration associated with some stimuli and cardiac acceleration with other inputs, scrutiny of the monograph fails to confirm Pratt's report.[14] On the other hand, certain of the kymographic records presented by Canestrini appear to indicate that heart-rate deceleration occurs with warm milk in the mouth, even though he fails to comment to this effect.

If it can shown that visual patterns which infants prefer are accompanied by decelerating heart rates while those not so preferred are not, and if certain changes in ongoing auditory input

[14] I am indebted to Professor William Gerler, now of Southern Illinois University and whose first language was German, for checking and corroborating my own scrutiny of the Canestrini monograph.

bring decelerating heart rates while others bring accelerating heart rates, it might open the way for information about preferences for auditory inputs in neonates. A still unpublished paper by Kagan and Lewis (1964) reports positive relationships between visual fixation times and cardiac deceleration for highly attentive infants at six months of age, but none for infants who are minimally attentive. One of the "if" hurdles may thus have been jumped; yet since the subjects were already six months old, their attention may derive from the attractiveness of the recognitively familiar.

Attractiveness of Recognitive Familiarity

In our own laboratory, Dr. Ina Uzgiris and I are concentrating on the effects on psychological development of the circumstances the infant encounters. We have started with the hypotheses that (1) objects becoming recognitively familiar become attractive, and (2) objects and persons responsive to an infant's action become attractive. In our first experiment, the strategy consisted in placing two mobiles over the cribs of infants between three and five weeks old—usually nearer four weeks. One mobile was unresponsive: it hung from a stand that rested on the floor. Another was intended to be responsive: it was attached to a pole and clamped to the crib so that the infant might make it move by shaking his body or legs. The two mobiles were separated by some ten inches, about a foot above the infant's eyes, their right-left positions alternating from child to child. We assumed that the babies would look at and become familiar with these mobiles as they lay awake. Yet, to ensure that all spent at least some time looking at them, we asked their mothers to find each day two periods of about fifteen minutes to place the awake and satisfied babies in their cribs. No mother reported difficulty in establishing such "looking times" after the babies were about six weeks old.

After the mobiles had been placed for approximately four weeks, tests of preference were made between the two familiar ones, and between each familiar one and a strange one. The mobiles were then taken away for about forty-eight hours. When they were returned, the preference tests were repeated. At this time, the preferred familiar mobile was paired with a strange one first; then, the unpreferred familiar mobile was paired with the strange one; and, finally, the two familiar mobiles were paired with each other.

The first test of preference for the two familiar mobiles was for ten minutes, with the two mobiles reversed after five minutes. The tests of preference between the familiar mobiles and the strange one were for four minutes, with each pair reversed as to side after two minutes. Preference consisted of fixating one of the mobiles in a test pair for more time than the other.

It should be noted that three roles exist for the mobiles: responsive familiar, unresponsive familiar, and strange. Three different mobiles were used: one consisting of three yarn tassels hung from a circle or triangle of homogeneous color, one with three boxes hung from the circle or triangle, and one with three umbrellas. Each was to serve equally often in each role. In the exploratory phase of the experiment, each served in each role, but not equally often. Later, an equalization was made.

In the exploratory experiment (Hunt & Uzgiris, 1965), 25 infants participated, but 6 were dropped for extreme side preferences, and the data for 4 others were incomplete. The results from the remaining 15 infants are clearly consonant with the hypothesis. All 15 preferred the preferred familiar mobile over the strange one, and 12 of the 15 preferred the unpreferred familiar mobile over the strange one.

Evidence concerning the hypothesis that preference goes to the responsive mobile over the stable or unresponsive one is less clear. Although many cribs were so solid that such young infants could not move them or the mobiles attached, some infants successfully moved the mobiles by shaking themselves or their legs. The infant would lie, looking up at the mobile hanging from the bar attached to his crib, and shake himself. When the mobile moved, he would laugh and watch until the motion stopped; then he would shake himself again and laugh at the responsive motion of the mobile. Mothers liked this arrangement because the game kept their infants preoccupied for a half-hour or more at a stretch. Various infants preferred various mobiles, but each who succeeded in moving his "responsive" mobile also preferred it over the unresponsive one. Whether this indicates preference for motion contingent to the infant's action or merely preference for things that move is not clear, nor is it easy to make clear.

When this experiment was extended so that each mobile appeared equally often in each role, preference for familiar mobiles over strange ones continued to be highly significant, even though there were more instances in which the strange one was preferred (Uzgiris & Hunt, 1965). Also, an analysis of variance showed that the infants had highly significant preferences among these three kinds of mobiles. However, this is largely the result of low preference for the umbrella mobile. The finding corroborates Berlyne's and Fantz's findings of general pattern preferences among very young infants.

Particular Experiences and Developmental Transitions

For theory and for educational technology, a key issue is the relationship of various kinds of experience to various developmental transitions. The issue raises many questions. Let me ask some and comment on a few.

Will infants' encounters with interesting and varied visual patterns hasten development of visual acuity, hitherto presumed almost entirely a matter of predetermined maturation?

Will encounters with a variety of visual and auditory patterns hasten the development of intentional efforts to regain perceptual contact with them in general, or is the effort specific to individual patterns repeatedly encountered? This asks whether the most useful formulation is of general stages of development or of stages in the organism's interaction with specific situations. Uzgiris (1964) has found that, while it remains true that with any given test-material the ordinality of conserving volume implies conservation of both weight and quantity and that conserving weight implies conservation of quantity, it is also true that children may conserve weight with one test-material while hardly conserving mere quantity with another material. Such a finding suggests the existence of considerable situational specificity. Considerable situational specificity is also suggested by Smedslund's (1964) relatively low level of intercorrelations among measures of various concrete operations. Situational specificity suggests that general stages of development may be an artifact of an infant's encountering a number of situations at about the same rate. If stages are general, moreover, they may acquire their generality, after the fashion of Harlow's (1949) learning sets, from encountering given kinds of situations over and over in a variety of settings.

Will encountering various visual and auditory patterns sufficiently motivate an infant to develop locomotion, or must he encounter situations which respond to his locomotor effort? This is relevant to the issue of the primacy of receptor inputs. Several lines of evidence suggest that the attractiveness of recognitive familiarity is important in the instigation and guidance of early infantile action, but it is also very likely that action must occur and get direct, responsive informational reinforcement.

Atypical Evidence of Receptor Primacy

Evidence consonant with the hypothetical role of intrinsic motivation in psychological development, and especially within the notion of receptor primacy, comes from unusual sources. One source is the success of Suzuki's method of teaching Japanese toddlers to play the violin (see Kendall, 1959). Beginning midway in the first year, simple melodies tape-recorded by excellent violinists are played repeatedly in the infant's hearing, especially as he is going to sleep. The mother is also taught to play a few of these melodies on the violin, and as the infant reaches toddlerhood, she is instructed to play these during his times of play and interaction. When the toddler takes the initiative and attempts to imitate his mother's violin-playing, when it is clear that he wants to play, he is given a small violin of his own and shown how to handle the bow and how to control pitch by placing his fingers on the strings. This may occur even before he is three years old. Important for our theoretical purposes are the avid interest and rapidly gained skill with which these toddlers learn. Paul Rolland (personal communication), President of the National Association of String Teachers, reports that many of the five- and six-year-olds taught by Suzuki's method have better technique and get better tone from their instruments than typical American violin students at the high school or even at the college level. Thus, it appears that the development, by repeated listening, of an image of melodies expertly played is of great importance both in getting fun from playing the instrument and in gaining the motor control that produces sound of high quality.

Another unusual source is the work of O. K. Moore (1964). Moore (personal communication) has observed an unusually high level of motor control in the writing of young children who, presumably, have developed images of letters from seeing them and hearing them repeatedly in their work with the "talking" electric typewriter invented by Richard Kobler of the Thomas A. Edison Research Laboratory. This motor control appeared after three- and four-year-olds had for several months spent some fifteen or twenty minutes a day striking the keys of the typewriter, seeing the letters produced thereby, and hearing them pronounced. When the children were given chalk at a blackboard, they soon discovered some of their scribbled patterns looked like the letters they had seen: a vertical straight line might look like the letter *l*, and a circular loop might look like the letter *o*. Often this discovery came with a verbalization to the effect that "I can make the letters with the chalk." Thereafter, making letters became a game. Noting what appeared to be chalk-written letters of unusual quality, Moore had judges estimate the ages of the children who had made them. The judges were teachers and a child psychologist, all highly familiar with the writing of school children. According to their judgments, these three- and four-year-olds with no special training in writing *per se* were making letters typical of school children seven, eight, or even nine years old. Such observations, despite the lack of nice experimental control, give credence to the hypothesis of receptor primacy, to the theory that the receptors build images which then serve as standards for motor skills.

This hypothesis would imply that infants who hear a great deal of human talk would vocalize more than infants who do not hear the human voice. Rheingold, Stanley, and Cooley (1962) have found that the motor response of touching a ball becomes more frequent when touching it closes a circuit that presents a brief motion-picture sequence with music, but this is a Skinnerian reinforcement. If the receptor-primacy hypothesis is correct, infants presented tape-recorded sounds should vocalize more than infants without such priming. Moreover, if repeatedly hearing given, tape-recorded phonemic patterns makes those patterns attractive, infants should make something approximating those sounds rather than others. The theorizing I present here suggests such investigative issues that might otherwise be overlooked. Investigation could disprove the hypothesis or call for its correction. This is the heuristic value of such theorizing.

Summary and Final Comment

In this paper, I have (1) outlined the answers given by the theory which has dominated the behavioral sciences for more than half a century to the eight motivation questions that I have identified; (2) synopsized both the conceptual and evidential bases for holding that a system of motivation inheres within the informational interaction of organisms with their circumstances; (3) presented a tentative hypothesis of the role of such motivation in the psychological development of human infants; and (4) indicated some issues, some methodological suggestions, and a few data relevant to the hypothesis or resulting from experimentation suggested by it.

The answers outlined to the eight motivation questions can be said to have been dominant within the theorizing of behavioral scientists during the past half-century because they have figured in the physiology stemming from the work of Claude Bernard (*i.e.*, Cannon, 1915; Richter, 1927; etc.), in both psychoanalytic psychology and the psychology deriving from the animal laboratories, and even in the conceptions of human nature in the economic and social theory of Marx and Engels (see Venable, 1945). In putting the springs of action entirely within the domains of biochemical interaction with the environment or sex and outside the domain of informational interaction with the environment, these dominant answers have been highly dissonant with the conceptions of these springs of human action assumed by our political, legal, and educational institutions. While the conception of intrinsic motivation is considerably different from the ancient conception of rationality, the idea that a basic source of motivation is inherent within the organism's informational interaction with its circumstances is far more consonant with the motivational assumptions of our political, legal, and educational institutions than has been this recently traditional view. Before too many efforts are made to revise our institutions to make them consonant with the answers to motivation questions in the theorizing recently dominant in the behavioral sciences, the implications of the newer evidence should be carefully weighed. The hypothetical role of motivation intrinsic within the operation of the eyes and ears in psychological development gives new meaning to the notion of organism-environment interaction and points to a radically changed conception of the role of experience in the development of both intelligence and motivation. The hypothetical role of intrinsic motivation in development suggests also that those observers of children who, at the turn of this century, thought they saw there a "spontaneous interest in learning" were perhaps less duped than their critics. A "thirst for knowledge" may, with proper early experience, become more than a figure of speech.

REFERENCES[15]

Allport, F. H. *Social psychology*. Boston: Houghton Mifflin, 1924.

Allport, G. W. Historical background of modern social psychology. In G. Lindzey (Ed.), *Handbook of social psychology*. Vol. 1. Cambridge, Mass.: Addison-Wesley, 1954. Pp. 3–56.

Allport, G. W. *Becoming: basic considerations in a psychology of personality*. New Haven: Yale Univ. Press, 1955.

Amsel, A. The role of frustrative nonreward in noncontinuous reward situations. *Psychol. Bull.*, 1958, 55, 102–119.

[15] The dates given in the text following the authors' names are, to the best of my knowledge, the original dates of publication. These are listed at the ends of the citations. The other date in each citation identifies the edition available to me.

Amsel, A., & Roussel, J. Motivational properties of frustration: I. Effect on running response of the addition of frustration of the motivational complex. *J. exp. Psychol.*, 1952, 43, 363–368.

Angell, J. R. The province of functional psychology. *Psychol. Rev.*, 1907, 14, 61–91.

Ashby, W. R. *Design for a brain.* New York: Wiley, 1952.

Attneave, F. Some informational aspects of visual perception. *Psychol. Rev.*, 1954, 61, 183–193.

Baldwin, J. M. *Mental development in the child and in the race: methods and processes.* (3rd ed.) New York: Macmillan, 1906. Originally published in 1895.

Bean, C. H. An unusual opportunity to investigate the psychology of language. *J. genet. Psychol.*, 1932, 40, 181–202.

Berlyne, D. E. The influence of the albedo and complexity of stimuli on visual fixation in the human infant. *Brit. J. Psychol.*, 1958, 49, 315–318.

Berlyne, D. E. *Conflict, arousal, and curiosity.* New York: McGraw-Hill, 1960.

Bexton, W. H., Heron, W., & Scott, T. H. Effects of increased variation in the sensory environment. *Canad. J. Psychol.*, 1954, 8, 70–76.

Binet, A. *Les idées modernes sur les enfants.* Paris: Ernest Flamarion, 1909. Cited in G. D. Stoddard, The I. Q.: its ups and downs. *Educ. Rec.*, 1939, 20, 44–57.

Brown, J. S. Problems presented by the concept of acquired drives. In M. R. Jones (Ed.), *Current theory and research in motivation: a symposium.* Lincoln: Univ. of Nebraska Press, 1953. Pp. 1–21.

Bruner, J. S. On perceptual readiness. *Psychol. Rev.*, 1957, 64, 123–152.

Bruner, J. S. The course of cognitive growth. *Amer. Psychologist*, 1964, 19, 1–15.

Bruner, J. S., & Potter, Mary C. Interference in visual recognition. *Science*, 1964, 144, 424–425.

Bühler, Charlotte. *The first year of life.* (Trans. by P. Greenberg & Rowena Ripin) New York: John Day, 1930.

Bühler, Charlotte, & Hetzer, Hildegard. Inventar der Verhaltungsweisen des ersten Lebensjahres. *Quel. Stud. Jugkd.*, 1927, 5, 125–250.

Butler, R. A. Discrimination learning by rhesus monkeys to visual exploration motivation. *J. comp. physiol. Psychol.*, 1953, 46, 95–98.

Butler, R. A. Incentive conditions which influence visual exploration. *J. exp. Psychol.*, 1954, 48, 19–23.

Butler, R. A. The differential effect of visual and auditory incentives on the performance of monkeys. *Amer. J. Psychol.*, 1958, 71, 591–593.

Callaway, E. III, & Dembo, D. Narrowed attention: a physiological phenomenon that accompanies a certain physiological change. *Arch. Neurol, Psychiat.*, 1958, 79, 74–90.

Canestrini, S. Über das Sinnesleben des Neugeborenen. *Monogr. Ges. Neurol. Psychiat.*, No. 5, 104. Berlin: Springer, 1912.

Cannon, W. B. *Bodily changes in pain, hunger, fear and rage.* (Rev. ed.) New York: Appleton, 1929. Originally published in 1915.

Carmichael, L. The development of behavior in vertebrates experimentally removed from influence of external stimulation. *Psychol. Rev.*, 1926, **33**, 51–58.

Charlesworth, W. R. The instigation and maintenance of curiosity behavior as a function of surprise versus novel and familiar stimuli. *Child Develpm.*, 1964, **35**, 1169–1186.

Chow, K. L. Further studies on selective ablation of associative cortex in relation to visually mediated behavior. *J. comp. physiol. Psychol.*, 1952, **45**, 109–118.

Cofer, C. N., & Appley, M. H. *Motivation: theory and research.* New York: Wiley, 1964.

Conant, J. B. *On understanding science.* New York: New American Library (Mentor No. 68), 1951.

Cremin, L. A. *The transformation of the school: progressivism in American education, 1876–1957.* New York: Knopf, 1962.

Cruze, W. W. Maturation and learning in chicks. *J. comp. Psychol.*, 1935, **20**, 371–409.

Darling, F. *Wild country.* London: 1938. Cited by Thorpe, 1956.

Darrow, C. W. Differences in the physiological reactions to sensory and ideational stimuli. *Psychol. Bull.*, 1929, **26**, 125–201. (a)

Darrow, C. W. Electrical and circulatory responses to brief sensory and ideational stimuli. *J. exp. Psychol.*, 1929, **12**, 267–300. (b)

Davis, R. C. Response patterns. *Trans. N. Y. Acad. Sci.*, 1957, 19, (Ser. II), 731–739.

Davis, R. C., & Buchwald, A. M. An exploration of somatic response patterns: stimulus and sex differences. *J. comp. physiol. Psychol.*, 1957, **50**, 44–52.

Davis, R. C., Buchwald, A. M., & Frankmann, R. W. Automatic and muscular responses and their relation to simple stimuli. *Psychol. Monogr.*, 1955, **69**, No. 20 (Whole No. 406).

Dember, W. N., Earl, R. W., & Paradise, N. Response by rats to differential stimulus complexity. *J. comp. physiol. Psychol.*, 1957, **50**, 514–518.

Dennis, W. Infant development under conditions of restricted practice and of minimum social stimulation. *Genet. Psychol. Monogr.*, 1941, **23**, 143–189.

Dennis, W. Causes of retardation among institutional children: Iran. *J. genet. Psychol.*, 1960, **96**, 47–59.

Dennis, W. The effect of supplementary experiences upon the behavioral development of institutional infants. *Child Develpm.*, 1965, **36**, in press.

Desmedt, J. E. Auditory-evoked potentials from cochlea to cortex as influenced by activation of the efferent olivo-cochlea bundle. *J. acoust. Soc. Amer.*, 1962, **34**, 1478–1483.

Dewey, J. The theory of emotion. *Psychol. Rev.*, 1894, **1**, 553–569; continued in 1895, **2**, 13–32.

Dewey, J. The reflex arc concept in psychology. *Psychol. Rev.*, 1896, **3**, 357–370.

Dewey, J. *The child and the curriculum.* Chicago: Univ. of Chicago Press (Phoenix Books P3), 1960. Originally published in 1902.

Dollard, J., & Miller, N. E. *Personality and psychotherapy: an analysis in terms of learning, thinking, and culture.* New York: McGraw-Hill, 1950.

Drury, Marjorie B. Progressive changes in nonfoveal perception of line patterns. *Amer. J. Psychol.*, 1933, **45**, 628–646.

Earl, R. W. Problem solving and motor skill behaviors under conditions of stimulus complexity. Unpublished doctoral dissertation, Univ. of Michigan, 1957.

Fantz, R. L. Pattern vision in young infants. *Psychol. Rec.*, 1958, **8**, 43–48.

Fantz, R. L. The origin of form perception. *Sci. Amer.*, 1961, **204** (5), 66–72.

Fantz, R. L. Pattern discrimination and selective attention as determinants of perceptual development from birth. To be published in Aline H. Kidd & Jeanne L. Rivoire (Eds.), *Perceptual development in children.* New York: International Universities Press, 1965.

Fenichel, O. *The psychoanalytic theory of the neuroses.* New York: Norton, 1945.

Festinger, L. *A theory of cognitive dissonance.* Evanston, Ill.: Row, Peterson, 1957.

Fex, J. Auditory activity in centrifugal and centripetal cochlear fibres in cats. *Acta. Physiol. Scand.*, 1962, **55** (Supplement 189).

Fox, S. S. Self-maintained sensory input and sensory deprivation in monkeys: a behavioral and neuropharmacological study. *J. comp. physiol. Psychol.*, 1962, **55**, 438–444.

Freeman, G. L. The relationship between performance level and bodily activity level. *J. exp. Psychol.*, 1940, **26**, 602–608.

Freud, Anna. *The ego and the mechanisms of defense.* (Trans. by C. Baines) New York: International Universities Press, 1946. Originally published in 1936.

Freud, Anna, & Burlingham, Dorothy. *Infants without families.* New York: International Universities Press, 1944.

Freud, S. Instincts and their vicissitudes. In *Collected Papers.* Vol. 4. London: Hogarth, 1927. Pp. 60–83. Originally published in 1915.

Freud, S. *New introductory lectures on psychoanalysis.* New York: Norton, 1933.

Freud, S. *The problem of anxiety.* (Trans. by H. A. Bunker) New York: Norton, 1936. Originally published in 1926.

Freud, S. The interpretation of dreams. In A. A. Brill (Trans. & Ed.), *The basic writings of Sigmund Freud.* New York: Modern Library, 1938. Originally published in 1900.

Freud, S. Three contributions to the theory of sex. In A. A. Brill (Trans. & Ed.), *The basic writings of Sigmund Freud.* New York: Modern Library, 1938. Originally published in 1905.

Freud, S. *Introductory lectures on psychoanalysis.* (Trans. by Joan Riviere) (2nd ed.) London: Allen & Unwin, 1940. Originally published in 1917.

Froebel, F. *The education of man.* (Trans. by W. N. Hailman) New York: Appleton, 1892. Originally published in 1826.

Galambos, R. Suppression of auditory nerve activity by stimulation of efferent fibers to the cochlea. *J. Neurophysiol.*, 1956, **19**, 424–429.

Gesell, A., *et al. The first five years of life.* New York: Harper, 1940.

Gorman, J. J., Cogan, D. G., & Gellis, S. S. An apparatus for grading the visual acuity of infants on the basis of optic nystagmus. *Pediatrics*, 1957, **19**, 1088–1092.

Grégoire, A. *L'apprentissage du langage: les deux premières années.* Paris: Droz, 1937.

Grégoire, A. *L'apprentissage du langage: II. la torisieme année et les années suivantes.* Paris: Droz, 1947.

Haber, R. N. Discrepancy from adaptation level as a source of affect. *J. exp. Psychol.*, 1958, **56**, 370–375.

Hall, M. *New memoire one the nervous system.* London, 1843.

Harlow, H. F. The formation of learning sets. *Psychol. Rev.*, 1949, **56**, 51–65.

Harlow, H. F. Learning and satiation of response in intrinsically motivated complex puzzle performance by monkeys. *J. comp. physiol. Psychol.*, 1950, **43**, 289–294.

Harlow, H. F. Motivation as a factor in the acquisition of new responses. In M. R. Jones (Ed.), *Current theory and research in motivation.* Lincoln: Univ. of Nebraska Press, 1953. Pp. 24–49.

Haywood, H. C. Relationships among anxiety, seeking of novel stimuli, and level of unassimilated percepts. *J. Pers.*, 1961, **29**, 105–114.

Haywood, H. C. Novelty-seeking behavior as a function of manifest anxiety and physiological arousal. *J. Pers.*, 1962, **30**, 63–74.

Haywood, H. C. Differential effects of delayed auditory feedback upon palmar sweating, heart rate, and pulse pressure. *J. speech hearing Res.*, 1963, **6**, 181–186.

Haywood, H. C., & Hunt, J. McV. Effects of epinephrine upon novelty preference and arousal. *J. abnorm. soc. Psychol.*, 1963, **67**, 206–213.

Hebb, D. O. On the nature of fear. *Psychol. Rev.*, 1946, **53**, 259–276.

Hebb, D. O. *The organization of behavior.* New York: Wiley, 1949.

Hebb, D. O. Drives and the C.N.S. (conceptual nervous system). *Psychol. Rev.*, 1955, **62**, 243–254.

Hebb, D. O., & Riesen, A. H. The genesis of irrational fears. *Bull. Canad. Psychol. Ass.*, 1943, **3**, 49–50.

Hebb, D. O., & Thompson, W. R. The social significance of animal studies. In G. Lindzey (Ed.), *Handbook of social psychology.* Vol. 1. Cambridge, Mass.: Addison-Wesley, 1954. Chap. 15.

Hediger, H. *Wild animals in captivity.* London, 1950. Cited by Thorpe, 1956.

Heinroth, O. Beitrage zur Biologie, namentlich Ethologie un Physiologie der

Anatiden. *Verhandl. V. Int. Ornithol. Kongr.,* 1910, 589–702. Cited by Thorpe, 1956.

Helson, H. Adaptation-level as frame of reference for prediction of psychophysical data. *Amer. J. Psychol.,* 1947, **60,** 1–29.

Helson, H. *Adaptation-level theory.* New York: Harper & Row, 1964.

Hendrick, I. The discussion of the "instinct to master." *Psychoanal. Quart.,* 1943, **12,** 561–565.

Hernandez-Péon, R., Scherrer, H., & Jouven, M. Modification of electric activity in cochlear nucleus during "attention" in unanesthetized cats. *Science,* 1956, **123,** 331–332.

Heron, W., Doane, B. K., & Scott, T. H. Visual disturbances after prolonged perceptual isolation. *Canad. J. Psychol.,* 1956, **10,** 13–18.

Hess, E. H. Ethology: an approach toward the complete analysis of behavior. In R. Brown, E. Galanter, E. H. Hess, & G. Mandler, *New directions in psychology.* New York: Holt, Rinehart, & Winston, 1962. Pp. 157–266.

Hollingworth, L. S., & Cobb, M. V. Children clustering at 165 I. Q. and children clustering at 145 I. Q. compared for three years in achievement. *Yearb. nat. Soc. Stud. Educ.,* 1928, **27,** Part II, 3–33.

Holt, E. B. *Animal drive and the learning process.* New York: Holt, 1931.

Hull, C. L. *Principles of behavior.* New York: Appleton-Century-Crofts, 1943.

Hunt, J. McV. Experience and the development of motivation: some reinterpretations. *Child Develpm.,* 1960, **31,** 489–504.

Hunt, J. McV. *Intelligence and experience.* New York: Ronald Press, 1961.

Hunt, J. McV. Piaget's observations as a source of hypotheses concerning motivation. *Merrill-Palmer Quart.,* 1963, **9,** 263–275. (a)

Hunt, J. McV. Motivation inherent in information processing and action. In O. J. Harvey (Ed.), *Motivation and social interaction: cognitive determinants.* New York: Ronald Press, 1963. Chap. 3. (b)

Hunt, J. McV. Montessori revisited. Introduction to *The Montessori Method.* New York: Shocken Books, 1964.

Hunt, J. McV. Traditional personality theory in the light of recent evidence. *Amer. Scientist,* 1965, **53,** 80–96.

Hunt, J. McV., & Quay, H. C. Early vibratory experience and the question of innate reinforcement value of vibration and other stimuli: a limitation on the discrepancy (burnt soup) principle in motivation. *Psychol. Rev.,* 1961, **68,** 149–156.

Hunt, J. McV., & Uzgiris, Ina C. Cathexis from recognitive familiarity: an exploratory study. To be published in the monograph honoring J. P. Guilford and based on papers presented at the APA (1964), 1965.

Igel, G. J., & Calvin, A. D. The development of affectional responses in infant dogs. *J. comp. physiol. Psychol.,* 1960, **53,** 302–305.

Inhelder, Bärbel, & Piaget, J. *The growth of logical thinking from childhood to adolescence: an essay on the construction of formal operational structures.* (Trans. by Anne Parsons & S. Milgram) New York: Basic Books, 1958. Originally published in 1955.

Irwin, O. C. Research on speech sounds for the first six months of life. *Psychol. Bull.*, 1941, 38, 277–285.

Irwin, O. C. Development of speech during infancy: curve of phonemic frequencies. *J. exp. Psychol.*, 1947, 37, 187–193.

Itard, J. M. G. *The wild boy of Aveyron.* (Trans. by George & Muriel Humphrey) New York: Appleton-Century-Crofts, 1932. Originally published in 1801.

Jacobsen, C. F., Wolfe, J. B., & Jackson, J. A. An experimental analysis of the functions of the frontal association areas in primates. *J. nerv. ment. Dis.*, 1935, 82, 1–14.

James, W. *Principles of psychology.* New York: Holt, 1890. 2 vols.

Jersild, A. T., & Holmes, Frances B. *Children's fears.* New York: Teachers College, Columbia Univ., 1935. (Child Develpm. Monogr. 20)

Jones, H. E., & Jones, Mary C. Fear. *Childh. Educ.*, 1928, 5, 136–143.

Kagan, J., & Lewis, M. Studies of attention in the human infant. Unpublished paper (1964) cited in Walters & Parke.

Keller, Helen A. *The story of my life.* New York: Grosset & Dunlap, 1911. Originally published in 1903.

Kelly, G. A. *The psychology of personal constructs.* New York: Norton, 1955. 2 vols.

Kendall, J. A report on Japan's phenomenal violinists: outline of talent education method—Shinichi Suzuki. *Violins & Violinists*, 1959, 20, 241–244.

Kiernan, C. C. Positive reinforcement by light: comments on Lockard's article. *Psychol. Bull.*, 1964, 62, 351–357.

Klüver, H. Visual functions after removal of the occipital lobes. *J. Psychol.*, 1941, 11, 23–45.

Köhler, W. *The mentality of apes.* (Trans. by Ella Winter) New York: Vintage Books, 1959. Originally published in 1924.

Lacey, J. I. Psychophysiological approaches to the evaluation of psychotherapeutic process and outcome. In E. Rubenstein & M. B. Parloff (Eds.), *Research in psychotherapy.* Washington, D.C.: Amer. Psychol. Ass., 1959. Pp. 160–208.

Landis, C., & Hunt, W. A. *The startle pattern.* New York: Farrar & Rinehart, 1939.

Lashley, K. S. The accuracy of movement in the absence of excitation from the moving organ. *Amer. J. Physiol.*, 1917, 43, 169–194.

Latif, I. The physiological basis of linguistic development and of the ontogeny of meaning: I and II. *Psychol. Rev.*, 1934, 41, 55–85 & 153–170.

Leaton, R. N., Symmes, D., & Barry, H. Familiarization with the test apparatus as a factor in the reinforcing effect of change in illumination. *J. Psychol.*, 1963, 55, 145–151.

Leuba, C. Toward some integration of learning theories: the concept of optimal stimulation. *Psychol. Rep.*, 1955, 1, 27–33.

Lewis, M. M. *Infant speech: a study of the beginnings of language.* (2nd ed.) New York: Humanities Press, 1951.

Lilly, J. C. Mental effects of reduction of ordinary levels of physical stimuli on intact, healthy persons. *Psychiat. Res. Rep.*, 1956, **5**, 1–9.

Lindsley, D. B. Psychophysiology and motivation. In M. R. Jones (Ed.), *Nebraska symposium on motivation: 1957*. Lincoln: Univ. of Nebraska Press, 1957. Pp. 44–104.

Lockard, R. B. Some effects of light upon the behavior of rodents. *Psychol. Bull.*, 1963, **60**, 509–529.

Lorenz, K. Der Kumpan in der Umwelt des Vögels. *J. Ornith.*, 1935, **83**, 137–214 & 289–413. Cited by Thorpe, 1956.

Lorenz, K. Über den Begriff der Instinkthandlung. *Folia Biotheretica*, 1937, **2**, 17–50. Cited by Thorpe, 1956.

Lundin, R. W. *An objective psychology of music*. New York: Ronald Press, 1953.

Lynip, A. W. The uses of magnetic devices in the collection and analyses of the preverbal utterances of an infant. *Genet. Psychol. Monogr.*, 1951, **44**, 221–262.

McCall, R. B. Stimulus change in light-contingent bar-pressing. *J. comp. physiol. Psychol.*, 1965, **59**, accepted and scheduled for No. 2.

McCarthy, Dorothea. Language development in children. In L. Carmichael (Ed.), *Manual of child psychology*. (2nd ed.) New York: Wiley, 1954. Chap. 9.

McClelland, D. C., Atkinson, J. W., Clark, R. W., & Lowell, E. L. *The achievement motive*. New York: Appleton-Century-Crofts, 1953.

McDougall, W. *An introduction to social psychology*. Boston: Luce, 1908.

McGraw, Myrtle B. *The neuromuscular maturation of the human infant*. New York: Columbia Univ. Press, 1943.

Mandler, G. The interruption of behavior. In D. Levine (Ed.), *Nebraska symposium on motivation: 1964*. Lincoln: Univ. of Nebraska Press, 1964. Pp. 163–221.

Maslow, A. H. *Motivation and personality*. New York: Harper, 1954.

Matthews, S. A., & Detwiler, S. R. The reaction of Amblystoma embryos following prolonged treatment with chloreton. *J. exp. Zool.*, 1926, **45**, 279–292.

Mead, G. H. *Mind, self, and society*. Chicago: Univ. of Chicago Press, 1934.

Meier, G. W., Fosher, D. P., Wittrig, J. J., Peeler, D. F., & Huff, F. W. Helson's residual factor versus innate S-R relations. *Psychol. Rep.*, 1960, **6**, 61–62.

Melton, A. W. Learning. In W. S. Monroe (Ed.), *Encyclopedia of educational research*. New York: Macmillan, 1941.

Miller, G. A., Galanter, E., & Pribram, K. H. *Plans and the structure of behavior*. New York: Holt, 1960.

Miller, N. E. Some reflections on the law of effect produce a new alternative to drive reduction. In M. R. Jones (Ed.), *Nebraska symposium on motivation: 1963*. Lincoln: Univ. of Nebraska Press, 1963. Pp. 65–112.

Miller, N. E., & Dollard J. *Social learning and imitation*. New Haven: Yale Univ. Press, 1941.

Mishkin, M. Visual discrimination performance following partial ablations of the temporal lobe: II. Ventral surface vs. hippocampus. *J. comp. physiol. Psychol.*, 1954, **47**, 187–193.

Montessori, Maria. *The Montessori method: scientific pedagogy as applied to child education in "The Children's House: with additions and revisions.* (Trans. by Anne E. George) New York: Frederick Stokes, 1912. Originally published in 1909.

Montgomery, K. C. A test of two explanations of spontaneous alternation. *J. comp. physiol. Psychol.*, 1952, **45**, 287–293.

Montgomery, K. C. Exploratory behavior as a function of "similarity" of stimulus situations. *J. comp. physiol. Psychol.*, 1953, **46**, 129–133. (a)

Montgomery, K. C. The effect of hunger and thirst drives upon exploratory behavior. *J. comp. physiol. Psychol.*, 1953, **46**, 315–319. (b)

Montgomery, K. C. The role of exploratory drive in learning. *J. comp. physiol. Psychol.*, 1954, **47**, 60–64.

Moore, H. T. The genetic aspect of consonance and dissonance. *Psychol. Rev. Monogr. Suppl.*, 1914, **17**, No. 2 (Whole No. 73), 1–68.

Moore, O. K. Autotelic responsive environments and exceptional children. Mimeographed paper, Rutgers Univ., 1964.

Morgan, C. L. *An introduction to comparative psychology.* (2nd ed.) London: Scott, 1909. Originally published in 1894.

Mowrer, O. H. On the psychology of "talking birds"—a contribution to language and personality theory. In O. H. Mowrer, *Learning theory and personality dynamics.* New York: Ronald Press, 1950. Chap. 24.

Mowrer, O. H. *Learning theory and behavior.* New York: Wiley, 1960.

Munsinger, H., & Kessen, W. Uncertainty, structure, and preference. *Psychol. Monogr.*, 1964, **78** (Whole No. 586), 1–24.

Munsinger, H., & Kessen, W. Stimulus variability and cognitive change. *Psychol. Rev.*, 1965, **72**, scheduled for November.

Myres, A. K., & Miller, N. E. Failure to find learned drive based on hunger: evidence for learning motivated by "exploration." *J. comp. physiol. Psychol.*, 1954, **47**, 428–436.

Newell, A., Shaw, J. C., & Simon, H. A. Elements of a theory of human problem solving. *Psychol. Rev.*, 1958, **65**, 151–166.

Nichols, I., & Hunt, J. McV. A case of partial bilateral frontal lobectomy: a psychopathological study. *Amer. J. Psychiat.*, 1940, **96**, 1063–1083.

Nissen, H. W. A study of exploratory behavior in the white rat by means of the obstruction method. *J. genet. Psychol.*, 1930, **37**, 361–376.

Osgood, C. E. The nature and measurement of meaning. *Psychol. Bull.*, 1952, **49**, 197–237.

Padilla, S. G. Further studies on the delayed pecking of chicks. *J. comp. Psychol.*, 1935, **20**, 413–443.

Pavlov, I. P. *Conditioned reflexes.* (Trans. by G. V. Anrep) London: Oxford Univ. Press, 1927.

Piaget, J. *Play, dreams, and imitation in childhood.* (Trans. of *La formation du symbole chez l'enfant* by C. Gattegno & F. M. Hodgson) New York: Norton, 1951. Originally published in 1945.

Piaget, J. *The origins of intelligence in children.* (Trans. by Margaret Cook) New York: International Universities Press, 1952. Originally published in 1936.

Piaget, J. *The psychology of intelligence.* (Trans. by M. Piercy & D. E. Berlyne) Paterson, N.J.: Littlefield, Adams & Co., 1960. Originally published in 1947.

Pratt, K. C. The neonate. In L. Carmichael (Ed.), *Manual of child psychology.* (2nd ed.) New York: Wiley, 1954. Chap. 4. Originally published in 1946.

Pribram, K. H. Neocortical function in behavior. In H. F. Harlow & C. N. Woolsey (Eds.), *Biological and biochemical bases of behavior.* Madison: Univ. of Wisconsin Press, 1958. Pp. 151–172.

Pribram, K. H. A review of theory in physiological psychology. *Annu. Rev. Psychol.*, 1960, 11, 1–40.

Ramsay, A. O. Familial recognition in domestic birds. *Auk*, 1951, 58, 57–58. Cited by Thorpe, 1956.

Razran, G. The observable unconscious and the inferable conscious in current Soviet psychophysiology: interoceptive conditioning, semantic conditioning, and the orienting reflex. *Psychol. Rev.*, 1961, 68, 81–147.

Rheingold, Harriet L., Stanley, W. C., & Cooley, J. A. Method for studying exploratory behavior in infants. *Science*, 1962, 136, 1054–1055.

Ribble, Margaret A. Infantile experience in relation to personality development. In J. McV. Hunt (Ed.), *Personality and the behavior disorders.* New York: Ronald Press, 1944. Chap. 20.

Richter, C. P. Animal behavior and internal drives. *Quart. Rev. Biol.*, 1927, 2, 307–343.

Rickers-Ovsiankina, Maria. Die Wiederaufnahme unterbrochener Handlungen. *Psychol. Forsch.*, 1928, 11, 302–375.

Riesen, A. H. The development of visual perception in man and chimpanzee. *Science*, 1947, 106, 107–108.

Riesen, A. H. Plasticity of behavior: psychological aspects. In H. F. Harlow & C. N. Woolsey (Eds.), *Biological and biochemical bases of behavior.* Madison: Univ. of Wisconsin Press, 1958. Pp. 425–450.

Rogers, C. R. *Client-centered therapy.* Boston: Houghton Mifflin, 1951.

Romanes, G. C. *Animal intelligence.* New York: Appleton, 1883.

Rose, J. E., & Woolsey, C. N. The relations of thalamic connections, cellular structure and evocable electrical activity in the auditory region of the cat. *J. comp. Neurol.*, 1949, 91, 441–466.

Ruckmick, C. A. *The psychology of feeling and emotion.* New York: McGraw-Hill, 1936.

Schachter, S., & Latané, B. Crime, cognition, and the autonomic nervous system. In D. Levine (Ed.), *Nebraska symposium on motivation: 1964.* Lincoln: Univ. of Nebraska Press, 1964.

Schachter, S., & Singer, J. E. Cognitive, social and physiological determinants of emotional state. *Psychol. Rev.*, 1962, **69**, 379–399.

Schachter, S., & Wheeler, L. Epinephrine, chlorpromazine, and amusement. *J. abnorm. soc. Psychol.*, 1962, **65**, 121–128.

Schaffer, H. R., & Emerson, Peggy E. The development of social attachments in infancy. *Monogr. Soc. Res. Child Develpm.*, 1964, **29**, No. 3 (Serial No. 94).

Schlosberg, H., & Stanley, W. C. A simple test of the normality of twenty-four distributions of electrical skin resistance. *Science*, 1953, **117**, 35–37.

Schneirla, T. C. An evolutionary and developmental theory of biphasic processes underlying approach and withdrawal. In M. R. Jones (Ed.), *Nebraska symposium on motivation: 1959*. Pp. 1–43.

Schneirla, T. C. Aspects of stimulation and organization in approach/withdrawal processes underlying vertebrate behavioral development. In D. H. Lehrman, R. Hinde, and Evelyn Shaw (Eds.), *Advances in the study of behavior*. New York: Academic Press, 1964.

Schulte, R. H. The effect of drugs and experience on preference for stimulus variability. Unpublished doctoral dissertation, Univ. of Illinois, 1964.

Scott, J. P. Social behavior, organization, and leadership in a small flock of domestic sheep. *Comp. Psychol. Monogr.*, 1945, **18** (4), 1–29.

Sears, R. R., Maccoby, Eleanor E., & Levin, H. *Patterns of child rearing.* Evanston, Ill.: Row, Peterson, 1957.

Sears, R. R., Whiting, J. W. M., Nowlis, V., & Sears, P. S. Some child-rearing antecedents of aggression and dependency in young children. *Genet. Psychol. Monogr.*, 1953, **47**, 135–234.

Sechenov, I. M. Reflexes of the brain. In *Sechenov's selected works.* Moscow-Leningrad: State Publications House, 1935. Originally published in 1863.

Séguin, E. *Idiocy and its treatment by the psychological method.* Albany, N.Y.: Teachers College, Columbia Univ., 1907. Originally published in 1866.

Sharpless, S., & Jasper, H. H. Habituation of the arousal reaction. *Brain*, 1956, **79**, 655–680.

Shirley, Mary M. *The first two years: a study of 25 babies.* Vol. 2. *Intellectual development.* Inst. Child Welf. Monogr. Ser., 1933, No. 7, 513 ff. (Minneapolis: Univ. of Minnesota Press)

Skeels, H. M. Some preliminary findings of three follow-up studies on the effects of adoption on children from institutions. *Children*, 1965, **12** (1), 33–34.

Skeels, H. M., & Dye, H. B. A study of the effects of differential stimulation on mentally retarded children. *Proc. Amer. Ass. ment. Def.*, 1939, **44**, 112–136.

Skinner, B. F. Are learning theories necessary? *Psychol. Rev.*, 1950, **57**, 193–216.

Skinner, B. F. *Science and human behavior.* New York: Macmillan, 1953.

Skinner, B. F. The experimental analysis of behavior. *Amer. Scientist*, 1957, **45**, 343–371.

Smedslund, J. Concrete reasoning: a study of intellectual development. *Monogr. Soc. Res. Child Develpm.*, 1964, **29**, No. 1 (Serial No. 93), 1–39.

Spitz, R. A. Hospitalism: an inquiry into the genesis of psychiatric conditions of early childhood. *Psychoanal. Stud. Child*, 1945, **1**, 53–74.

Spitz, R. A. Hospitalism: a follow-up report. *Psychoanal. Stud. Child*, 1946, **2**, 113–117.

Spitz, R. A., & Wolf, K. M. The smiling response: a contribution to the ontogenesis of social relations. *Genet. Psychol. Monogr.*, 1946, **34**, 57–125.

Stirnimann, F. Über das Farbenemphinden Neugeborener. *Ann. Paedia.*, 1944, **163**, 1–25.

Suchman, J. R. Inquiry training in the elementary school. *Sci. Teacher*, 1960, **27**, 42–47.

Taylor, D. W. Toward an information processing theory of motivation. In M. R. Jones (Ed.), *Nebraska symposium on motivation: 1960*. Lincoln: Univ. of Nebraska Press, 1960. Pp. 51–78.

Thorndike, E. L. Animal intelligence. *Psychol. Rev. Monogr. Suppl.*, 1898, **2**, No. 8.

Thorpe, W. H. The learning ability of birds. *Ibis*, 1951, **93**, 1–52 & 252–296.

Thorpe, W. H. *Learning and instinct in animals*. London: Methuen, 1956.

Tolman, E. C. The determiners of behavior at a choice point. *Psychol. Rev.*, 1938, **45**, 1–41.

Tolman, E. C. A stimulus-expectancy need-cathexis psychology. *Science*, 1945, **101**, 160–166.

Tomkins, S. The psychology of knowledge. Invited address, Div. 8, Amer. Psychol. Ass., Los Angeles, September, 1964; mimeographed.

Uzgiris, Ina C. Situational generality of conservation. *Child Develpm.*, 1964, **35**, 831–841.

Uzgiris, Ina C., & Hunt, J. McV. A longitudinal study of recognition learning. Paper presented at Soc. Res. Child Develpm., Minneapolis, March, 1965.

Venable, V. *Human nature: the Marxian view*. New York: Knopf, 1945.

Walker, E. L. Psychological complexity as a basis for a theory of motivation and choice. In D. Levine (Ed.), *Nebraska symposium on motivation: 1964*. Lincoln: Univ. of Nebraska Press, 1964. Pp. 47–95.

Walters, R. H., & Parke, R. D. The role of the distance receptors in the development of social responsiveness. To be published in L. P. Lipsitt & C. C. Spiker (Eds.), *Advances in child development and behavior*. Vol. 2. New York: Academic Press, 1965.

Warren, R. P., & Pfaffmann, C. Early experience and taste aversion. *J. comp. physiol. Psychol.*, 1958, **51**, 263–266.

Watson, J. B., & Rayner, R. Conditioned emotional reactions. *J. exp. Psychol.*, 1920, **3**, 1–14.

White, B. L., & Castle, P. W. Visually exploratory behavior following post-natal handling in human infants. *Percept. mot. Skills*, 1964, **18**, 497–502.

White, B. L., Castle, P. W., & Held, R. Observations on the development of visually directed reaching. *Child Develpm.*, 1964, **35**, 349–364.

White, R. W. Motivation reconsidered: the concept of competence. *Psychol. Rev.*, 1959, **66**, 297–333.

White, R. W. Competence and the psychosexual stages of development. In M. R. Jones (Ed.), *Nebraska symposium on motivation: 1960*. Lincoln: Univ. of Nebraska Press, 1960. Pp. 97–141.

Wiederhold, M. L. Effects of efferent pathways on acoustic evoked responses in the auditory nervous system. S.M. thesis, Department of Electrical Engineering, Massachusetts Institute of Technology, June, 1963.

Wiener, N. *Cybernetics*. New York: Wiley, 1948.

Woodworth, R. S. Reinforcement of perception. *Amer. J. Psychol.*, 1947, **60**, 119–124.

Yoshii, N. K., & Tsukiyama, K. EEG studies on conditioned behavior of the white rat. *Jap. J. Physiol.*, 1952, **2**, 186–193.

Zeigarnik, B. Das Behalten von erledigter und unerledigter Handlungen. *Psychol. Forsch.*, 1927, **9**, 1–85.

Ethnocentric and Other Altruistic Motives[1]

DONALD T. CAMPBELL

Northwestern University

When one who is not a specialist in human motivation is invited to address this esteemed symposium, his assignment must be to broaden the symposium's coverage by examining the relevance to motivational theory of his research, no matter how remote such relevance might seem. In my case, this moves me far from the usual excellent range of topics.

My current research, in collaboration with the anthropologist Robert A. LeVine, is on the cross-cultural study of ethnocentrism. Supported by a grant from the Carnegie Corporation, we are enabling cooperating anthropologists to spend an extra two months in the field to collect specialized data on intergroup relations, outgroup stereotypes, social-distance requirements vis-à-vis neighboring peoples, ingroup self-adulation, and other aspects of ethnocentrism. Background materials thought to be predictive of degrees of ethnocentrism are also being collected. An eighty-page field manual has been prepared to guide the data collection and to make the information as comparable as possible from culture to culture. Earlier and longer versions of the field manual have already been used among the Eskimos and Indians of northern Canada, in two groups in the Eastern New Guinea highlands, and among the Embu and Gusii of Kenya. For the Gusii, I was privileged to join Professor LeVine last spring in a three-month

[1] This paper is a product of the Cooperative Cross-Cultural Study of Ethnocentrism, supported by a grant from the Carnegie Corporation of New York to Northwestern University. Professor Robert A. LeVine, Anthropology and Human Development, University of Chicago, is co-director of the project.

period of field work among a group which he had extensively studied some six years earlier. Eventually, we hope to have data collected on some fifty traditional societies. We hope in this way to get numerous independent instances of indigenous inter-group relations and attitudes before these are covered over by the diffusion of the European pattern of nationalism. While the data are being collected for use in quantitative cross-cultural hypothesis testing in the tradition of Murdock (1949) and Whiting and Child (1953), they will also be reported in a series of ethnographic monographs on regional intergroup relations.

    We hope to be able to use these data in a comparative testing of the adequacy of various social-science theories insofar as they have implications for the arena of our data collection. These are theories that can be used to predict what sorts of groups are more ethnocentric (e.g., their child-rearing practices, their au-thority structure, their societal-complexity level, etc.); or theories that predict for any ingroup the outgroup toward which it will focus the most ethnocentric hostility; or theories that predict the content of the stereotyped images which groups will hold of one another. More than half of these theories are primarily psycho-logical in origin and thus have explicit motivational components. Such theories include frustration-aggression-displacement theory, authoritarian personality theory, self-esteem theory, perception theory, projection theory, identification theory, and reinforce-ment and generalization theory.

    But it is not only the psychological theories that have moti-vational components. Theories stated at the societal level imply those individual motivational processes that are requisite to their operation, even though these are not always spelled out. It is this source of motivational theory that receives attention in the present paper. Thus, while this research stems from the problem of prejudice typical of psychology's social psychology, it has moved into the arenas of sociology and anthropology, and for the sake of the breadth of this symposium, it is as a social scientist rather than a psychologist *per se* that I will write.

    The essay that follows is not typical of my participation in social psychology. And its motivation includes more than an altruistic desire to broaden the symposium's coverage. It involves a self-directed protest against the overly individualistic assumption as to human motivation which is dominant in social psychology today. This assumption can be called *skin-surface hedonism*, the notion that all human activity has as its goal the pleasurable activation of taste receptors and other erogenous zones, the reinforcements of food, sex, and pain avoidance. Thus Thibaut and Kelley (1959) and Homans (1961) and numerous others put forth a social psychology deriving group processes and structures entirely from the self-centered concern of the actors as to "What's there in it for me?"—a mutual back scratching on the part of fundamentally selfish organisms. I teach such a course myself, in which the principles of social psychology are organized around a loosened set of Hullian symbols, the formula $S \times D \times K \times H \rightarrow R$, and I was tempted to make my presentation here on the form whch Hull's K takes when so used, on acquiring K through observation and linguistic instruction, and on the utility of using the concept of negative K as well as positive K.

Such approaches seem to me to be appropriate applications of the strategy of deliberate initial oversimplification. We make our first model of rat and man as simple as possible. We scrupulously examine how far we can go with these few assumptions. We add parameters only when the data clearly force them upon us. The course of the development of the Hullian formula is this: an initial $S \rightarrow R$ became, step by step, $S \times H \rightarrow R$, then $S \times D \times H \rightarrow R$, and then $S \times D \times K \times H \rightarrow R$, as forced by specific findings. It is already more complex than this, but still a very drastic oversimplification. But we repeatedly forget that it is a deliberately oversimplified view we are using, or, if we do not forget it, our students do. Thus we contribute to or symtomatize an attitudinal climate in which many young people feel guilty if caught in an altruistic act, as if violating some higher ethic to "don't be a sucker" or "look out first for Number One." Thus I occasionally look at our teaching in social psychology with the revulsion that "this is *not* man as I know him." In such a mood the only social-psychology text I can find which portrays social man adequately is Asch (1952). Perhaps this is because Asch has put accuracy of description ahead of theoretical simplicity and rigor—something we eschew in the otherwise worthy strategy of deliberate oversimplification in theory building.

Perhaps I am manifesting that humanist's protest which in so many former reductionists betokens sentimental senility and the presence of maturing children old enough to take one's theories as recipes for life. Such scientifically irrelevant motives are hard to keep out, but they are not involved solely on the humanist's side. If, as I believe, the social sciences need open-minded individuals who are willing to question the culturally given, they are apt to recruit persons who are not only willing but eager to do so. Practitioners of the strategy of deliberate oversimplification are apt to have a scientifically irrelevant enjoyment of an iconoclasm which affronts cultural beliefs and a view of man's nature which deflates and demeans. However, humanist's protest though this essay be in part, it attempts to keep some standing with iconoclast and reductionist by showing the termite to share whatever nobility it ascribes to man.

REALISTIC-GROUP-CONFLICT THEORY

There have recently been a number of explicit reactions against psychologizing in the explanation of intergroup conflict. Abel (1941), White (1949), Bernard (1957a, 1957b), Newcomb (1960), and Faris (1962) have explicitly affirmed the inadequacy and irrelevancy of psychological explanations, usually with the frustration-aggression-displacement theory as an example. Some quotations will illustrate this point of view: "Warfare is a struggle between social organisms, not individuals. Its explanation is therefore social or cultural, not psychological" (White, 1949, p. 132). "To attempt to explain war by appeal of innate pugnacity would be like explaining Egyptian, Gothic, and Mayan architecture by citing the physical properties of stone" (White, 1949, p. 131). "Explaining the forces which lead a particular individual to become a warrior, or a soldier to be pugnacious and aggressive, no more explains why that individual's tribe or nation is fighting another nation than knowledge of the chemical composition of a boulder reveals the reasons why it rolls down hill when pushed" (Newcomb, 1960, p. 321). "Many prominent and influential investigators of intergroup interaction made an early choice of the wrong path in seeking the explanations in the processes of individual psychology and psychoanalysis. . . . Part of the difficulty appears to lie in defects of knowledge and theory in the above fields, but the more important part stems from failure to recognize the nature of collective processes" (Faris, 1962, p. 43).

Most of those who have rejected psychological explanations have espoused a point of view which is here called the realistic-group-conflict theory. This theory assumes that group conflicts are rational in the sense that groups do have incompatible goals and are in competition for scarce resources. Such "realistic" sources of group conflict are contrasted with those psychological theories which see intergroup conflicts as displacements or projective expressions of problems that are essentially intragroup or intra-individual in origin. Among those who have in some degree articulated the realistic-group-conflict point of view are Sumner (1906), Davie (1929), White (1949, 1959), Sherif (1953, 1961), Coser (1956), Bernard (1957a, 1957b), Newcomb (1960), and Boulding (1962). Not all of these eschew psychological explanations; for example, Coser and Boulding do not, nor does Sherif, except for the displacement-projective ones. But for all, realistic sources of group conflict are a primary emphasis. Much of the elegant elaboration of the theory has to do with the course of conflicts, with the formation of coalitions, with the optimal strategies in conflict, with relative payoffs, and with other features not transferable to the present setting (viz., Bernard, 1957a, 1957b; Boulding, 1962). Many other features, more descriptive than deductive perhaps, are highly relevant and are enumerated below. This enumeration is not completely parsimonious in that some principles are but more explicit spellings-out of other more general ones.

1. *Real conflict of group interests causes intergroup conflict.* Intergroup conflict is most intense where the real conflict of interests is greatest and where the conflicting parties have the

most to gain by victory. Since reasonable a priori statements can be made about the real conflict of interests between the groups in any area, this can be spelled out in terms of a number of more specific propositions. However, this will not be done immediately, because more economy of presentation will be achieved if a number of intermediate propositions linking threat and conflict to ethnocentrism are presented first.

2. *Real conflict of interests, overt, active, or past intergroup conflict, and/or the presence of hostile, threatening, and competitive outgroup neighbors, which collectively may be called "real threat," cause perception of threat.* This proposition is usually implicit, but it is needed for the inclusion of Sherif and much of Coser and more generally for the prediction from group-level phenomena to the corresponding sentiments of individual ingroup members. With this causal sequence in mind, the subsequent principles could be stated either in terms of real threat or in terms of perceived threat, or they could be stated as separate principles in both terms. As most characteristic of the literature being surveyed, the real-threat statement has been employed, with perceived threat implicit, except where perceived threat has other sources.

3. *Real threat causes hostility toward the source of threat.* While often left implicit as too obvious to need stating, this is a characteristic proposition of realistic-group-conflict theory. Sherif (1953; 1961, p. 45) states it in terms of the dislike of an outgroup emerging as a result of perceived threat or the perception of the outgroup as in conflict with the ingroup. The proposition implies a correlational relationship between degrees of threat and degrees of hostility. Sherif (1961, p. 45) makes this explicit, stating that the more important the goal competed for, the more hostility; the greater the value which is being threatened and the greater the perceived interference with goal attainment, the greater the hostility.

4. *Real threat causes ingroup solidarity.* This is the most recurrent and explicit proposition of the theory. White gives typical expression of it: "An international event at Pearl Harbor transformed a listless disgruntled mass of conscripts into a spirited

fighting force. It would make more sense to say that it is war that breeds martial spirit than to argue that pugnacious instincts cause wars" (1949, p. 133). Sumner becomes a realistic-group-conflict theorist on this point: "The exigencies of war with outsiders are what make peace inside, lest internal discord should weaken the we-group for war. These exigencies also make government and law in the ingroup, in order to prevent quarrels and enforce discipline" (1906, p. 12). This is one of Sherif's most emphasized points (1953, p. 196; 1961, p. 21), stated as the principal that the presence of a negatively related outgroup increases ingroup solidarity. This is likewise Coser's (1956, pp. 87–95) strongest theme, among the many well-articulated principles he presents. On this point he is able to cite Simmel, Sorel, Marx, Sumner, and many others. Other theorists stating this principle are Lewis (1961), Murphy and Kasdan (1959), and Boulding (1962, pp. 162–163). We can make no pretense to comprehensive citation of this most ubiquitous principle. For example, Dahrendorf (1964, p. 58) makes this application of it: "It appears to be a general law that human groups react to external pressure by increased internal coherence. In the East-West conflict, each society finds itself in such a position of pressure from without ... [which] may lead the liberal societies of the West to restrict internal liberties in the name of resistance to totalitarian pressure ... [resulting in] the paradoxical possibility that democracy can be destroyed while it is being protected." Rosenblatt (1964) has provided a number of additional citations to this point (Alexander, 1951, p. 208; Berkowitz, 1962, pp. 188–191; Clark, 1938; Hayes, 1926, chap. 7; Murdock, 1931; Myers, 1962; Pillsbury, 1919, chap. 3; Royal Institute of International Affairs, 1939; Simpson & Yinger, 1958, pp. 114, 339; Williams, 1947, p. 58).

5. *Real threat causes increased awareness of own ingroup identity.* This is stated in Coser's (1956, pp. 104–110) terms, but for convenience it can also be used to cover the accentuation of the distinctness and superiority of ingroup customs. Sherif emphasizes that threat and intergroup competition cause the exaggeration of ingroup virtues and the magnification of outgroup

vices (1961, pp. 21, 38, 45, 46, 143). Leach (1954) has illustrated in great detail how factional conflict can lead to otherwise disfunctional and artificial preservation of linguistic differences quite inconsistent with historical, racial, residential, or cultural antecedents. The reactivation of traditional languages under conditions of conflict, as in the Irish effort to re-establish Gaelic, are symptoms of this same principle. Sumner seems also to have had this in mind, though he uses ethnocentrism rather than external threat to represent the causal forces involved: "Ethnocentrism leads a people to exaggerate and intensify everything in their own folkways which is peculiar and which differentiates them from others. It therefore strengthens the folkways" (1906, p. 13).

6. *Real threat increases the tightness of group boundaries.* This principle is elucidated by Coser (1956, pp. 95–104). For convenience we will interpret tightness of group boundaries to refer not only to actual boundary marking, wall building, guard posting, traveler stopping, shibboleth usage, etc., but also, in a more figurative sense, to social-distance maintenance. Sherif has noted the effect of group competition on social distance (1961, p. 46).

7. *Real threat reduces defection from the group.* This point of Coser's (1956, pp. 95–104) specifies one aspect of ingroup solidarity.

8. *Real threat increases punishment and rejection of defectors.* This specific solidarity-maintaining mechanism of vengeance against renegades and apostates is noted by Coser (1956, pp. 67–72).

9. *Real threat creates punishment and rejection of deviants.* This solidarity mechanism of reduced tolerance for loyal innovators, revisionists, and heretics has been noted by both Coser (1956, pp. 70–71, 100–101) and Sherif (1961). Rokeach (1960, pp. 378–388) provides an extensive theoretical and empirical study of the effects of threat on dogmatism. At the level of threat to ingroup (in contrast to threat to individual persons), his most relevant evidence comes from a historical analysis of the degree of dogmatism found in papal encyclicals over a 1,200-year period.

The more real the threat, the greater the dogmatism, expressed by both the severity of punishment specified for deviators and the absolutism of the pronouncement.

10. *Real threat increases ethnocentrism.* The above points may be summarized by saying that the realistic-group-conflict theorists generate the whole syndrome of ethnocentrism from the reaction to conflict and threat from outgroups.

11. *False perception of threat from an outgroup causes increased ingroup solidarity and hostility toward the outgroup.* While the realistic-group-conflict theorists focus on real threat, they also note that the principles are subject to exploitation by leaders or those controlling communications media in a way which makes conflict and hostility toward outgroups a projective symptom of intragroup problems rather than a product of intergroup conflict. Thus Coser (1956, pp. 105–106) states that leaders may seek out an enemy or create a ficticious one just to preserve or achieve ingroup solidarity. This is certainly one of the most ubiquitous observations on the exploitative opportunism of nationalistic politics. White has stated it thus: "Hostility toward a foreign power or toward a minority group within a society is often an effective means of unifying a nation. In times of national emergency or crisis, therefore, a nation may attempt to achieve inner unity and solidarity by fomenting hostility towards a foreign power—an old trick—or against a minority group within its gates—also an old trick" (1949, p. 137). Boulding (1962, p. 162) notes the principle. Rosenblatt (1964), in a review of parallel principles in ethnocentrism and nationalism, provides these citations: Alexander (1951, p. 281), Allport (1933, chap. 7), Bay et al. (1950, pp. 8, 93 ff.), Braunthal (1946, chap. 4), Gilbert (1950, pp. 28–30), Hayes (1926, chap. 3), Hertz (1944, p. 218), Machiavelli (1947, p. 65), Murdock (1931), Pillsbury (1919, chap. 3), Royal Institute of International Affairs (1939), Simpson and Yinger (1958, p. 114), Skinner (1959, p. 8), and Znaniecki (1952, pp. xiv–xv).

These basic propositions lead to more specific predictions which the data being collected by the Cooperative Cross-Cultural

Study of Ethnocentrism might optimistically be hoped to test. These will be listed here but not expanded upon, as they are not central to the development of the present argument:

The weakest group in a local cluster should be the most ethnocentric.

In cross-cultural correlations, the weaker groups should be less ethnocentric.

Groups within regional clusters should tend to be homogeneous in strength and ethnocentrism.

The more dissimilar an ingroup's economy from that of its outgroups, the less ethnocentric it should be.

The ingroup should show the least ethnocentric hostility toward the outgroup with the least similar economy.

Groups exploiting natural resources in short supply should be more ethnocentric than groups utilizing abundant resources.

Those groups with the most movable wealth should be the most ethnocentric.

Those groups most isolated from other groups should be least ethnocentric.

The farther an island is from the nearest land or other islands, the more likely it is to be divided into two conflicting groups.

The nearer outgroups should be the targets for more ethnocentric hostility than more remote ones.

The strongest and most threatening outgroup should be the target of the most ethnocentric hostility from an ingroup.

The more ethnocentric the ingroup, the more it should perceive outgroups as strong, aggressive, and effective rather than despising them as weak, cowardly, stupid, and lazy.

PSYCHOLOGICAL PROCESS FROM SOCIAL-LEVEL FUNCTIONALITY

In the frustration-aggression-displacement analysis of intergroup hostility, social processes are derived from functional mechanisms at the individual level. In contrast, in the realistic-group-conflict theory, the functionality is at the group level, but with inevitable implications for psychological processes.

The observation that outgroup threat to the ingroup increases individual hostility toward the outgroup and individual loyalty to the group is certainly one of the most agreed-upon observations of descriptive, non-experimental social science. It is so ubiqui-

tously observed, including our own personal experiences in wartime, as to seem to need no explanation. Yet it is not predictable
from the individualistic hedonism of modern learning theory,
Lewinian topology, cognitive-congruity theory, or psychoanalysis,
particularly when attention is called to individual willingness
to fight and die for the ingroup.

This willingness to risk death for group causes is, of course,
a rare commodity in peacetime and in sophisticated society. As
descriptions of the nonlethal character of much primitive war
show (Davie, 1929; Turney-High, 1949), it may also be a rare
commodity in more tradition-bound societies. Yet it is present,
and it is one of the things which makes lethal war possible. Even
the urban sophisticates, whose daily experiences leave them
unable to believe that such motives exist, find themselves willing
to die for novel causes, if not for shopworn ones. And such willingness to die bears little relation to the likelihood of success of
the cause in question. For substantial minorities, if not majorities, the mottoes "better a dead hero than a live coward,"
"better a dead ingrouper than a live outgrouper," "better a dead
Ibo than a live Yoruba," "better a dead Moslem than a live
Christian," "give me liberty or give me death," and "better
dead than red" are genuine sentiments to be backed by action.
So ubiquitous (if not universal) is this attitude, so important
is its role in making wars possible, that one joins Freud in agree-
ing that it must be something basic in man's social nature.
Agreement with Freud as to the importance of the problem does
not of course commit one to his solution of postulating a generally disfunctional death wish. Instead, one looks to the obvious
group-level functionality of such attitudes.

This motivational feature is being seriously neglected in
modern social-science discussions of the causes of war. Wars
may not be born in the minds of men, but the minds of men, the
nature of man, make wars possible. And among the many aspects
of that nature, the altruistic willingness for self-sacrificial death
in group causes may be more significant than the tendency for
covetous hostility toward outgroup members.

One aspect of the American scene calling attention to this

motivational feature is the regularly greater domestic popularity of international belligerency as opposed to international conciliation. Thus during the 1960 presidential elections, Kennedy held an initial advantage over Nixon because Nixon had inherited the Eisenhower "small military budget" position, allowing Kennedy to pose as the more bellicose, the more internationally intransigent. Nixon suffered under this unfair disadvantage all summer until, on the Quemoy and Matsu Islands issue, he was at last able to trick Kennedy into taking the more conciliatory stand. Pushing this issue, Nixon rapidly gained in popularity, coming close to overtaking Kennedy, who, however, on the Cuba issue, was finally able again to monopolize the more bellicose stand. An analysis of this and other American campaigns would no doubt show that the candidate who took the more bellicose position never felt the need for apologizing or feeling defensive about it, while the one with the more conciliatory attitudes inevitably felt that his loyalty was in question and that explanations were needed.

Similarly, it is probably true that in Kennedy's fluctuations of international stance while in office, he was more popular during the more belligerent periods. After the Cuba crisis of October, 1962, it was politically opportune to pillory those who had advocated the more moderate course, while those who had advocated irresponsibly aggressive approaches went unscathed: "there is apparently no penalty for recklessly truculent counsel in our national life, but ... there remains a constant hazard for the man who tries to seek tolerable alternatives. ... One is tempted to ask why there has been so little public agitation about the identity of those who recommended air attacks and so large an effort to picture Stevenson as the sinner in the affair" (Wechsler, 1963, pp. 16, 17). We judge this state of affairs to be made possible by this basic aspect of the ethnocentric syndrome.

There is a tendency in functional theory in sociology to regard pointing to a function as equivalent to explaining, an implicit assumption that groups will have those characteristics which make them function best. However, if a blatant teleology is to be avoided, a selective-survival evolutionary model needs to be made explicit: in a long history in which groups and individuals have varied widely and in which only some have survived, the surviving groups will tend to have those social customs and genes which have furthered survival in intergroup conflict. Note that both biological and sociocultural evolution may be involved.

DRIVES, INCENTIVES, AND REINFORCERS AS INTERNALIZED ECOLOGICAL CORRELATIONS

While there is a too-frequent tendency to stop the analysis as though a prime mover had been found whenever a drive or other motive has been hypothesized, most contributors to the physiology of motivation in the Nebraska Symposia on Motivation would no doubt interpret the particular neural and endocrine mechanisms they describe as end products of an evolutionary process. Thus the drive of thirst and the reinforcing effect of drinking water are the innate internalizations of the value of water in maintaining vital processes. Thus the reinforcing effect of sweets, including saccharin, represents the approximate truism that such substances are more nourishing than others. This instance points out the manner in which an only partial ecological correlation becomes exaggerated into a rigid rule of selection when internalized. It also indicates the important fact that the truths, the ecological correlations mapped in motivational systems, have only a retrospective validity. If the environment has changed radically, they may no longer have survival value. Thus the increased availability of manufactured sweets and the lower caloric output required in modern environments have made the reinforcing value of sugar disfunctional. Note also that had saccharin been abundantly present in the past environment of vertebrates and man, the sense-organ system would no doubt have evolved an ability to discriminate saccharin from nutritive sweets.

Modern research in the physiological psychology of motivation has fragmented our earlier view of one general drive and drive-reduction. Instead, we now have a steadily lengthening list of quite specific instigator and reinforcement sense-organ and effector subsystems. But for each, a past survival relevance can be assumed—each reflects some partial truth about organism-environment relations. This holds for the innate pains and aversions as well as for the innate incentives and reinforcers.

In the continuing expansion of our catalog of drives, incentives, and reinforcers, we will continue to work at the experimental behavioral and physiological level. We may indeed not be too far from the day when a skillful anatomist may be able to diagnose an as yet uncataloged motive by tracing neuron pathways in the brain. Another approach is to study organism-ecology relationships and to posit motivational syndromes to correspond to the strong survival functions which are available for exploitation. Although this is more problematic and presumptive, I believe that it merits examination as a supplementary approach. It will be employed in what follows.

To work from opportunity to mechanism runs the risk of teleology or tautology, which can only be avoided by a probabilistic interpretation of blind mutation and selective retention processes and by acceptance of limits to the generalization. The greatness of Darwin's contribution was not, of course, the concept of evolution of the complex from the simple or of the origin of diverse species from a common progenitor; rather, it was his concept of "natural selection," whereby the exquisite fit of organism to environmental opportunity could be explained by the differential propagation of blind, haphazard variation without recourse to teleology, plan, or external guidance. In this differential propagation, the organism's structure came to map the environment and to exploit its opportunities in ways as deterministically comprehensible as the learning of a maze pattern by the trial and error of a blind rat (Campbell, 1959, 1960). To work from maze shape to rat running path or from environmental opportunity to organismic structure requires the assumption that among the innumerable responses blindly emitted or among the innumerable genetic mutations over the eons, some will occur that will be enough more appropriate than others to lead to a differential reinforcement or differential survival rate. This will obviously not be so where the required variation is at a great variation distance from the prior adaptive form or response repertory. Thus we could design a maze which a blind rat would never learn because of its reluctance to explore in open space, where wall contact must be lost. Similarly, many highly functional organic forms may never have been evolved because they were too many mutation steps from existing forms. Only where each mutation step contributes a selection advantage can a complex form like the eye evolve. Nonetheless, modern evolutionary theorists argue that all ecological niches (opportunity patterns) that are near to prior forms will tend to be filled. Thus when Darwin's finches (Lack, 1947) landed on the Galápagos Islands, they found the ecological niches for woodpeckers, robins, and flycatchers unfilled and hence evolved finch-based imitations of these various forms. Similarly, there are ecological niches for herbivores, and these create an ecological niche for carnivores, and thus the marsupials in Australia have evolved to fill all these niches, including a remarkably wolf-like marsupial predator. It is the selective retention from among innumerable variations that makes the environment appear to cause or to shape organic form and behavioral repertory. It is the bias placed by the environment upon the blind or quasi-random variations which makes the extremely unlikely adaptive variant almost inevitable in the long course of evolution.

Convergent evolution, those cases in which evolutionary sequences starting from quite different origins converge on common form and function, testify with particular clarity to the existence of an advantageous ecological niche. Thus winged flight has been independently invented by pterodactyls, birds, bats, and insects. Thus the eye has been developed in strikingly similar form by vertebrates and the cephalopod octopus. The great selective advantage of these forms is obvious.

THE SURVIVAL VALUE OF SOCIAL ORGANIZATION

A convergent evolution on a complex pattern of social coordination that we may call "urban" has repeatedly occurred. In such "urban" social life there occur these features: an apartment-house mode of residence, a nonperishable food produced and stored in surplus, a full-time division of labor, including members who do no food producing themselves, being fed by others, and with one of the first occupational specialties being professional soldiers. Such urban civilizations have apparently arisen independently several times in the course of human history (Steward, 1955a, 1955b), as in Egypt, Mesopotamia, China, India, Peru, and Mexico. If we keep the list of common features at this minimal level, the convergence repeatedly occurs among the social insects (Allee, Emerson, Park, Park, & Schmidt, 1949).

Not once but several times have solitary cockroach-like species evolved into social termites. Quite independently, the social ants have shown a convergence on the same pattern of stored foods and worker and soldier castes. Although ants and bees are closer relatives than ants and termites, their common progenitors were solitary species, not social. In all cases, the social forms appear to have come later than the solitary ones, representing a superior adaptation. Solitary forms with social progenitors are certainly rare, if ever occurring. This repeated convergence points to a very strong survival value in the pattern of social coordination. And while sociocultural evolution (Campbell, 1965) is involved in one case and biological evolution in the other, one would expect parallel individual motivations to exist, supporting the social functions. In the following paragraphs, some of the advantages or economies of social life are noted, with hypotheses as to the individual values or motives that would sustain their operation.

Economy of Cognition

From the standpoint of a psychologist interested in cognitive processes, one of the most obvious economies of social life is the economy of cognition, i.e., of processes whereby the trial-and-error explorations of one member serve to save others the trouble of entering the same blind alleys. In the social insects and man, such survival-relevant processes are readily observable, mediated by both observation and linguistic instruction. Asch (1952; Campbell, 1961) has called attention to the essential role played in social life of willingness to make use of the observations reported by others and, correspondingly, of reporting one's own observations so that others can depend upon them. Two requisite values emerge. On the one hand, there is a requirement of honesty by communicators. On the other hand, there is a requirement of trust in communication. These are presumably universal values in human societies.

The economy of cognition is clearly shown in the scouting activities of the social insects, in which the trial-and-error encounter of a food supply by one worker leads to a direct loco-motion to the food by the other workers. In the ants, this may be mediated by a scented backtracking. In the honeybees, it is achieved by a functionally linguistic instruction. Through the wagging dance described by Frisch (1950), the successful scout indicates the range and course, so that the other worker bees can fly directly to the new food source. Here, too, honesty and trust, or their functional equivalents, are required. Hives with scout bees that keep the good news to themselves or dance of non-existent treasures or give erroneous bearings undoubtedly occur from time to time and fail to survive. Similarly, trust, gullibility, and belief, or their functional equivalents, are required of the recipients of the messages and have survival value even if the recipients are occasionally deceived. The ecological pressure of the economy of cognition keeps honesty and trust as effective values. It is hard to see how it can be exploited without them.

At a more primitive level, this economy of cognition can be seen as operating through those mechanisms which enable ani-mals to profit from the misfortunes of their fellows. The squeal of the caught rabbit brings no big-brother rabbits to the rescue and is thus of no value to the squealer, but it does enable other rabbits to learn from his mistakes. The ape's dread of dead and dismembered ape bodies (Hebb, 1946) can be interpreted as serving a similar function.

Economy of Specialization and the Division of Labor

Ubiquitous in complex social life is the specialization of tasks and the division of labor. A minimal economic requirement is transportable foodstuffs, but the large-population division-of-labor complexes seem to have been built up only around food-stuffs that are not only transportable but also storable without spoilage (Forde, 1934, p. 418; Steward, 1955a, 1955b). Requisite values related to this complex include industriousness, surplus production, hoarding, abstinance from indulgence, and obligation to share.

Economy of Mutual Defense

This selective criterion received great emphasis from Kropotkin (1902, 1924) in his effort to revise the erroneously individualistic hedonism assumed by the early interpreters of Darwin. The concentrated defensive or offensive efforts of many individuals make them effective in instances where they would all be vanquished in a series of one-at-a-time encounters with the same foe. The requisite values are loyalty, altruistic willingness to sacrifice self for the group, etc. A division of labor along these lines allows for soldier castes with special armaments which interfere with food-producing work.

The ubiquity of the professional soldier among all of the early human cities and among the termites and ants is probably related to the need to protect the stored food supply from pillaging. This, rather than the need for the soldiers to keep the peasants enslaved, provides the common denominator crossing insect and human forms.

BIOLOGICAL VERSUS SOCIOCULTURAL EVOLUTION

In the case of the termites, it is biological evolution which is involved, and the individual motives which support the social system may thus be regarded as innate (although complexly so, in that it is an environmental difference in infancy which differentiates workers from soldiers and triggers to development one of the two quite separate motivational patterns which are potential in a genetic endowment identical for both). In the case of urban civilization, sociocultural evolution is involved, a selective retention of customs developing without necessary change in biological structure. Thus the human motives corresponding to urban civilization—the honesty, trust, hoarding, sharing, bravery, and loyalty—might well be regarded as acquired motives instilled in each new generation by social-indoctrination processes.

The dominant position in social psychology is of course to regard them as such. This by no means detracts from their importance nor contradicts the importance of social-level function in determining individual motivation.

From a biological point of view, however, it is hard to see how this could be purely so. The innumerable genes as mutation loci, the complex and indirect effects of each, the heterozygosity within and genetic variability between human groups, make likely genetic differences affecting the social-coordination function. Undoubtedly, the great increases in population ensuing from urban life and agriculture differentially propagated certain genetic combinations. The survival value of the economy of cognition, manifest in the learning of language, undoubtedly led to a genetic evolution of the capacity to learn language—though not a genetic inheritance of a specific language. Waddington (1960) has suggested that the great survival advantage of learned culture has led to an innate predisposition toward such learning, a deference to adult lore on the part of children which he finds the basis of the ethical sense in man. In a similar way, any mutations furthering in man a capacity for ingroup identification, outgroup hostility, and ethnocentric self-sacrificial loyalty would have had a past survival value.

While cities are clearly a social invention, not universal in man, groups and group life have a different status. Man's primate progenitors were undoubtedly social animals with a cooperative band life, even if not a complex division of labor. And the motives and values which have been enumerated above had survival value at this protohuman level as well as in urban agricultural life. The tremendous survival value of being social makes innate social motives as likely on a priori grounds as self-centered ones. These concepts are, of course, far from new. Darwin (1871) emphasized the survival value of social life and the probability that man's moral sense and group loyalty had instinctive bases rather than being learned modifications in the service of selfishness. Karl Pearson (1887, 1897) eloquently advocated this same point of view in criticism of those who, as Kidd and Spencer, drew their political conclusions solely from the implications of individual competition, neglecting selection at the group level.

These are heretical comments for a contemporary social psychologist. Social psychologists are perforce environmentalists in their research, for it is environments that can be manipulated and have been manipulated by the social forces we study. We are environmentalists because the genetic emphasis has been pre-empted by those who would minimize the effects of social experience and exaggerate the role of inherited individual differences, the right of inherited social rank, etc. (Pastore, 1949; Hofstadter, 1955). Furthermore, we have more than enough work cut out for ourselves dealing with the principles of environmental effect. These reasons should not, however, lead us to take a stand denying biological bases for social motives. The implications of genetic theory are such that in order to claim it irrelevant, one would have to develop specific theories as to why the normal processes of genetic selection had not taken place.

There is still in general psychology, as well as in social psychology, a great preference for the *tabula rasa* assumption. In part, this may get a specious justification from a feeling that it is more parsimonious to say "it is learned" than to say "it is inherited." From the evolutionary sequence, the reverse seems to be the case—in the more primitive organisms, coordinated behavior is instinctive which in the higher forms has to be learned. It is easier to design a machine that will perform a given act than to design one that will learn to perform it. The feeling of greater parsimony comes from a hidden vestige of dualism. We are loath to interpret a nonspecific general attitude or value as innate because we find it so hard to imagine how an inherited nervous system could be designed that would provide for such reactions. The anatomical problem is indeed great. But it is not eliminated when we say it is learned, for each learned habit, value, or general orientation is just as fully embodied in physiological differentia as is any instinct.

Both sociologists and psychologists today give precedence to the psychological in explaining the social. On psychological grounds we can predict that aggregates of persons become more and more a social group the longer they are left together, definite movement in this direction occurring in a two-hour small-groups laboratory session. Thus the development of group consensus or norms is presaged by a number of psychological mechanisms. Principles of observational learning and/or conformity lead to the prediction that on those problems discussed and reacted to, the person-to-person similarity will increase. Principles of cognitive dissonance predict that those members expressing the most dissident opinions will have the most persuasive messages addressed to them because of the motivating effects their discordant opinions have on their listeners. This furthers the homogenization of opinion. Increased interaction under normal conditions increases interpersonal liking, thus generating a group loyalty, etc. Even a division of labor or a turn taking can be predicted from the mutually extinguishing effects of responses that produce collisions. In such a manner, group processes can be predicted from principles of individual psychology.

A thorough study of the individual psychology of termite workers, queens, and soldiers would in a similar way lead us to predict, on the basis of purely individual motives and reactions, the emergence of collaborative effort, mutual feeding and grooming, group reaction to an invasion of ants, etc. But in this latter case we would not be tempted to view the group-level product as an incidental implication of processes basically individual— we would instead see the individual motivations as being what they are just because of the group functionality and its survival value. May not the same be said—in part at least—for the individual psychological motivations of the human being?

Rationalistic social-contract theories that saw social life as an intelligent decision on the part of totally selfish hedonistic calculators who had a prior solitary existence was pseudoanthropology, even in Rousseau's time, and is not accepted as descriptive in anthropology or sociology today. Nor did it ever explain the selfless behavior which makes lethal wars possible. Yet most psychologists approach social behavior with some such model in mind (e.g., Thibaut & Kelley, 1959; Homans, 1961).

AMBIVALENCE AS OPTIMAL COMPROMISE

This is not to portray man as a purely social, purely altruistic animal. If man has altruistic motives, these are certainly mixed with the purely selfish. In this, man is no doubt a much less social animal than is the soldier or worker termite, as Freud noted. He says of human social life: "Civilization is a process in the service of Eros whose purpose is to combine single human individuals, and after that, families, then races, peoples, nations, into one great unity, the unity of mankind. . . . But man's natural aggressive instinct, the hostility of each against all and of all against each, opposes this program of civilization. . . . The struggle between Eros and Death, between the instinct of life and the instinct of destruction . . . is what all life essentially consists of, and the evolution of civilization may therefore be simply described as the struggle for life of the human species" (Freud, 1930; 1961, p. 122). He then contrasts the social animals: "Why do our relatives the animals not exhibit any such cultural struggle? We don't know. Very probably some of them—the bees, the ants, the termites—strove for thousands of years before they arrived at the state institutions, the distribution of functions, and the restrictions upon individuals, for which we admire them today. It is indicative of our present state that we should not think ourselves happy in any of these animal states, nor in any of the roles assigned by them to the individual" (Freud, 1930; 1961, p. 123). Henry (1955) makes an analogous distinction: "the crucial difference between insect societies and human ones is that whereas the former are organized to achieve homeostasis, the organization of the latter seems to guarantee and specifically provide for instability."

One essential difference between man and termite lies in the genetic unit of selection at the biological level. For the social insect, all individuals but the queen are sterile and are genetically identical. Selective survival relevant to evolution is solely at the group level. Thus group coordination and group survival are the only contributors to genetic change. For man, there is genetic differentiation and selection at the individual level. Thus there is selection both of tendencies leading one man to survive at the expense of another fellow ingroup member as well as tendencies leading one group to survive at the expense of another group. This dual selective system gets ensconced in man as a fundamental ambivalence between egoism and altruism, an ambivalence which the termite is spared. (A parallel analysis can, of course, be made of the duality of learning settings, in which man is reinforced both for cooperative effort and for self-seeking.) It is on this basis that the frustration-aggression-displacement theory of outgroup hostility becomes compatible with the altruism of realistic-group-conflict theory.

The presence in moral codes, proverb sets, and motivational systems of opposing values is often interpreted as discrediting the value system by showing its logical inconsistency. This is a misapplication of logic, and in multiple-contingency environments, the joint presence of opposing tendencies has a functional survival value. Where each of two opposing tendencies has survival relevance, the biological solution seems to be an ambivalent alternation of expressions of each rather than the consistent expression of an intermediate motivational state. Ambivalence, rather than averaging, seems the optimal compromise. William James has stated the point well:

> Since any entirely unknown object may be fraught with weal or woe, *nature implants contrary impulses to act on many classes of things*, and leaves it to slight alternations in the conditions of the individual case to decide which impulse shall carry the day. Thus greediness and suspicion, curiosity and timidity, coyness and desire, bashfulness and vanity, sociability and pugnacity, seem to shoot over into each other as quickly, and to remain in as unstable equilibrium, in the higher birds and mammals as in man [James, 1890, p. 392].
>
> Curiosity and fear form a couple of antagonistic emotions liable to be awakened by the same outward thing, and manifestly both useful to their possessor. The spectacle of their alternation is often amusing enough, as in the timid approaches and scared wheelings which sheep or cattle will make in the presence of some new object they are investigating. I have seen alligators in the water act in precisely the same way towards a man seated on the beach in front of them—gradually drawing near as long as he kept still, frantically careening back as soon

as he made a movement. Inasmuch as new objects *may* be advantageous, it is better that an animal not absolutely fear them. But inasmuch as they may also possibly be harmful, it is better that he should not be quite indifferent to them either [James, 1890, p. 429].

Schneirla, in this symposium (1959), has similarly emphasized the functionality of opposing motive sets.

Applied to our present problem, we can interpret altruistic, self-sacrificial ethnocentric motives as ambivalently balanced with the own-skin-saving self-centered ones. The normal peace-time exigencies of life are such that the altruistic ethnocentric components are rarely tapped, and the self-centered ones predominate. But the two sets of motives are not mutually exclusive, even though they are often ambivalently incompatible in expression. Altruism and self-seeking can coexist just as do exploratory curiosity and fear of the novel.

IMPLICATIONS

The wisdom produced by evolutionary processes—be they biological or sociocultural—is retrospective. While it is true that an evolutionary orientation gives a social scientist more respect for the adaptedness and adaptiveness of social custom and superstition than is possessed by the usual social psychologist, such respect can only be based upon the assumption that the aspects of the environment which shaped such form and function have not changed. Where the environment has changed fundamentally, the evolutionary product may be fundamentally disfunctional. Thus the presence of nuclear weapons may be judged a change in the environment so fundamental as to make ethnocentric loyalty and the willingness to risk one's own life in the process of attacking the outgroup no longer have the group survival value which they once had.

For an evolutionary process to take place, there need to be variations (as by mutation, trial, etc.), stable aspects of the environment differentially selecting among such variations and a retention-propagation system rigidly holding on to the selected variations. The variation and the retention aspects are inherently at odds. Every new mutation represents a failure of reproduction of a prior selected form. Too high a mutation rate jeopardizes the preservation of already achieved adaptations. There arise in evolutionary systems, therefore, mechanisms for curbing the variation rate. The more elaborate the achieved adaptation, the more likely are mutations to be deleterious, and therefore the stronger the inhibitions on mutation. For this reason, we may expect to find great strength in the preservation and propagation systems, which will lead to a perpetuation of once-adaptive traits long after environmental shifts have removed their adaptedness. While this has been stated in biological form, a similar expectation would hold for the products of sociocultural evolution (Campbell, 1965). For this reason, those who work on the design of political structures for the elimination of war should probably build so that the system will work even if man continues to be a being with stupidly provincial ethnocentric loyalties.

Viewing man's "animal soul" as basically selfish, viewing what is emotional, primitive, and irrational in man as autistic, we have tended to see the altruistic as moral, as the imposed achievement of civilization. Under a broader framework we must now, in some cases, be willing to see altruistic social motives as irrational and immoral, or at least amoral.

SUMMARY

A survey of sociological theories of intergroup conflict shows an impressive consensus for the proposition that outgroup threat to an ingroup increases ingroup solidarity and ethnocentric self-sacrificial loyalty. While such a reaction has had obvious group survival value in the past history of man, it is not readily derivable from the skin-surface hedonism characteristic of psychological theory. Consideration of the great competitive advantage of social life over solitary life leads to the expectation that biological and sociocultural evolution would have produced in both man and termite motivational dispositions furthering group life and reflecting its advantages, as in the economy of cognition, division of labor, and mutual defense. In some respects at least, man should be regarded as basically a social animal, with individual dispositions reflecting that fact. Because the wisdom of evolution is retrospective, social motivations such as are found in ethnocentrism may be judged disfunctional in a changed environment. In any event, the identification of the social and altruistic with the normatively moral should be held in abeyance.

REFERENCES

Abel, T. The element of decision in the pattern of war. *Amer. sociol. Rev.*, 1941, **2**, 853–859.

Alexander, F. *Our age of unreason.* (Rev. ed.) Philadelphia: Lippincott, 1951.

Allee, W. C., Emerson, A. E., Park, O., Park, T., & Schmidt, K. P. *Principles of animal ecology.* Philadelphia: Saunders, 1949.

Allport, F. H. *Institutional behavior.* Chapel Hill: Univ. of North Carolina Press, 1933.

Allport, G. W. *The nature of prejudice.* Cambridge, Mass.: Addison-Wesley, 1954.

Asch, S. E. *Social psychology.* New York: Prentice-Hall, 1952.

Bay, C., Gullvag, I., Ofstad, H., & Tonnessen, H. *Nationalism: a study of identifications with people and power.* Oslo: Institute for Social Research, 1950.

Berkowitz, L. *Aggression: a social psychological analysis.* New York: McGraw-Hill, 1962.

Bernard, J. The sociological study of conflict. In J. Bernard *et al., The nature of conflict.* Paris: UNESCO, 1957. Pp. 33–117. (a)

Bernard, J. Parties and issues in conflict. *J. confl. Resol.*, 1957, **1**, 111–121. (b)

Boulding, K. E. *Conflict and defense: a general theory.* New York: Harper, 1962.

Braunthal, J. *The paradox of nationalism.* London: St. Botolph, 1946.

Campbell, D. T. Methodological suggestions from a comparative psychology of knowledge processes. *Inquiry*, 1959, **2**, 152–182. Reprinted in A. Rapoport, L. Bertalanffy, & R. L. Meier (Eds.), *Yearb. Soc. gen. syst. Res.*, 1961, **6**, 15–29.

Campbell, D. T. Blind variation and selective retention in creative thought as in other knowledge processes. *Psychol. Rev.*, 1960, **67**, 380–400.

Campbell, D. T. Conformity in psychology's theories of acquired behavioral dispositions. In I. A. Berg & B. M. Bass (Eds.), *Conformity and deviation.* New York: Harper, 1961. Pp. 101–142.

Campbell, D. T. Social attitudes and other acquired behavioral dispositions. In S. Koch (Ed.) *Psychology: a study of a science.* Vol. 6. *Investigations of man as socius.* New York: McGraw-Hill, 1963. Pp. 94–172.

Campbell, D. T. Variation and selective retention in sociocultural evolution. In R. W. Mack, G. I. Blanksten, & H. R. Barringer (Eds.), *Social change in underdeveloped areas: a reinterpretation of evolutionary theory.* Cambridge, Mass.: Schenkman, 1965, in press.

Campbell, D. T., & LeVine, R. A. A proposal for cooperative cross-cultural research on ethnocentrism. *J. confl. Resol.*, 1961, 5, 82–108.

Clark, S. D. Canadian national sentiment and imperial sentiment. In H. F. Angus (Ed.), *Canada and her great neighbor.* Toronto: Ryerson, 1938. Pp. 225–248.

Coser, L. A. *The functions of social conflict.* Glencoe, Ill.: Free Press, 1956.

Dahrendorf, R. The new Germanies. *Encounter*, 1964, 22, 50–58.

Darwin, C. *The descent of man and selection in relation to sex.* London: J. Murray, 1871. Chap. 4. The moral sense.

Davie, M. R. *The evolution of war.* New Haven: Yale Univ. Press, 1929.

Faris, R. E. L. Interaction levels and intergroup relations. In M. Sherif (Ed.), *Intergroup relations and leadership.* New York: Wiley, 1962. Pp. 24–45.

Freud, S. *Civilization and its discontents.* London: Hogarth, 1930. Standard ed., Vol. 21, 1961.

Frisch, K. von. *Bees, their vision, chemical sense, and language.* Ithaca: Cornell Univ. Press, 1950.

Forde, C. D. *Habitat, economy, and society: a geographical introduction to ethnography.* London: Methuen, 1934.

Gilbert, G. M. *The psychology of dictatorship.* New York: Ronald Press, 1950.

Hayes, C. J. H. *Essays on nationalism.* New York: Macmillan, 1926.

Hebb, D. O. On the nature of fear. *Psychol. Rev.*, 1946, 53, 259–276.

Hebb, D. O., & Thompson, W. R. The social significance of animal studies. In G. Lindzey (Ed.), *Handbook of social psychology.* Cambridge, Mass.: Addison-Wesley, 1954. Pp. 532–561.

Henry, J. Homeostasis, society, evolution: a critique. *Scient. Month.*, 1955, 81, 305.

Hertz, F. *Nationality in history and politics.* New York: Oxford Univ. Press, 1944.

Hofstadter, R. *Social Darwinism in American thought.* (Rev. ed.) Boston: Beacon Press, 1955. (1st ed., Univ. of Philadelphia Press, 1944)

Homans, G. C. *Social behavior: its elementary forms.* New York: Harcourt, Brace, & World, 1961.

James, W. *Principles of psychology.* Vol. 2. New York: Holt, 1890.

Kropotkin, P. *Mutual aid: a factor in evolution.* New York: Doubleday, Page, 1902.

Kropotkin, P. *Ethics: origin and development.* New York: Dial Press, 1924. (Tudor, 1947)

Lack, D. *Darwin's finches.* Cambridge, Eng.: Cambridge Univ. Press, 1947.

Leach, E. R. *Political systems of highland Burma.* London: G. Bell, 1954.

Lewis, W. H. Feuding and social change in Morocco. *J. confl. Resol.*, 1961, 5, 43–54.

Lorenz, K. *Das sogenannte Böse: zur Naturgeschichte der Aggression.* Vienna: Borotha-Schoeler, 1963.

Machiavelli, N. *The Prince.* New York: Crofts, 1947.

Murdock, G. P. Ethnocentrism. In E. R. A. Seligman (Ed), *Encyclopedia of the social sciences.* Vol. 5. New York: Macmillan, 1931. Pp. 613–614.

Murdock, G. P. *Social structure.* New York: Macmillan, 1949.

Murphy, R. F., & Kasdan, L. The structure of parallel cousin marriage. *Amer. Anthropolgist,* 1959, **61**, 17–29.

Myers, A. Team competition, success, and the adjustment of group members. *J. abnorm. soc. Psychol.,* 1962, **65**, 325–332.

Newcomb, W. W. Toward an understanding of war. In G. E. Dole & R. L. Carneiro (Eds.), *Essays in the science of culture.* New York: Crowell, 1960. Pp. 317–336.

Pastore, N. *The nature-nurture controversy.* New York: King's Crown Press, Columbia Univ., 1949.

Pearson, K. The moral basis of socialism. In *The ethic of free thought.* London: T. Fisher Unwin, 1887. Pp. 317–345.

Pearson, K. Socialism and natural selection. In *The chances of death.* London: Edward Arnold, 1897. Pp. 103–139.

Pillsbury, W. B. *The psychology of nationality and internationalism.* New York: Appleton, 1919.

Rokeach, M. *The open and closed mind.* New York: Basic Books, 1960.

Rosenblatt, P. C. Origins and effects of group ethnocentrism and nationalism. *J. confl. Resol.,* 1964, **8**, 131–146.

Royal Institute of International Affairs. *Nationalism.* London: Oxford Univ. Press, 1939.

Schneirla, T. C. An evolutionary and developmental theory of biphasic processes underlying approach and withdrawal. In M. R. Jones (Ed.), *Nebraska symposium on motivation: 1959.* Lincoln: Univ. of Nebraska Press, 1959. Pp. 1–42.

Sherif, M., & Sherif, C. W. *Groups in harmony and tension.* New York: Harper, 1953.

Sherif, M., Harvey, O. J., White, B. J., Hood, W. R., & Sherif, C. W. *Intergroup conflict and cooperation: the robbers cave experiment.* Norman: Institute of Group Relations, Univ. of Oklahoma, 1961.

Simpson, G. E., & Yinger, J. M. *Racial and cultural minorities.* (Rev. ed.) New York: Harper, 1958.

Skinner, G. W. The nature of loyalties in rural Indonesia. In G. W. Skinner (Ed.), *Local, ethnic, and national loyalties in village Indonesia.* New Haven: Yale Univ. Southeast Asia Studies, 1959. Pp. 1–11.

Steward, J. H. *Theory of culture change: the methodology of multilinear evolution.* Urbana: Univ. of Illinois Press, 1955. (a)

Steward, J. H. (Ed.). *Irrigation civilizations: a comparative study.* Washington, D.C.: Pan American Union, 1955. (b)

Sumner, W. G. *Folkways.* New York: Ginn, 1906.

Thibaut, J. W., & Kelley, H. H. *The social psychology of groups.* New York: Wiley, 1959.

Turney-High, H. H. *Primitive war*. Columbia: Univ. of South Carolina Press, 1949.

Waddington, C. H. *The ethical animal*. London: Allen & Unwin, 1960.

Wechsler, J. A. The brothers Alsop and Adlai Stevenson. *The Progressive*, 1963, **27** (3), 14–18.

White, L. A. *The science of culture: a study of man and civilization*. New York: Farrar, Strauss, 1949.

White, L. A. *The evolution of culture: the development of civilization to the fall of Rome*. New York: McGraw-Hill, 1959.

Whiting, J. W. M., & Child, I. L. *Child training and personality*. New Haven: Yale Univ. Press, 1953.

Williams, R. M. Jr. *The reduction of intergroup tensions*. New York: Social Science Research Council, 1947. No. 57.

Znaniecki, F. *Modern nationalities*. Urbana: Univ. of Illinois Press, 1952.

Motivation in an Informational Psychology

J. P. GUILFORD

University of Southern California

It is probably unnecessary for me to begin by disclaiming any profound knowledge in the field of motivation, since it is probably known that this subject is not my prime area of specialization or even a strong secondary one. It is true that I have devoted some attention to studies of what I have chosen to call "hormetic" traits (of needs, interests, and attitudes) by the approach of factor analysis and that a chapter on these matters was included in my book on personality (Guilford, 1959a).

In some recent attempts toward the generation of general psychological theory (Guilford, 1961), I have also made some remarks concerning motivation in some considerations growing out of my analytical studies of human intellectual abilities. These remarks concerned particularly some views on the phenomenon of reinforcement in learning. In the course of reflection upon the many intellectual abilities or functions that have been differentiated, I have developed a conception that has been called an "informational psychology," which belongs in the category of cognitive theory (Guilford, 1962).

The decision was to devote this paper primarily to a consideration of how the problems of motivation appear from an informational point of view. In this connection, it is important to consider, also, what behavioral phenomena need to be accounted for, from any point of view. I shall take advantage of the opportunity to express some views regarding traditional theories of motivation. In connection with some background information concerning the nature of the informational psychology that I have in mind, I shall consider how it could account for some of the phenomena of motivation that have been matters of concern for other theories.

WHY PSYCHOLOGY NEEDS THE CONCEPT OF MOTIVATION

In spite of the fact that a psychologist now and then suggests that, in view of the glaring lack of agreement on the nature of motivation, it is time we replace the concept, the intelligent man on the street would not sanction such a move. For him, motives, when identified in particular instances of behavior, answer the practical question, the "why" of the behavior. The policeman who wants to put his finger on the right suspect and the judge and the jury who decide on the criminal's fate all think very much in terms of determining forces behind the criminal act. All those who deal directly with the behavior of others and who want to understand them give very high status to information about their desires and intentions. Very likely you have heard the story of the two psychiatrists who met on the street. Dr. A greeted his acquaintance with "Good morning, Dr. X," to which Dr. X replied, "Good morning. How are *you* this morning?" After passing, Dr. A turned to his companion, asking, "Now what do you think he meant by that?"

It is when we try to go behind and underneath the manifestations of what are popularly called "motives" that we find a nest of very baffling questions. The many investigators and thinkers about the subject, each coming at it from his own personal angle, remind one of the proverbial blind men and the elephant. I heard a poet say recently that sometimes after the blind men have given their views, the elephant walks away; there is no more elephant. I doubt that the motivation elephant will walk away; the problems under that heading are too real and too important.

Things To Be Accounted For

It is not only a matter of psychologists having only limited personal views of the phenomena of motivation; it is also true that the phenomena to be accounted for are themselves quite heterogeneous, even though they have somehow been coralled under the same label. Perhaps we should not attempt to account for all those phenomena by means of the same principle or set of principles. The things to be accounted for are well known to the members of this symposium, but for clarity of further discussion, it should pay to set them out explicitly.

Spontaneous behavior.—The behaviorist's original program for a completely objective psychology envisaged behavior as being a matter of the environment, which is all outside the organism's skin, applying stimuli and the organism reacting to those stimuli. But it was obvious almost immediately that much overt behavior could not be traced to environmental stimuli; much of it is spontaneous and apparently not externally aroused. If not externally instigated, then it must be internally instigated. The problem is then to determine the internal sources. The sources could be in the body but outside the nervous system or they could be inside the nervous system. If from inside the nervous system, they could arise from non-nervous tissue, such as the blood, or from nervous tissue itself. Such reasoning has guided physiological studies designed to pinpoint the sources of internally aroused behavior.

Variations of energy.—There are certain limited circumstances under which the energy or vigor of an overt response bears direct relation to the energy of the instigating stimulus, but it is obvious that the correlation is not very high. Stimuli of low energy can often trigger activity with a high degree of energy. Some stimuli are much more arousing than others, and the organism behaves at higher levels of activation at some times than at others, as shown in terms of levels of enthusiasm, speed, or power. Such phenomena are usually subsumed under the concept of motivation.

Direction of effort.—There is apparently less unanimity to the effect that motives have directing features, that they determine where sense organs are directed and where energies are turned. In this connection, there is sometimes talk of goals, sometimes not. Some writers speak unhesitatingly of purposiveness; some shrink from any suggestion of teleology. In these days of cybernetics and guided missiles, it should be much easier to accept the idea that behavior runs its course toward the achievement of goals. A guided missile is given a target or goal, and any deviation in its course is self-corrected to bring it back on course. It can thus have the distinct appearance of purposive behavior.

At any rate, organisms behave as if they were seeking certain environmental conditions, of safety, of comfort, of pleasurable stimulation, and of release from pain or unpleasant stimuli. They keep acting until those conditions are achieved, then cease further action of that kind. They also show choices between stimuli and between possible courses of action. It is not so very difficult, as a rule, to distinguish between ends in their behavior and means-to-end activity.

Incentives and values.—It is often recognized that environmental objects and events acquire motivational properties, for example, the cathexes of Freudian psychology, the valences of Lewin, and the incentives of Hull. Both positive and negative values are taken into consideration: attractions and repulsions. The way in which objects and events acquire incentive value and the roles of those values in determining behavior provide numerous problems.

Other motivational problems.—There are a number of other aspects of behavior that bear rather direct relations to motivation. Of these, more generally recognized are the phenomena of reinforcement, frustration, and conflict. Most learning theory gives a prominent place, if not a key role, to reinforcement. How shall reinforcement be interpreted and just how does it operate to effect fixation of learned behavior? What, precisely, happens when the organism's efforts toward reaching a goal are thwarted? What are the sources and consequences of conflicts? As we all know, the literature on these subjects is mountainous.

SOME VIEWS ON PRESENT CONCEPTIONS

I would feel rather presumptuous in making evaluative remarks regarding a field of which I know so little, except for some encouragement I find in the recent book by Cofer and Appley (1964). After a most thorough examination of the subject, they sum up the situation by saying: "It is clear that a comprehensive, definitive psychology of motivation does not yet exist" (p. 808).

This statement gives me courage to offer a few thoughts on some of the views.

First, it occurs to me that, as in so many other areas in the subject matter of psychology, we fall into the semantic trap of assuming that one concept, such as "motivation," surely indicates a unified thing. We have suffered from the same kind of error in our attitudes toward other concepts, such as reasoning, problem solving, creative imagination, and intelligence. On the one hand, a consequence may be failure to analyze where we should do so, as in connection with the nonmotivational concepts that I have just mentioned. Another consequence, as in connection with the concept of motivation, has been the all too common tendency to overgeneralize. We come out with such conclusions as those beginning with "All motivation is _____." All motivation is drive; all motivation is homeostasis; all motivation is activation level; all motivation is the hedonic aspect of behavior; all motivation is self-actualization; and so on. Such generalizations also reflect a common overemphasis on the urge for parsimony, to the extent that we attempt to find the simplest possible explanation in terms of a single key concept. Too many psychologists, like the wise men of old, are apparently in search of the philosopher's stone!

As we find many different kinds of intellectual functions, which should also mean that we shall have to recognize different kinds of learning phenomena, we should consider whether all the kinds of phenomena now enjoying a home under a single label of motivation actually call for a single explanation. Neal Miller (1961) appears to be entertaining the same question. Before attempting to force all the various phenomena now recognized under motivation into a single mold, it might well pay to reconsider seriously that whole range of phenomena to see whether theories of lesser scope are more appropriate. With some of the more restricted areas of behavior accounted for separately, a theory of larger scope might appear as a means of welding the lesser theories together, as, eventually, there must be encompassing behavioral theory, such as Hull and others have attempted.

The Question of Taxonomy of Motives

Where formerly psychologists and others often made an effort to draw up lists of instincts, more recently, but not so often, they have instead sometimes attempted to draw up lists of motives: innate and acquired, primary and secondary. There is much value in having such lists; they answer the question of *what* things exist in an area or aspect of behavior, and they keep us aware of the range or scope of phenomena in that area.

Following the lead of Hull and his very neat theory and taking cues from what could be learned about motives from the study of rats and other lower animals, the prevailing taxonomy became exceedingly limited. It is true that with the recognition of secondary drives the way was opened to a much greater scope, but the taxonomic effort stopped very much with the drives that could be considered primary, and even among these, only food hunger, thirst, and pain, to all of which behavior is aversive, were given much attention.

Not discounting at all the value of studies of these three primary motives in the behavior of rats and the implications that can be drawn in the way of hypotheses regarding human motivation, many of us have recoiled at the idea that man also lives with similar limitations. For example, it has especially been regarded necessary to support the thesis that man has an innate desire to acquire knowledge (White, 1961; Berlyne, 1962). From my undergraduate days in philosophy courses under Hartley Burr Alexander, I remember that he often quoted Aristotle, I believe it was, as saying, "All men, by nature, desire to know." A number of investigators have provided evidence for an innate curiosity drive, even in rats (for example, Montgomery, 1951). It has even been suggested that rats have a problem-solving motive (Havelka, 1956). After considering the results in general on the behavior of flatworms and annelids, Jacobson (1963) came to the general conclusion that their behavior, including motivational aspects, seems to be far more complex than common behavior theory would suggest.

Self-Actualization Theory

If the Hullian view of motivation goes far to one extreme,

the self-actualization view goes far in the opposite direction. Most views other than that of self-actualization rest upon the axiom that Darwin's principle of survival is the ultimate test of behavior and they seem to assume that no additional principle is needed. Application of the survival principle leads naturally to the concepts of adaptation and adjustment. Threats to survival arise and the organism attempts to remove those threats. More specifically, conditions of depletion and of discomfort come about and something is done to neutralize those conditions. Maintenance of homeostasis or equilibration are common descriptions of these events. Life is just one sequence of upsets of equilibrium and efforts to restore equilibrium.

Somehow, I have never been able to accept this simple, generalized picture of motivated behavior. Conservation of life there must be; this no one can deny. But it is rather apparent that the organism also does things that upset its own equilibrium as well as to restore it. Growth itself requires this, and only in this way can many of the new and higher states of equilibrium be achieved. Only in this way can many improvements occur. What constitutes improvement, of course, depends upon what we recognize as values, but I think all of us would agree that it is better to be men than mice, better to be supermen than cavemen. The principle of survival alone could hardly bring about such improvements. Amoebae have survived for millions of years; they have passed the test of survival and continue to do so. What is the goal in addition to survival? Frankly, I do not know. But it may be expressed fairly well in the words from a popular song: "You can be better than you are."

For reasons just indicated, I must confess that the self-actualization view has considerable general appeal, but from a scientific point of view, it leaves very much to be desired. One must decry its vagueness and its looseness of concepts that lack empirical reference. I feel very uncomfortable when I read about it. The view is largely in the category of philosophical speculation rather than scientific theory. This does not prohibit its application in the technology of psychotherapy, for in technologies, the pragmatic test of "Does it work?" is regarded as sufficient. And in the field of psychotherapy, unfortunately, almost any procedures, based upon quite heterogeneous types of theories, seem to work well enough to yield partial reinforcements. And as I understand it, partially reinforced behavior is more difficult to extinguish in the face of lack of evidence. Thus, technology may offer little in the way of tests of a theory. There is a long way to go, yet, in putting self-actualization theory to empirical test.

Cybernetic Views

It would seem that the best hope at present for putting purposive or goal-seeking aspects of motivation, including self-actualization, into scientifically respectable form is through an application of the kind of thinking demonstrated by the discipline of cybernetics. Cybernetics, as most of you are aware, deals with self-regulating systems, as in automated procedures and in computer operations. Such systems call our attention to the importance of information transmission. In automated devices, as in living organisms, there is a clear distinction between two functions of energy. There is the energy that carries out the various operations, where work must be done, and there is the energy that has control functions, where triggering and release of much greater quantities of energy are involved. There is also a sensing mechanism for detecting the nature of actions accomplished, supplying feedback information, and there are devices for effecting the necessary corrections to keep the system operating toward its goal.

Goals are pre-set. In the case of self-regulating machines, the pre-setting is imposed by the builder and the operator. In the case of the living organism, goals are basically determined intrinsically, and their sources provide some of the problem in the general area of motivation. The emphasis upon information transmission and upon a need for an operational kind of analysis is congruent with what I am suggesting as an informational type of psychology.

BACKGROUND OF AN INFORMATIONAL PSYCHOLOGY

As I indicated earlier, I was led into efforts toward psychological theory through experience in analyzing intelligence into component abilities by means of factor analysis. This experience covers the past sixteen years at the University of Southern California, four years of wartime experience in the investigation of components of aptitude for aviation flying personnel, and two years before that in my connection with the Bureau of Instructional Research here at the University of Nebraska, on top of an interest in intelligence testing dating back to graduate-student days.

Structure-of-Intellect Theory

Beginning about ten years ago, when the number of recognized intellectual abilities approached about forty, efforts were initiated to put some kind of logical order and system into the growing list, the consequence of which, by 1959, was the morphological model baptized as the "structure of intellect," an illustration of which can be seen in Figure 1 (Guilford, 1959b). The model, in the form of a three-dimensional matrix, is a cross-classification of the abilities, first, according to five major kinds

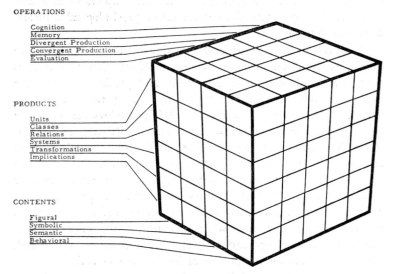

OPERATIONS

Cognition
Memory
Divergent Production
Convergent Production
Evaluation

PRODUCTS

Units
Classes
Relations
Systems
Transformations
Implications

CONTENTS

Figural
Symbolic
Semantic
Behavioral

Fig. 1. Model for the structure of intellect (I am indebted to Dr. Ralph Hoepfner for designing this version of the model).

of *operations*—cognition, memory, divergent production, convergent production, and evaluation; second, according to four major kinds of *contents* (categories of information)—figural, symbolic, semantic, and behavioral; and third, according to six kinds of *products* of information—units, classes, relations, systems, transformations, and implications.

Formal definitions of the fifteen categories of factors will not be presented here; a few illustrations should suffice to indicate their general characters. Reference to Figure 2 will show examples of the four major kinds of information (content) in the segment representing memory storage. At the left are a number of visual objects having only figural properties of color, shape, and size. Even letters, to those who are not familiar with the Roman alphabet, have figural properties only. When recognized as letters, they also become symbolic elements. A combination of them, as in a syllable or a word, becomes a symbolic unit. When a printed word is not only recognized as a familiar symbolic entity but also conveys meaning, that meaning is semantic content and the idea is a semantic unit. The expressive face and hands at the right stand for behavioral or psychological information that they suggest.

Each cell in the cubical model in Figure 1 represents a unique ability or function, unique by reason of its conjunction of a particular kind of content, operation, and product. To test the ability to cognize symbolic units, we may present anagrams, such as HRIAC, RESEV, and RECNAT, to see how efficiently the examinee can see familiar words: CHAIR, VERSE, and CANTER. To test the ability identified as divergent production of semantic systems, we may give a test in which the examinee must produce a number of organized four-word sentences in a limited time. To test the ability of convergent production of behavioral systems, we may present in random order four pictures from a cartoon sequence, where the proper sequence is determined by the feelings and actions of the characters concerned, asking the examinee to put them in the correct order.

In support of the validity of the model as a heuristic device, I can report that since its first conception in this form, about

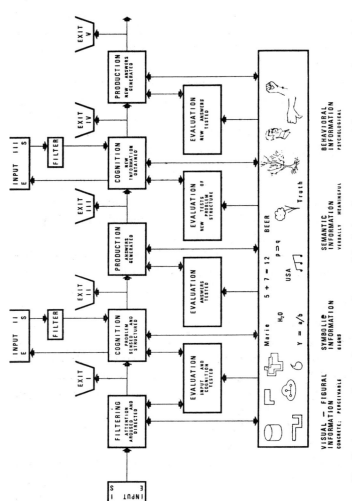

Fig. 2. An operational, data-processing model designed to represent the events in typical problem solving, which also means that it applies in a wide range of behavior. "E" and "S" at "Input" indicate environmental and somatic sources, respectively.

thirty additional distinguishable intellectual abilities, each with its unique combination of a certain operation, content, and product, have been recognized, a few from scattered sources in the literature but mostly from our own aptitudes research. The last twenty were found on the basis of hypotheses deduced from the model, and about fifteen others are at present under investigation.

Of special interest to us here are certain categories and certain concepts pertaining to the model. At first it might be thought that the intellectual abilities and the intellectual functions which they imply are concerned with means to ends rather than with ends or goals and hence that they have little significance for the understanding of motivation. But proposals for general cognitive theory of behavior have by no means been unknown, and attempts to give cognitive interpretations to some motivational phenomena have been actively defended. The remainder of this paper will be an effort in these directions.

From the standpoint of psychological theory, the most striking thing about the collection of intellectual functions and the model in which they are organized is the prominence of information. Ten of the fifteen categories of abilities—four kinds of content and six kinds of product—pertain to information; only five pertain to operations performed on information. As I have said a number of times before, the picture suggested of the functioning organism is that of an agent that processes information.

Information is defined in most general terms as "that which the organism discriminates." Discriminations are made most sharply along the lines of the different kinds of content and next in terms of different kinds of product. Further discriminations are made within any one combination of content and product. Since discriminations, as indicated by differential reactions, may be made unconsciously as well as consciously, there is no reason for labeling this informational view as "mentalistic," one of the "bad" words for several decades but fortunately losing some of its negative valence.

An Informational View of Learning

Any theory of behavior that has general scope must attempt to account for learning. From the point of view under discussion, so far as intellectual functioning is concerned—and this covers a very great range of behavior—learning is the emergence of new information. It is discovery; it is the achievement of new discriminations; it is the formation of new products or the revision of old ones. This view avoids the issue of whether or not changes in behavior must involve associations in order to qualify as learning. As a matter of fact, it goes well beyond the time-honored association principle and substitutes for it the six products of information.

Probably closest to the traditional concept of association is the product of implication. Implications can be fairly well equated to expectancies, anticipations, and perhaps Thorndike's concept of "belongingness." The logical paradigm is stated in the form "If A, then B." But a psychological implication has something further, in the way of a psychological event, that holds A and B together or leads the organism, having the one item of information, to expect the other with a certain degree of confidence or conviction based upon probabilistic aspects of exposure or possible congruencies due to the properties of the things connected.

But it is in connection with reinforcement that motivational matters become relevant, even crucial, in fixing the newly acquired information to any degree in memory storage. I have suggested (Guilford, 1961) that the key to reinforcement is to be found in the operation of evaluation. As nearly as we can tell from the dozen evaluation abilities that we have demonstrated and the kinds of tests that it takes to demonstrate them, evaluation is a process of deciding whether or not cognized information satisfies certain criteria or requirements.

There was a time when the definition was broad enough to justify extending it more broadly to decisions regarding goal satisfactions. That was during my more optimistic period, when it was expected that evaluation as conceived in structure-of-intellect (SI) theory would account for most interpretations of reinforcement. Feedback information of various kinds was thought to provide the operating basis of evaluation. For example, it would account for such concepts as Thorndike's "confirming reaction," "knowledge of results," the hedonistic view, with pleasure and pain serving as "go" and "stop" signals, and even for drive reduction.

However, more recent findings on the better tests of evaluative abilities suggest that the criteria involved in SI evaluation abilities are rather limited to a few criteria of the logical type, such as identity of products and consistency between products of information. It may yet be found that other kinds of criteria for evaluation do function in some areas of information. For example, esthetic criteria may be relevant to abilities for judging goodness of figural information, and ethical criteria may apply in the area of behavioral information. Behavioral information involves cognition of the states of mind of other individuals from sensory cues transmitted by those individuals. It is possible that other sets of evaluative abilities will be found, involving nonlogical criteria for judgment and decision. It would seem that evaluation is too broad to be confined to the logical criteria of identity and consistency and minor variations of these conditions.

Cognition of Internal States

The mention of pleasure and pain and of drive reduction, as feedback information involved in reinforcement, suggests a more general informational status for feelings and emotions, drives and motives. We not only know, but we know that we know. And we know that we have feelings, needs, and desires. Much of this kind of information is less well structured than information arising from our exteroceptors, probably for the reason that in our psychological development we have lacked the opportunity for corrective feedback information such as we obtain from manipulation of things in our external environment. But such as it is, information arising from internal sources may constitute a domain of its own, perhaps parallel to the present behavioral category in the SI model. Whether a full set of twenty-four distinguishable abilities will be found to apply is problematical, but there may be some structuring, in the form of products, and some or all of the five major kinds of operations may apply.

An Operational Model of Behavior

The structure-of-intellect model is sometimes referred to as being "static," which I suppose is intended to be a reflection on its usefulness, if not on its validity. Personally, I have never been much moved by the distinction between "static" *versus* "dynamic," although the former is generally regarded as one of the "bad" words and the latter as one of the "good" words. The model is intended as a taxonomy of behavior and, as such, serves to answer the questions about *what* functions exist. It is readily admitted that something more is needed to answer questions of how and why, but I have always felt that taxonomic questions need to be answered first, with the answers to them providing a foundation on which further enlightenment is built.

An Informational Problem-Solving Model

In recent months I have given attention to a new type of model that is in the operational category and hence has more "dynamic" aspects. It was designed to give a generalized picture of what goes on in problem solving, but since most behavior has some problem-solving aspects, the model should have rather general application as a paradigm of behavior, including motivational aspects. I shall present a brief account of the model and mention some of the ways in which motivational phenomena fit into the picture. It will be obvious that I am far from having a comprehensive theory of motivation.

The model (see Figure 2) reflects some of the traditional views about various essential events in problem solving—awareness that a problem exists, analysis or structuring of the problem, suggestion of alternative solutions, and testing of the possible solutions. The general picture is that of a system within which there is flow of information (as indicated by the arrows), which is coded and recoded in various forms, with inputs and outputs, which means that the system is an open one.

One of the main features is the memory store, underlying all other operations, affecting all those operations and being affected by them. Input of information, from external environmental sources (E) and internal somatic sources (S), first faces a filtering hurdle, where selective steps occur. It is interesting that in the past twenty years the old mentallistic concept of "attention" has been rediscovered, under the more useful terms of "vigilance" and "filtering." Both of these concepts have strong motivational implications, as did the former "conditions of attention."

We shall skip over the event of recognizing that a problem exists for the moment. The operation of cognition, in its broadest sense, is simply knowing or understanding, but more technically stated it is being in possession of a product of information as distinct from other products. If the individual's cognized problem has any degree of complexity, the product is likely to be in the form of a system. Cognition depends heavily upon things in memory storage and may also depend upon evaluation. There may be some trial-and-error activity, with successive attempts at improving the cognized product and with successive evaluations of the attempts. Cognition of the problem provides what some have called a "search model," which serves as a pattern for the production of possible solutions, which rest upon information from memory storage.

There is evidently another filtering activity that prevents total recall and reduces the amount of retrieval of irrelevant information. One can conceive of the filter as having been set by the nature of the search model. Evaluation of the kind recognized in the SI abilities should occur most clearly when the produced solution is matched with the search model to determine whether or not the requirements of similarity and/or consistency have been met. It is not so certain that evaluation also serves the filtering function that was just mentioned.

It is even less certain that filtering at the point of input is also a matter of evaluation. According to the TOTE conception of Miller, Galanter, and Pribram (1960), in which there are fairly obviously some parallels between their concept of "test" and my concept of evaluation, no distinction is made between a test of input and a test of production. Some of our recent results suggest that there is a difference.

In our first major study of creative-thinking abilities, we hypothesized and we found a factor that could be identified as "sensitivity to problems," measured by tests that require the detection of defects and deficiencies in common objects and in social customs. Later, this ability was put in the cell in the SI model known as the "evaluation of semantic implications" (Guilford, 1959b). The defense for this was that seeing something wrong with an object is a matter of evaluating the implication that the object is all right or that seeing defects and deficiencies is an evaluation of implications.

I was somewhat uncomfortable about this logic and must now make a correction. A recent analysis (Nihira *et al.*, 1964) shows that another factor has a better claim for the spot for evaluation of semantic implications. Its tests provide inferences from given information, to be evaluated for consistency with that information. Inferences are obviously implications, and in these tests they have to be evaluated. Tests for the sensitivity-to-problems factor went together on another factor defined as the *cognition* of semantic implications. After all, being sensitive to a condition is a matter of cognition. Moving the factor of sensitivity to problems, the awareness of defects and deficiencies, from the evaluation category to the cognition category suggests that the initial test in the TOTE pattern is different from later tests.

Our other recent findings that evaluative abilities seem somewhat restricted with respect to the kinds of criteria of judgment Hoepfner *et al.*, 1964) also lead to some reservations as to the role of evaluation of this kind at the point of input of information. Although it could conceivably play a role there, as well as very much all along the way in problem solving, something more may well be required. That it is some kind of evaluative activity seems most reasonable. At this point in time, my conclusion is that some kind of evaluative activity, with feedback information contributing to it, runs through most behavior and that it has much relevance for theory of motivation. The chances seem to be that we shall have to go beyond or to extend the present SI model to make logical room for other kinds of evaluation.

Accounting for Some Other Motivational Phenomena

Thus far, most of the effort in this paper to show some relationship between information processing and motivational phenomena has been directed to accounting for reinforcement in learning. Reference was also made to the fact that affective experience could be regarded as evaluative information and that the phenomenon of need reduction could be so regarded. If need reduction can be regarded as information, we can also treat awareness of needs themselves as information, as well as emotional states in general. The input from the soma in the model in Figure 2 theoretically takes care of that possibility. The somatic input provides a running account of internal affairs, vague and ill-structured as that account is. This all sounds rather commonsensical, but this conception offers a challenge to learn more about which somatic cognitions are common, which ones are possible, and how they can become better structured and more contributory to general personal welfare.

The informational point of view has nothing particularly new in accounting for arousal level or activation level. Information of the internal-behavioral type (needs, feelings, emotions) can also discriminate different levels of vitalness or urgency connected with a situation, and activation levels can be stepped up or not in accordance with that information. Such rationalizing does nothing more than express in new language psychological knowledge we already have.

In connection with goal-directed behavior, it can be said that there is goal information and that this is in the form of the product of implication. Human goals are almost entirely developed by experience in the form of anticipated values, and anticipations are implications. I note that Cofer and Appley (1964) come out of their reviews of the facts and thinking on motivation with a strong emphasis upon anticipation, which can be readily interpreted in informational language. They speak of an *anticipation-arousal mechanism* and an *anticipation-invigoration mechanism*, which I understand them to mean as accounting for the goal-setting phenomenon and the activation level–setting phenomenon, respectively. Whether or not they would accept the idea that these concepts support an informational view, I think that they supply significant links in such a theory.

Summary

Lacking anything in the way of a fully worked-out theory of motivational phenomena from the standpoint of an informational psychology, this paper has first reminded the reader of the various phenomena somewhat loosely housed under the broad concept of motivation. It has ventured to offer some evaluative views of traditional efforts at theorizing, questioning whether we are yet ready for a single, comprehensive theory.

A brief account was given of the background information, derived from investigations of human intellectual abilities or functions, that has led to a somewhat general psychological theory that emphasizes types of information and conceives of the organism as an information-processing agent. Two models, one taxonomic and the other operational, were presented to represent the structure of the theory.

Aspects of the models that have some promise for accounting for some of the phenomena of motivation are the operation of evaluation, which has the general function of indicating whether or not aspects of behavior satisfy criteria of "goodness" of some kind; the category of behavioral information that is hypothesized to describe what is popularly known as "self-knowledge"; and the informational product of implication, which describes or accounts for the anticipatory character of goal-seeking behavior.

REFERENCES

Berlyne, D. E. Uncertainty and epistemic curiosity. *Brit. J. Psychol.*, 1962, 53, 27–34.
Cofer, C. N., & Appley, M. H. *Motivation: theory and research.* New York: Wiley, 1964.
Guilford, J. P. *Personality.* New York: McGraw-Hill, 1959. (a)

Guilford, J. P. Three faces of intellect. *Amer. Psychologist*, 1959, **14**, 469–479. (b)

Guilford, J. P. Factorial angles to psychology. *Psychol. Rev.*, 1961, **68**, 1–20.

Guilford, J. P. An informational view of mind. *J. psychol. Researches*, 1962, **6**, 1–10.

Havelka, J. Problem-seeking behavior in rats. *Canad. J. Psychol.*, 1956, **10**, 91–97.

Hoepfner, R., Guilford, J. P., & Merrifield, P. R. A factor analysis of the symbolic-evaluation abilities. *Rep. psychol. Lab.*, No. 33. Los Angeles: Univ. of Southern California, 1964.

Jacobson, A. L. Learning in flatworms and annelids. *Psychol. Rev.*, 1963, **60**, 74–94.

Miller, G. A., Galanter, E., & Pribram, K. H. *Plans and the structure of behavior.* New York: Holt, 1960.

Miller, N. E. Implications for theories of reinforcement. In D. E. Sheer (Ed.), *Electrical stimulation of the brain.* Austin: Univ. of Texas Press, 1961. Pp. 575–581.

Montgomery, K. C. The relation between exploratory behavior and spontaneous alternation in the white rat. *J. comp. physiol. Psychol.*, 1951, **44**, 582–589.

Nihira, K., Guilford, J. P., Hoepfner, R., and Merrifield, P. R. A factor analysis of the semantic-evaluation abilities. *Rep. psychol. Lab.*, No. 32, Los Angeles: Univ. of Southern California, 1964.

White, R. W. Motivation reconsidered: the concept of competence. *Psychol. Rev.*, 1961, **66**, 297–333.

Indexes

Subject Index

Adaptation level, 216–217
  optimal standards of, 217–220
  tranquilizer effects on, 224–225
Anxiety,
  theories of, 212–213
Arousal levels,
  optimal, 223–224
Associationism, 9–14
Base response,
  effects of, 146–148
Behavior,
  directional properties of, 82–84
  & extrinsic forces, 194–197
  & motivation, 7–8
  motivational-reward model of, 3–5
  motivational unit of, 17–18
  processes of, 2
  S-R conception of, 8–14
Behavior change,
  & intrinsic motivation, 226–231
Behavior therapy, vii
Cognition,
  economy of, 298–299
Cognitive dissonance, 195, 208, 213–214
Cognitive theory,
  & informational psychology, 313
Computer processing,
  & cortical functions in human thought, 204–207
  & human thought, 203–207
Conditioning, 10
  classical, 173–176

Convergent evolution,
  & social organization, 297–298
Developmental transitions,
  & experiences, 266–267
Development of knowledge,
  principles of, 31–34
Drive,
  defined, 15
  energizing conceptions of, 15
  primary & secondary, 19–20
  & reward, 16
Drive stimulus,
  defined, 15
Ecological-organism interaction, 295–297
Emotional arousal,
  & frustration, 208
  studies of, 208–209
Emotional motives, 105
  as lower-level processes, 69, 71–73
  continuum with physiological motives, 66–68
  & emotional processes, 67–68
  in higher species, 68–69
  & perceptual processes, 73–75
  phylogenetic antiquity of, 72–73, 77–80
  & physiological motives, 64–66
Emotional processes,
  defined, 25–26
Emotions,
  as conscious experiences, 53–56
  as disrupting processes, 56–57
  as strong experiences, 37

Author Index